W9-BUI-074

18,618

LB
1715   Weil
.W369   Social models
1978   of teaching

DATE DUE

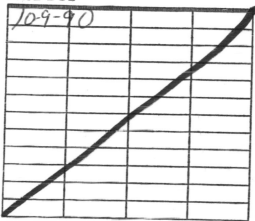

10-9-90

Social models of teaching
LB1715.W369 1978   18618

Weil, Marsha
        VRJC/WRIGHT LIBRARY

MARSHA WEIL and BRUCE JOYCE

SOCIAL

MODELS OF TEACHING

EXPANDING YOUR
TEACHING REPERTOIRE

VERNON REGIONAL
JUNIOR COLLEGE LIBRARY

PRENTICE-HALL, INC., ENGLEWOOD CLIFFS, NEW JERSEY 07632

Library of Congress Cataloging in Publication Data

WEIL, MARSHA.
    Social models of teaching.
    (Expanding your teaching repertoire)

    Includes bibliographical references and index.
    1. Teachers, Training of.   2. Teachers—In-service
training.   I. Joyce, Bruce R., joint author.
    II. Title.   III. Series.
LB1715.W369   371.1'46   77-5448
ISBN 0-13-815944-0
ISBN 0-13-815936-X pbk.

This book is dedicated to our parents

GRACE AND MITCHELL LEWIS
URSULA AND LOUIS JOYCE

©1978 by Prentice-Hall, Inc., Englewood Cliffs, New Jersey 07632

*All rights reserved. No part of this book may be reproduced
in any form or by any means
without permission in writing from the publisher.*

PRINTED IN THE UNITED STATES OF AMERICA

10   9   8   7   6   5   4   3   2   1

PRENTICE-HALL INTERNATIONAL, INC., *London*
PRENTICE-HALL OF AUSTRALIA PTY. LIMITED, *Sydney*
PRENTICE-HALL OF CANADA, LTD., *Toronto*
PRENTICE-HALL OF INDIA PRIVATE LIMITED, *New Delhi*
PRENTICE-HALL OF JAPAN, INC., *Tokyo*
PRENTICE-HALL OF SOUTHEAST ASIA PTE. LTD., *Singapore*
WHITEHALL BOOKS LIMITED, *Wellington, New Zealand*

CONTENTS

FOREWORD

One thing that researchers seem to agree upon in defining a good teacher is that he or she be flexible. Marsha Weil and Bruce Joyce's Models of Teaching program widens the range of strategies available to the teacher. Having many strategies to apply appropriately may not necessarily make a good teacher, but it will contribute to the *craft* of instruction. The *art* of instruction each person must supply for himself or herself.

The three strategies addressed in this volume are aimed at facilitating democratic processes and creating a more humane society. Other volumes present teaching skills designed to develop an individual's self-understanding and ability to process information.

Careful thought about fostering a democratic and humane society has never been needed more than at the present time. The material presented here is designed for the thoughtful teacher. It is based on solid philosophical, social, and psychological rationales. The "why" as well as the "how" is addressed. Each model—Simulation, Role Playing, and Jurisprudential—is anchored on a solid theoretical base. Then examples of teaching behavior are presented. This is followed by suggested ways the teacher might practice the strategy discussed. Finally, methods of evaluation are offered. Although the presentation is structured, it leaves room for teachers to improvise and be creative.

This book and its supporting materials provide a wealth of resources that may be used by teachers at many levels; the authors, through flexible organization, have made it easy to do this. Guided by their teachers, preservice teachers will be able to enter the classroom with confidence if they have at their command two or three strategies with which they feel comfortable. Working cooperatively with their colleagues at their own pace, practicing teachers will enlarge their repertoire by drawing upon this bank of materials. Graduate students in curriculum and instruction will find many concrete cases to be analyzed and critiqued. Teacher educators, recognizing the diversity of learners within a pluralistic society, will appreciate the useful alternatives to meet the needs of individuals. The Models of Teaching program suggests alternatives and provides ways of developing flexibility. Finally, although it may be heretical, I strongly suggest the values of these protocols to professors of history, philosophy, economics, and to other academicians interested in bringing new life to their classrooms.

The resource potential of the materials treated here reflects the regard in which the authors hold all teachers. It is apparent that they consider teaching a *profession* and value teachers as unique individuals, each of whom possesses special qualities that might be enhanced through an orderly learning process. These are indeed *teaching* materials. They do their job in a climate of creativity, joy, and humor, while communicating respect for the intelligence of the person charged with helping others to learn. Those who use the book as a guide will embark upon an adventure that will reward not only themselves, but those they teach.

Carolyn L. Ellner

Claremont Graduate School

ACKNOWLEDGMENTS

We owe an enormous debt to a large number of colleagues and students throughout the United States. At Teachers' College, Columbia University, Rhoada Wald, Michael McKibbin, Michael Feller, Christina Gullion, Kathryn O'Donnell, Clark Brown, Robert Gower, Jill Levine, Kay Vandergrift, Joseph Kelly, Gene Rude, Deane Flood, Daisy Reed, Sam Stewart, Charlie Abate, plus many teachers, school administrators, professors, and researchers helped us develop and test the early versions of what ultimately became these materials. Karl Schmidt, then of Science Research Associates, worked very closely with us and with Drs. Wald and McKibbin to build the first widely disseminated materials. David Hunt, Ed Sullivan, Joann Greenwood, Joyce Noy, Roma Reid and others at the Ontario Institute for Studies in Education helped to structure and conduct some of the most important training research we were able to do and helped us embark on the first research with children.

Roger Pankratz of Western Kentucky University, Carolyn Ellner of the Claremont Graduate School of Education, Pat Murphy of the University of Minnesota, Greta Morine-Dershimer of the Far West Laboratory, Paul and Margaret Collins of the California State University of Hayward worked individually and together with us in developing and testing teacher training ideas relevant to this Models of Teaching series. Christopher Clark, Penelope Peterson, Ronald Marx,

Jane Anton, and Janet Crist-Witzel of the Stanford Center for Research and Development in Teaching helped harden our ideas and conducted a series of investigations with us that advanced our thinking.

National Teacher Corps, especially William Smith, James B. Steffenson, and Paul Collins, helped us greatly. Their colleagues, Art Brill, Jack Ether, Dan Ganeles, Bev Elender, and Jan Hillson provided many interesting ideas and in many ways opened up new areas of research and development before we had perceived them ourselves.

Floyd Waterman of the University of Nebraska, Rupert Trujillo of the University of New Mexico, Bud Meyers of the University of Vermont, Berj Harootunian of Syracuse University, and Chet Hill and Dave Marsh of the University of Southern California also worked with us in a variety of ways. Members of the Allendale School staff in Pasadena, California, including Alma Hill and Elsa Brizzi, advanced our thinking about the adaptation of *Models of Teaching* to multicultural settings; Claudia Ulbrecht, Jennifer Bird-in-Ground, Muata, and Joel Morine contributed imaginative demonstration lessons.

The Bureau of Educational Professions Development supported some of the most difficult early work; we are especially indebted to Allen Schmeider for his counsel and advice during that period. The present materials were piloted in the Corps Member Training Institute of National Teacher Corps. Drs. Smith, Waterman, Pankratz, and McKibbin, Paul Collins, Jim Steffensen, and Beryl Nelson were powerful colleagues during that experience. The National Education Association piloted the training of teachers to operate teacher centers based on *Models of Teaching*. John Leeke of the NEA staff and Ruth Foster of the Omaha Public Schools were especially helpful to us during that experiment.

Finally, we acknowledge with gratitude the contributions of the people who developed the concepts around which the various models are based: Fannie Shaftel, Professor Emeritus of Stanford University, Richard Suchman, Bill Gordon of Synectics Incorporated, Donald Oliver of Harvard University, James P. Shaver of the University of Utah, and other colleagues are gratefully acknowledged.

Marsha Weil
Bruce Joyce

Supplementary audio-visual materials to accompany this text can be ordered from:

Dr. Bruce Joyce
Center for Research and Development in Teaching
Stanford University
Stanford, California 94305

INTRODUCTION

A POINT OF VIEW ABOUT TEACHING

How do we think of ourselves as professional teachers and educators? We are responsible for many types of instruction, for helping our students grow in self-awareness and in their ability to relate to others, for clarifying values, for promoting moral development, and for a host of other objectives. Our responsibilities can conveniently be described in three categories: responsibility for the personal growth of our students, responsibility for their social development and preparation for national and world citizenship, and responsibility for their mastery of academic subjects, including the basic skills of reading and computation that are so essential to contemporary life. In order to accomplish these objectives we work in schools, and within these in classrooms, learning centers, and libraries. Much of our contact with students is formal: they are assembled in classes to take one or more courses from us. But we have much informal contact with them as well. In addition, we teachers work either relatively alone or in teaching teams, perhaps with paid and volunteer aides assisting us.

To carry out these multiple responsibilities, we are required to engage in several professional roles, often simultaneously. We are counselors, facilitators, instructional managers, curriculum designers, academic instructors, evaluators of instruction, and, reluctantly, disciplinarians. To fill these roles, we draw on a variety of models

1

of teaching. There are presently available to us many alternatives for organizing and carrying out learning experiences, some formal and traditional and others casual and emergent.

Our initial preparation for teaching is relatively brief, considering the diverse responsibilities and the complexity of our roles. The preparation we receive prior to entering the classroom takes place in university courses and in the relatively short apprenticeship that we call "student teaching" or "internship."

When we begin our teaching, we perceive only dimly that we must master multiple roles. Gradually, as we get our bearings, we begin to see teaching as a cluster of differing roles and responsibilities. We then seek alternative ways to fulfill our tasks as teachers, and we begin to broaden our perspective on the nature of teaching. Finally, we spend the greater part of our professional lives attempting to improve our competence and to sharpen our skills. As we become more professional, we try to expand the ways we can be meaningful to our students—we master more roles.

The authors see the development of professional competence in teaching as an increased ability to play the various assigned roles more effectively. Our point of view is that a large part of this competence consists in mastering a repertoire of approaches to teaching that can be used to carry out these roles. We believe that competence is expanded in two ways: first, by increasing the *range of teaching strategies* that we are able to employ; second, by *becoming increasingly skillful* in the use of each of these strategies.

Different roles *require* different teaching strategies. In our earlier book, *Models of Teaching* (1972), we described our search for teaching strategies that are based on defendable theories about how people learn, grow, and develop. Some of these theory-based models of teaching are more appropriate to some objectives than to others. For example, some are specially tailored to help students grow in self-awareness and strength of self-concept. Others are more appropriate for improving human relations in the classroom and helping students clarify their social values. Yet others are more appropriate for the mastery of subject matter. Some models of teaching are quite narrow in their focus, and others are useful for a wide variety of purposes.

A model of teaching consists of guidelines for designing educational activities and environments. It specifies ways of teaching and learning that are intended to achieve certain kinds of goals. A model includes a rationale, a theory that justifies it and describes what it is good for and why; the rationale may be accompanied by empirical evidence that it "works." In *Models of Teaching*, we deliberately selected models representing different frames of reference toward educational goals and methods. That book was written for the purpose of helping teachers explore a variety of philosophical and psychological positions, which they could then make come to life in the classroom.

We discovered models of teaching in many sources. Educators, psychologists, sociologists, systems analysts, psychiatrists, and many others have all developed theoretical positions about learning and teaching. Curriculum development projects, schools and school districts, and organizations representing particular curriculum areas or disciplines have also developed a large number of approaches to teaching and learning. The task of selection began with compiling a very long list of sources of models. Included were the works of counselors and therapists such as Erikson

(1950), Maslow (1962), and Rogers (1951), as well as those of learning theorists such as Ausubel (1963), Bruner (1966), and Skinner (1957); developmental psychologists such as Hunt (1971), Kohlberg (1966), and Piaget (1952); and philosophers such as Broudy (1965), Dewey (1916), and James (1899). Curriculum development in the academic subjects provided many examples, as did group dynamics. Patterns of teaching from great experimental schools such as Summerhill made their way onto our list. Altogether, more than eighty theorists, schools, and projects were identified, far more than any teacher would be able to master during a career.

Gradually, we began to group the models on the basis of their chief emphases—the ways they approached educational goals and means. We eventually organized them into four families:

1. Social Interaction Models. These emphasize the relationships of the individual to society or to other persons. They focus on the processes by which reality is socially negotiated. Consequently, with respect to goals, models from this orientation give priority to the improvement of the individual's ability to relate to others, the improvement of democratic processes, and the improvement of the society. It must be stressed that the social-relations orientation does not assume that these goals constitute the *only* important dimension of life. While social relations may be emphasized more than other domains, social theorists are also concerned with the development of the mind and the self, and the learning of academic subjects. (It is the rare theorist in education who is not concerned with more than one aspect of the learner's development, or who does not use more than one aspect of the environment to influence the learner's development.)

2. Information Processing Models. The second large family of models share an orientation toward the information processing capability of students and toward the systems that can improve their information processing capability. Information processing refers to the ways people handle stimuli from the environment, organize data, sense problems, generate concepts and solutions to problems, and employ verbal and nonverbal symbols. Some information processing models are concerned with the ability of the learner to solve problems, and thus emphasize productive thinking; others are concerned with general intellectual ability. Some emphasize the teaching of strategies derived from the academic disciplines. Again, however, it must be stressed that nearly all models from this family are also concerned with social relationships and the development of an integrated, functioning self.

3. Personal Models. The third family share an orientation toward the individual and the development of selfhood. They emphasize the processes by which individuals construct and organize their unique reality. Frequently, they focus on the emotional life of the individual. It is expected that the focus on helping individuals to develop a productive relationship with their environment and to view themselves as capable persons will produce richer interpersonal relations and a more effective information processing capability.

4. Behavior Modification Models. This fourth type of model has evolved from attempts to develop efficient systems for sequencing learning tasks and shaping behavior by manipulating reinforcement. Exponents of reinforcement theory, such as Skinner (1957), have developed these models and operant conditioning as their central mechanism. They are frequently referred to as behavior modification theories because they emphasize changing the external behavior of the learners and describe them in terms of visible behavior rather than underlying and unobservable behavior. Operant conditioning has been applied to a wide variety of goals, in education and other areas, ranging from military training to the improvement of interpersonal behavior and even to therapy. It is represented by a large number of models, some of which are media-oriented (such as programmed stategies) and some of which are oriented to interactive teaching (such as the use of tokens to shape social behavior).

These families of models are by no means antithetical or mutually exclusive. The actual prescriptions for developing the instructional activities and learning environments that emerge from some of them—even those classified in different families—are remarkably similar. Also, within the families, models share many features with respect both to goals and to the kinds of means they recommend. All educational activities evoke different meanings in different people. In this sense, everything we do is personal. Similarly, most of our experiences, especially educational ones, involve some intellectual or information processing activity.

Over the years, we have discussed our original classifications with many of our colleagues, agreeing with many of their objections and rethinking our position. In this text, we have reclassified a few of the models. In general, we feel it is the basic framework of families that has become a powerful intellectual tool for teachers and curriculum planners, rather than the specific classification of individual models. However, we have made an effort to classify models according to the most prominent goal or features that distinguish them from another family.

In this three-volume series, we are concerned only with models from the information processing, social, and personal families. It seemed to us that there are presently available several excellent sources on the adaptation of behavior modification and its variations to the classroom. We therefore decided to concentrate on models that are less available in the literature. Models from these three families are listed in Figures 1A-1C.

To us, growth in teaching is the increasing mastery of a variety of models of teaching and the ability to use them effectively. Some philosophies of teacher education maintain that a teacher should master a single model and utilize it well. We believe that very few teachers are so limited in capacity. Most of us can quite easily develop a repertoire of six or eight models of teaching, which we can use in order to carry out our roles. We should choose our "basic" repertoire to meet the needs generated by our teaching assignment. Certain models are more appropriate for some curriculums than for others; that is, the curriculum helps define our role and the kinds of competencies that we need. For example, a secondary school science teacher of biology who is using Biological Sciences Study Committee materials will want to master the particular kind of inductive approach that fits best with those materials; an elementary school social studies teacher who is helping children study values may want to master one of the models appropriate to clarifying values and analyzing public issues. Once a teacher master the "basic" repertoire of models, he or she can then expand it by learning new models and by combining and transforming the basic ones to create new ones. In the midst of a social studies unit, a teacher may use a highly specific model to help children master map skills, and combine this model with group-dynamic models that help students attack social issues. A highly skilled performance in teaching blends the variety of models appropriately and embellishes them. Master teachers create new models of teaching and test them in the course of their work.

Model	Major Theorist	Mission or Goals for Which Most Applicable
Inductive Thinking Model Inquiry Training Model	Hilda Taba Richard Suchman	Designed primarily for development of inductive mental processes and academic reasoning or theory building, but these capacities are useful for personal and social goals as well.
Science Inquiry Model	Joseph J. Schwab (also much of the Curriculum Reform Movement of the 1960s)	Designed to teach the research system of a discipline, but also expected to have effects in other domains (sociological methods may be taught in order to increase social understanding and social problem-solving).
Concept Attainment Model	Jerome Bruner	Designed primarily to develop inductive reasoning, but also for concept development and analysis.
Developmental Model	Jean Piaget Irving Sigel Edmund Sullivan	Designed to increase general intellectual development, especially logical reasoning, but can be applied to social and moral development as well (see Kohlberg, 1966).
Advance Organizer Model	David Ausubel	Designed to increase the efficiency of information processing capacities to meaningfully absorb and relate bodies of knowledge.

Figure 1A. *The Information Processing Family of Models.*

Making Theories Practical

We did not make up the models of teaching you will learn here, nor did we invent the theories upon which they are based. Most of these ideas have been available to educators for many years. Our contribution has been to develop a way of making these theories operational, and to describe what teachers *do* when they teach according to one theory or another.

To translate a theory into practical teaching form, we employ a set of four concepts: *syntax*, *principles of reaction*, *social system*, and *support system*. The first two concepts are especially important in making a theory practical.

Syntax describes the model as a flow of actions. If teachers were to use the model, how would they begin? What would they do first, second, third? We describe syntax in terms of sequences of events, which we call *phases*. Each model has a distinct *flow* of phases—for example, present material to the learner, develop confronting situation—or, present organizing ideas to students, provide data sources. A comparison of the structural phasing of models reveals the practical differences

Model	Major Theorist	Mission or Goals for Which Most Applicable
Group Investigation Model	Herbert Thelen John Dewey	Development of skills for participation in democratic social process through combined emphasis on interpersonal (group) skills and academic-inquiry skills. Aspects of personal development are important outgrowths of this model.
Classroom Meeting Model (Social Problem-Solving)	William Glasser	Development of self-understanding and responsibility to oneself and one's social group.
Social Inquiry Model	Byron Massialas Benjamin Cox	Social problem-solving, primarily through academic inquiry and logical reasoning.
Laboratory Method Model	National Training Laboratory (NTL), Bethel, Maine	Development of interpersonal and group skills and, through this, personal awareness and flexibility.
Jurisprudential Model	Donald Oliver James P. Shaver	Designed primarily to teach the jurisprudential frame of reference as a way of thinking about and resolving social issues.
Role Playing Model	Fannie Shaftel George Shaftel	Designed to induce students to inquire into personal and social values, with their own behavior and values becoming the source of their inquiry.
Social Simulation Model	Sarene Boocock	Designed to help students experience various social processes and realities and to examine their own reactions to them.

Figure 1B. *The Social Family of Models.*

among them. An inductive strategy has a different phase and a different sequence than a deductive one.

Principles of reaction guide the teacher's responses to the learner; they tell the teacher how to regard the learner and respond to what he or she does. In some models, the teacher overtly tries to shape behavior by rewarding certain student activities and maintaining a neutral stance toward others. In other models, such as those designed to develop creativity, the teacher tries to maintain a nonevaluative, carefully equal stance so that the learners become self-directing. Principles of reaction provide the teacher with rules of thumb by which to "tune in" to the student and select appropriate responses to what the student does.

The social system provides a description of student and teacher roles and relationships and the kinds of norms that are encouraged. The leadership roles of the

Model	Major Theorist	Mission or Goals for Which Most Applicable
Nondirective Model	Carl Rogers	Emphasis on building the capacity for personal development in terms of self-awareness, understanding, autonomy, and self-concept.
Awareness Training Model	Fritz Perls	Increasing one's capacity for self-exploration and self-awareness. Much emphasis on development of inter-personal awareness and understanding, as well as body and sensory awareness.
Synectics Model	William Gordon	Personal development of creativity and creative problem-solving.
Conceptual Systems Model	David Hunt	Designed to increase personal complexity and flexibility.

Figure 1C. *The Personal Family of Models.*

teacher vary greatly from model to model. In some models, the teacher is a reflector or a facilitator of group activity; in others, a counselor of individuals; and in still others, a taskmaster. The concept of hierarchical relationships is explained in terms of the sharing of initiating activity by teacher and learner, the location of authority, and the amount of control over activity that emerges from the process of interaction. In some models, the teacher is the center of activity and the source of input— the organizer and pacer of the situation. Some models provide for relatively equal distribution of activity between teacher and student, whereas others place the student at the center. Finally, different models reward different student behaviors. In some, the students are rewarded for completing a job done or sticking to a pre-scribed line of inquiry; in others, the students' reward is knowing that they have learned something.

One way to describe a teaching model, then, is in terms of the degree of structure in the learning environment. That is, as roles, relationships, norms, and activities become less externally imposed and more within the student's control, the social system becomes less structured.

The support system refers to additional requirements beyond the usual human skills, capacities, and technical facilities necessary to implement a model. For example, a human relations model may require a trained leader; a nondirec-tive model may require a particular type of personality (exceedingly patient and supportive). If a model postulates that students teach themselves, with the role of the teacher limited to consultation and facilitation, what support is necessary? A classroom supplied only with textbooks would be limiting and prescriptive; addi-tional support in the form of books, films, self-instructional systems, travel ar-rangements, and the like is necessary. Support requirements are derived from two sources: the role specifications for the teacher and the substantive demands of the experience.

Those of you who have used our *Models of Teaching* text will notice that some descriptions of the model in the present book are slightly different from those in the earlier work. This is because, as we worked with different models, we gained greater ability to describe them and could incorporate more elements of the theory of a model into its basic set of activities. Therefore, we are now more precise about the events that take place within any given phase of activity. Occasionally, we have revised or expanded the phases of activity. In all cases, we are able to identify specific planning and teaching skills that facilitate the implementation of a model. We have learned and changed over the years!

Although we are delighted with our increased ability to describe initial teacher (and student) behaviors for each model, and although we feel this will greatly enhance easy and early mastery of each model, we offer a caution to our supporters, and to our critics. A model of teaching is not a simple fixed formula for completing a job. It provides definite ideas for creating an environment from which students are likely to learn certain kinds of things, but it has to become a flexible, fluid instrument that is modified to fit different types of subject matter and that responds to students who are different from one another.

There is an old saying that fencing coaches preach to their students: Treat the sword like a bird. If you hold it too tightly, you choke it! If you hold it too loosely, it will fly away! So it is with a model of teaching. If one uses it too rigidly, it becomes a blunt instrument. If one holds it too lightly, it dissolves and becomes undistinguishable from any other method of teaching. It fails to do its work!

Experience and Research with Models

Our impression from experience is that in-service teachers learn models of teaching that are new to them somewhat more easily and rapidly than do teachers-in-training or inexperienced teachers. This is probably because experienced teachers have more of the general competencies of teaching in hand and are more comfortable working with children during the first stages of practice with a new teaching approach.

In a series of research studies, we asked the question: How does the "natural" teaching style of teachers affect their ability to learn new models of teaching? The answer to this appears to be that teachers of nearly any style can master any of the models of teaching identified above with relatively little difficulty. Not everyone learns every model equally well or needs to use any given model regularly. However, nearly all teachers are capable of mastering the fundamentals of several models of teaching and of applying them effectively in the classroom.

Teachers very definitely have preferences for different models and use some more than others. We believe, however, that a range of approaches is needed. Once this is accepted, teachers who attempt to widen their repertoire will discover delights in some models of teaching that at first seemed unattractive.

Generally speaking, the time needed to learn new models of teaching shortens with each new acquisition. It takes several, perhaps five or six trials, for a teacher to be able to comfortably handle unfamiliar models in the classroom at first, but fewer trials are needed with each successive model.

Over the years, we have conducted a series of investigations into how people acquire and use models of teaching that are new to them. At this point, we believe that most of us first learn a model in a form appropriate for short lessons or units.

This "short form" is relatively rigid: we "follow the steps" (phases) of the model rather closely during the first practice sessions. With increasing practice, we learn to transform the model and expand it, adapting it to the kinds of things that we teach best, to the children being taught, and to the local conditions. In time, we learn to apply the model more effectively to curriculum materials and to combine it with other models of teaching, thereby incorporating it into the working repertoire. Following that, we gradually learn to teach the model to the children, helping them to make the model their own as part of their quest to "learn how to learn." For example, in science classes we help students learn to carry on inductive inquiry by themselves, our function as teachers becoming one of helping them learn rather than one of leading them through a sequence of learning steps.

To reiterate, the stages of mastering a model are: (1) learning how to apply it in some acceptable form; (2) expanding, embellishing, and transforming it to our own styles and curriculum; (3) applying its elements to the roles we play in our classroom; (4) combining it with other models; and (5) teaching it to the children themselves.

Some people quickly grasp the essential ideas and procedures of a model after reading brief introductory materials and viewing or experiencing a demonstration. We have found that approximating the sequence of activities of a model—its syntax —is not difficult in most cases. However, implementing a model in a way that truly reflects its theoretical underpinnings and fulfills all its potential objectives requires a deeper understanding. Consequently, we have chosen to err on the side of specificity in the explanation in our training systems. Some teachers, maybe most teachers, will not need the extent of explanation, illustration, and step-by-step training that our systems offer. They may be turned off by what is perceived as prescription. However, other teachers we have worked with prefer a highly structured training approach with many illustrations and examples.

We hope you do not take our effort to provide as much detail as we can as a belief that there is only one way to learn new models of teaching (or only one way to teach them). Our primary purpose, rather, is to provide something for everyone, something for an audience representing all grade levels, subject matter, and learning styles! When you feel ready to move on to the next steps in training, by all means do so. (We shall speak more about learning options later in this introduction).

Expanded Uses of a Model

We have mentioned that the goal in the initial stage of training (and throughout our training systems) is for teachers to use a model to develop short lessons, and to try these out several times with colleagues and small groups of students. The ultimate uses of a model extend far beyond the construction of the relatively short, isolated lessons that conveniently serve the training function.

A model can be used to guide learning activities extended over a long period of time, to diagnose and evaluate pupils, and to train students to use the model independently. Teachers can create many variations on each model, or they can take the "essence" of a model, dropping the syntax and phases, and perceptively use the key elements in an impromptu learning situation. Models can be designed into learning materials, and thereby become materials-mediated instead of teacher-mediated. (Programmed instruction, for example, is designed around Skinner's work.)

The models of teaching we present in these three books are applicable to all types of learning settings, both traditional and open. In open environments, self-directed, materials-mediated learning activities can be developed by designing them around the phases of the model. Students can work with one another, using key elements of the model. Bulletin boards can be based on one or more models of teaching. Learning centers can be developed around different models of teaching. For example, there can be an Inquiry Corner—or, alternatively, a Science Corner—that is based on the Inquiry Training Model. There can be a Concept Corner where students acquire concepts for many subject areas through concept attainment activities.

We touch on these expanded uses briefly in the last portion of each instructional system, but we do not train directly for them. We strongly urge small groups of teachers to brainstorm regarding the adaptation of models to different learning settings.

TRAINING TO LEARN A MODEL

The three books in this series are designed to help present and future teachers teach themselves a variety of models of teaching. One book presents teaching models from the information processing family; another presents models from the social family; and another, models from the personal family.

The Training Approach: Four Components

In these books, the materials for each model have been organized into four components: I) Describing and Understanding the Model; II) Viewing the Model; III) Planning and Peer Teaching; and IV) Adapting the Model. This organization reflects our belief about how one goes about training individuals to learn a complex performance behavior such as teaching (or tennis or computer programming or flying).

The notion is quite simple. First, you will read or hear a verbal description of the new model; this will give a general overview of the major operations and an explanation of the rationale, or theory, behind the activities included in the model. You need to become familiar with the goals of the model—that is, what its activities can and cannot accomplish—and with its key ideas. For example, if you were learning tennis, you would need to know at the onset that there are forehand shots, backhand shots, serves, lobs, and net play. You would also have to know something about scoring and about when the objective of the activity is accomplished—that is, about "games," "sets," and "matches." Learning a model of teaching is like learning to play tennis; at first, then, you would need a description of the activity—its objectives and key features. Component I of each model provides this.

Many of us prefer to see a demonstration of the activity. Demonstrations make words come alive, especially if the new activity is unfamiliar to us. So, in training for a model of teaching we move next to a demonstration, the model in action. In these learning systems, demonstration is accomplished through annotated transcripts of actual teaching sessions and/or through the optional use of audio tapes of lessons. In Component II of these models, you will find a transcript of a demonstration of the model, which we refer to as the *demonstration transcript.* In addition, you may have available a demonstration audio tape. In the exercises and activities, we shall be referring primarily to the demonstration transcript, but other forms of demonstration could also be used, or someone skilled in the model could conduct a live demonstration.

Finally, you practice. In tennis, you hit balls against a backboard or return "shots" from a ball-machine, spending hours, first on the forehand and then on the backhand, gradually learning more and more about the discrepancy between what you are doing and a *good* stroke. Similarly, in learning a model of teaching, you study and practice the *major elements* of a model several times before actually playing a game. Aspects of the theory are further explained and opportunity to apply your knowledge of them is provided through written exercises.

In Component III, it is time to move from practice to the "court." In teaching, this means planning and teaching an actual lesson. In tennis, it means playing one or two games at a time—not an entire match! In teaching, you select a topic, shape it according to the model, plan lessons, and teach them to a group of peers. Peer teaching is different from practice with children and has advantages over such practice when you are just trying out a model, namely that adult "learners" can coach you as you practice. Peer teaching gives you a chance to master the elements of the model before you try it with children, so that you are more surefooted when you do work with them.

After peer teaching, we suggest that you try the model with children, preferably small groups, but perhaps classroom-size groups. Again, these trials should be relatively short lessons or sets of lessons. Remember, at this point you are just sharpening your skills. (It is important to master the basics of your own tennis game before figuring out how to defend against such players as Chris Evert, Jimmy Connors, or Arthur Ashe! Or before learning how to play on different types of courts, such as grass, clay, and asphalt.) Mastering the basics comes before working out your own personal style, which surely will develop and be unique to you even though the model remains the same.

Finally, with the basic skills and activities in place, it is time to explore the model in the context of your actual teaching situation, your curriculum, and your students. It's time to think about the long-term goals of the model—for yourself, your subject area, and your students. You ask questions such as: How do I take the materials and curriculums I work with and enhance them with the model? How do I teach students to use a model over a long period of time? How do I develop variations on the basic model or incorporate elements of it into my style? How can I "stretch" a model so that it's not a cookie-cutter, thirty-minute lesson, but instead becomes a paradigm for many days and weeks of learning activities? How do I move from using the model of teaching as a guide for a short lesson to using it as guidelines for larger curricular sequences and, finally, for organizing the classroom as a learning environment? These questions are covered in Component IV, Adapting the Model.

In summary, the written materials (and the audio-visual materials, if available) are designed to help you 1) master the theory and basic elements of a model (describing and understanding the model), 2) provide demonstration (viewing the model), 3) initiate practice (planning and peer teaching), and 4) extend the model to your classroom setting and curricular planning (adapting the model). These components and their parts are listed in Figure 2.

COMPONENT I: DESCRIBING AND UNDERSTANDING THE MODEL

Materials	Activity
1. Theory and Overview	Reading
2. Theory in Practice	Reading
3. Taking Theory Into Action	Reading/Writing
4. Theory Checkup	Writing

COMPONENT II: VIEWING THE MODEL

Materials	Activity
1. Analyzing Teaching	Reading/Writing
2. Viewing the Lesson	Reading/Writing/Discussion

Optional Material	Optional Activity
3. Analyzing the Demonstration	Discussion/Writing

COMPONENT III: PLANNING AND PEER TEACHING

Materials	Activity
1. Selecting the Topic	Reading/Writing
2. Preparing and Organizing Materials	Reading/Writing
3. Determining Educational Objectives	Reading/Writing
4. Completing the Planning Guide	Writing
5. Peer Teaching	Teaching
6. Analyzing the Lesson	Discussion/Analysis

Optional Material	Optional Activity
7. Microteaching and Analysis	Teaching/Analysis

COMPONENT IV: ADAPTING THE MODEL

Materials	Activity
1. Curriculum Transformation	Reading
2. Long-Term Uses	Reading
3. Combining the Model With Other Models of Teaching	Reading

Figure 2. *Components of the Training System.*

Ways to Go Through the Training System: Options

We have provided options for two reasons: teachers differ in their learning styles and preferences, and training situations differ in their organizational possibilities, flexibility, and support systems. The major training options are three. They concern:

1. the sequence and order of components
2. the medium for demonstration of the model: written transcript, live, audio-filmstrip, or photostrip
3. the role of the trainer: self-instructional, group instruction with instructor as facilitator, and instructor-led presentations

Essentially, the material is self-instructional: you can work through it on your own (except for peer teaching), or with a group of colleagues. An instructor is not necessary. On the other hand, a knowledgeable instructor can greatly enhance the learning situation by serving as a facilitator and reactor. Our preference is for teachers to work in groups, selecting the models they wish to concentrate on and helping one another master them. However, the material can form the basis for preplanned workshops in which all participants study the same models.

Although this series is designed so that one first learns the theory of the model, then analyzes demonstrations of it, then practices it with peers, and finally practices it in the classroom, there are many alternative sequences, all equally viable. Some groups prefer to begin with demonstration. These people would like to see the model before they read about it. This makes perfectly good sense. In other groups, the beginning activity might be to appoint one teacher to demonstrate the model live with children or with those being trained. This requires that the demonstrator master the theory, read the transcript lesson, and practice the model so that he or she can introduce the training with the live demonstration. It is also possible to begin with curriculum materials, analyzing them to find which model of teaching is most appropriate and then concentrating on learning how to adapt the model to the curriculum materials. For example, most approaches to the teaching of reading are built upon a particular model of teaching or the combination of a few of them. Teachers of reading may prefer to begin with the models that underlie the curriculums they are using. For most of us, the "understanding first" sequence is the most comfortable (see Figure 3).

Many of us can handle abstract ideas only after we have experienced the concrete situation. We also do not like to perfect isolated skills without seeing the whole; we find that it's easier to go back to the task of mastering the basics when we have seen an example of the end product! For those who prefer a quick overview and then need to see a model of the activity before going further in training, we suggest another sequence. Figure 4 indicates a way of meeting these needs.

Some people (not the authors) like to go right to the tennis match before learning anything about the game. That is another alternative. It is possible to view a filmstrip and/or read the demonstration transcript before undertaking the Overview and Theory into Practice Steps (see Figure 5).

Flexibility in developing the training sequence will depend, of course, on

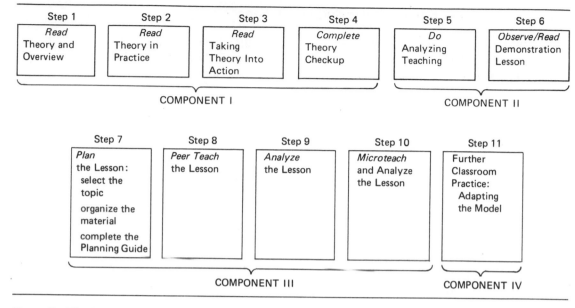

Step 1	Step 2	Step 3	Step 4	Step 5	Step 6
Read Theory and Overview	*Read* Theory in Practice	*Read* Taking Theory Into Action	*Complete* Theory Checkup	*Do* Analyzing Teaching	*Observe/Read* Demonstration Lesson

COMPONENT I ⌣_____⌣ COMPONENT II

Step 7	Step 8	Step 9	Step 10	Step 11
Plan the Lesson: select the topic organize the material complete the Planning Guide	*Peer Teach* the Lesson	*Analyze* the Lesson	*Microteach* and Analyze the Lesson	Further Classroom Practice: Adapting the Model

COMPONENT III ⌣_____⌣ COMPONENT IV

Figure 3. *The "Understanding First" Approach.*

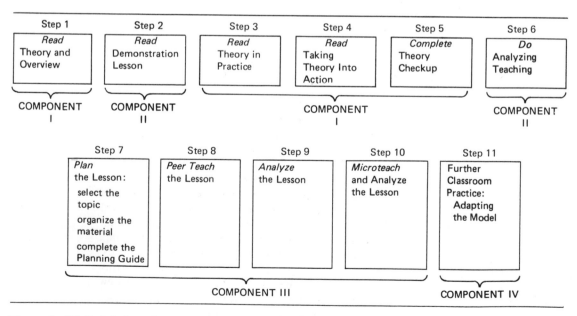

Step 1	Step 2	Step 3	Step 4	Step 5	Step 6
Read Theory and Overview	*Read* Demonstration Lesson	*Read* Theory in Practice	*Read* Taking Theory Into Action	*Complete* Theory Checkup	*Do* Analyzing Teaching

COMPONENT I ⌣ COMPONENT II ⌣ COMPONENT I ⌣ COMPONENT II

Step 7	Step 8	Step 9	Step 10	Step 11
Plan the Lesson: select the topic organize the material complete the Planning Guide	*Peer Teach* the Lesson	*Analyze* the Lesson	*Microteach* and Analyze the Lesson	Further Classroom Practice: Adapting the Model

COMPONENT III ⌣_____⌣ COMPONENT IV

Figure 4. *"A Quick Overview and the Real Thing" Approach.*

whether the materials are used on an individualized or an instructor-directed basis. However, we do want to alert both instructors and trainees that alternatives are possible!

In the early years of our work with models of teaching, we used to spend weeks of instruction on a single model, going deeply into the theory, the issues in the particular field of knowledge, and our own and our students' personal philosophy of education. Besides believing that these considerations were important for our students, we believed they were necessary for performance mastery. What we have learned in recent years is that initial training in a model can take place in a relatively short period of time—perhaps four to five hours from introduction through peer teaching. Teachers are quick to sense their own problems and correct their behavior. In the first planning and peer teaching sessions, they note their points of confusion. For clarification, they go back to the training materials, to their instructor, or to their colleagues. After that, it is *practice* and *more practice*! What teachers need is time to absorb the ideas, to master the skills, and to try out the model with many topics and pupils.

Discussions of the philosophy of learning and teaching underlying particular models, and questions concerning specific difficulties in applying the model in the classroom are more valid and are dealt with more meaningfully following some degree of practice with the model. This is less true with experienced teachers than with preservice students. Even so, we strongly advise *everyone* to get into practice as soon as possible. It has been amazing to us how much a satisfactory learning experience alters initial questions, concerns, and doubts, regardless of previous experience.

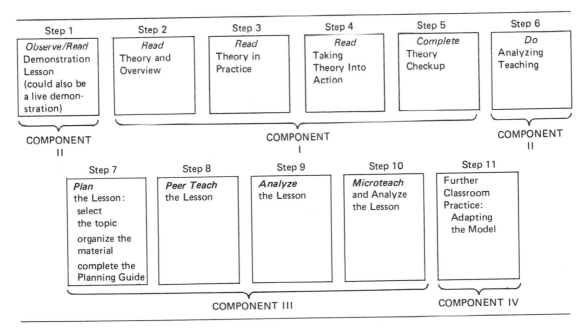

Figure 5. *"See the Real Thing First and Find Out Later" Approach.*

Everyone feels some insecurity in learning a new skill; however, we can almost promise that in four or five hours of earnest work, you will have enough initial competence in a model to, first, feel comfortable about your own strength and skill, and, second, to correct problem areas on your own and polish and shape the model in your own style!

This system is aimed almost exclusively at developing *initial clinical* (or performance) competence in a model. Although the overview materials discuss the philosophical and theoretical rationale for the model, we have not designed these materials to explore very many of the interesting issues surrounding these theories. We can imagine instructors supplementing practice in a model with readings and discussions on the philosophical, theoretical, or even empirical background and issues of a model.

Analysis of Teaching

One of the features of this training is the constant analysis of teaching that is included. We regard the analysis of teaching, not as an evaluation of teacher performance, but as a *feedback* tool, one that enables teachers to obtain reasonably objective information about their performance of the model of teaching and that provides guidelines for modifying teaching activities the next time.

In our training system, teaching analysis is introduced in the demonstration component. We have developed a Teaching Analysis Guide for each model that covers the major activities and principles of reaction for the phases in that model. The Guides usually consist of between fifteen and twenty questions and are first used in conjunction with the demonstration lessons. A more important use comes during peer teaching, when feedback is based on the Guide. A sample portion of a Teaching Guide appears in Figure 6.

The Guide is divided according to the phases of the model with a scale for analyzing important activities in each phase. Because every teaching situation is (and should be) sufficiently unpredictable that different teaching behaviors are necessary, we cannot be exact in measuring just how well any given teaching situation turns out; hence, the scale. We have grown more and more committed to the idea that once teachers have mastered the basics of a model, they should transpose and transform it, so that every model assumes a variety of forms. Thus, measuring competence and providing feedback should be flexible. There are standards of performance, but good performance appears in many forms. The Guide tells where to look for the essential competencies of each model and provides latitude so that different forms of competence can be identified.

Skills in Teaching

Two terms that you will come across in these books are *skill* (teaching skill) and *move*, by which we mean a particular teaching behavior that contributes to the effectiveness and uniqueness of that model. Asking a higher-order question, paraphrasing a student's comment, and summarizing the major points of a discussion are examples of teaching moves or skills. Sometimes a teaching skill is a single teacher comment or question, and sometimes it is a series of comments or questions.

During the course of a model or any thirty- or forty-minute learning activity,

PHASE TWO: Testing Concept Attainment

12. After the concept was agreed upon, did the teacher present additional exemplars and ask whether they contained the concept?	Thoroughly	Partially	Missing	Not Needed
13. Did the teacher ask the students to justify their answers?	Thoroughly	Partially	Missing	Not Needed
14. Were the students able to supply their own exemplars to fit the concept?	Thoroughly	Partially	Missing	Not Needed
15. Did the teacher ask the students to justify their exemplars by identifying the essential attributes?	Thoroughly	Partially	Missing	Not Needed

PHASE THREE: Analyzing Strategies

16. Did the teacher ask the students to describe the thinking processes they used in attaining the concept?	Thoroughly	Partially	Missing	Not Needed
17. Did the teacher ask the students to reflect on the role of attributes and concepts in their thinking strategies?	Thoroughly	Partially	Missing	Not Needed
18. Did the teacher ask the students to evaluate the effectiveness of their strategies?	Thoroughly	Partially	Missing	Not Needed

Figure 6. *Part of a Teaching Analysis Guide.*

the teacher (and students) exhibit hundreds of behaviors and many skills. Some models are dependent on how we master particular teacher skills. We have tried to identify and describe these skills. In addition to *interactive* teaching skills, we have identified critical *planning* skills. Some training approaches separate planning and teaching skills from teaching strategies. We prefer to introduce skills as part of the models and teach them in the context of the model, where the phases of activities provide guidelines as to when and how to use a particular skill.

WHAT IS IN THIS SYSTEM AND HOW TO USE IT

There are three books in this series. They cover description and understanding, demonstration, planning and peer teaching, and adaptation for models in the information processing, social, and personal families. Within each family, the models dealt with are:

Information Processing Family
      Concept Attainment Model(s)
      Inquiry Training Model
      Advance Organizer Model

Social Family
>   Jurisprudential Model
>   Simulation Model
>   Role Playing Model

Personal Family
>   Synectics Model
>   Nondirective Model

We repeat that these materials are designed to be used on a self-instructional basis, usually in a student-directed group with the instructor serving as a facilitator. We strongly urge that teachers share their learning of a model with one another. It's usually richer, more instructive, and more fun that way.

Component I:
Describing and Understanding the Model

The first of the four components of our training approach is Describing and Understanding the Model. This component consists of two readings and a Theory Checkup. The first reading (Theory and Overview) discusses the goals, assumptions, key ideas, and procedures (syntax) of the model. The second reading (Taking Theory Into Action) provides further discussion and illustration of the model's major concepts. Through short written exercises, you are given opportunities to apply these concepts and to identify any difficulties you may have. We have made a special effort to select the major ideas you will apply when you teach and to develop a strong training sequence for them. It is one thing to read about an idea in the overview and another to practice and apply it. We urge you to concentrate especially on this reading and to do so at the point in the training sequence that is the most appropriate for you.

Finally, the Theory Checkup enables you to check your understanding of the ideas discussed and illustrated in the three previous readings. The checkup is for your use only; it is not a test. If you did not grasp an item, you may want to reread the relevant pages in the readings. Some people may want to complete the Theory Checkup after the first reading; others may want to wait until they have finished the second reading. One way to view the checkup is as a guide to tell you what to concentrate on. It can also be viewed as a means of checking your understanding before going on to Components II and III. No doubt you will be better prepared for the Theory Checkup after you complete the second reading.

Component II: Viewing the Model

Component II (Viewing the Model) includes two learning activities. The first is reading the Teaching Analysis Guide and identifying any items that you do not understand. The second activity is reading the demonstration transcript. As you read the lesson, your attention is directed to the occurrence of the phases of the model. We suggest that you share your spontaneous reactions and comments with the group.

One thing to keep in mind is that there is no such thing as a "perfect" model.

There are always ways to enrich the lesson, or to improve a particular aspect. Besides, each of us have our preferred styles and expressions, which have nothing to do with the model per se. We have tried to select demonstrations that reveal the phases of the model and the major elements discussed in the text. Sometimes this does not happen, even in demonstration lessons. One of your jobs as an observer is to comment on those places in the lesson that may deviate (either by commission or omission) from your understanding of the model up to that point. Besides being critical, we'd like you to be attuned to the strengths of the lessons, the teacher moves that were particularly strong, the way the topic and material were designed for the model, and the way the lesson was organized for presentation. If there is time, you may want to read the model a second time, using the Teaching Analysis Guide as a format for analysis. Optional activities are included for use with audio tapes, where available, or with live demonstrations.

Component III: Planning and Peer Teaching

The activities in this component will guide you through the steps in planning a model lesson, which you will then peer teach to a small group of colleagues. The planning steps include topic selection, designing and organizing materials, and selecting behavioral objectives. Each step is discussed in terms of its unique features for the particular model you are studying. Special planning skills are taught in this part of the training program. A Planning Guide is provided to assist you in completing the various aspects of planning and to alert you to problem areas. Sample planning forms are provided for some of the models. In some cases, materials are provided from which to develop peer teaching lessons, in the event that you want to teach from them rather than use them as guides or suggestions. (Component IV also includes curriculum materials from which lessons may be planned.) We strongly urge you to select your own topics and prepare your own materials. This is one of the best ways to apply the ideas of the model and test your planning skills.

Peer teaching is just what the name suggests. It means that teachers practice teaching skills or models of teaching in groups, taking turns playing the role of the learners. Peer teaching accomplishes several things. First, it enables you to practice a new teaching strategy before you try it out with students. This gives you a chance to familiarize yourself with the structure of the model, to become more comfortable with it as you work it out in the classroom. It provides practice, not only in the actual teaching, but also in the planning for it. Translating material into new and unfamiliar models of teaching requires you to think differently about your teaching than you may have done before, and you need practice to become comfortable with the new approaches and moves.

A second benefit of peer teaching is that, because you do it with one another, you gain the kinds of feedback that fellow professional teachers can give. If a half-dozen teachers are practicing the same model and take turns teaching it, you can coach one another. Often, when you are in the role of student you see things that you do not see when you are in the role of teacher. Thus, you can avail yourselves of one another's professional opinion and coaching.

Third, peer teaching gets people working together to improve their classroom performance. It increases dialogue about the dynamics of teaching, gives a language for discussing the problems of teaching, and provides a warm and enriching exper-

VERNON REGIONAL
JUNIOR COLLEGE LIBRARY

ience in itself. Also, when you teach with others, you add their ideas to your own. When you see four or five people teaching the same model that you are trying to learn, you are exposed to new ideas about variations on that model, and so your learning is richer.

Being a Teacher in Peer Teaching. When you plan a lesson for your peers, you should plan one for their level. That is, you should select material that will be stimulating for your colleagues. This does not mean that you cannot select material that is also appropriate for children. Many concepts in mathematics, science, social science, and literature are fun for adults to learn again, especially when you see them highlighted by a fresh approach. Because of the constraints of time, most peer teaching lessons have to be relatively short—they are simulations of the kind of teaching we do with children. Make sure that there is enough time both to be taught and to provide feedback. Talk through your planning before beginning the model, describe the materials you are going to use, and be certain that everyone is oriented to the lesson.

Being a Learner in Peer Teaching. As learners in peer teaching, you should be yourselves. The best way to kill peer teaching is to "act the role of the child." You should permit yourselves to be engaged by your fellow teachers as you would if they were teaching a course or workshop, or engaging in any other kind of learning activity. However, not only are you learners to the teacher, but you are also learning yourselves, and you need to be in a position to provide feedback and coaching to the one who teaches. Thus, you need to familiarize yourselves thoroughly with the model before you begin, and perhaps to have copies of the Teaching Analysis Guide so that you can analyze the teaching as it goes along, in preparation for the feedback session.

Being an Observer in Peer Teaching. In a group of five or six, it is wise for one person to be the teacher, three or four to be the learners, and one person simply to assume the role of observer. The observer uses the Teaching Guide and should be in charge of the feedback session, helping the teacher analyze the teaching process and drawing from the learners their opinions and insights about what went on. In most cases the observer becomes the leader of the post-mortem.

Organizing the Peer Teaching. It is our experience that the most comfortable size for a peer teaching group is between five and seven. With that size, there are enough people to play the role of learner, someone is available to be observer, and the group is large enough to provide diverse opinions, yet small enough to conduct its business in a relatively short period of time. Optimally, the six or seven people are all studying the same model of teaching, learning the theory, viewing the demonstrations, and then taking turns as teachers in a series of peer teaching activities. If this is the case, then before each individual tries out the teaching with children, she or he will have taught the model at least once and seen it taught a half-dozen times. By the end of that period of time, they should all begin to feel extremely comfortable with the model and well aware of the role of the learner. One of the most artful aspects of learning the new model of teaching is to "feel" what the learners feel when they are introduced to the model. The more we can anticipate how children will react, the more we can prepare ourselves for their reactions and ease their way into the new role required by the model.

Microteaching. The last activity in the planning and peer teaching component is to teach the lesson to a small group of students—what we call microteaching. We

COMPONENT I: DESCRIBING AND UNDERSTANDING THE MODEL

1. The order in which the readings should be covered.
2. How much, if any, discussion to have about the material in Component I.

COMPONENT II: VIEWING THE MODEL

1. Reading/observing the model individually *or* as a group.
2. Whether to observe a live demonstration, read the demonstration transcript, or hear a taped lesson.
3. Whether to analyze the demonstration lesson using the Teaching Analysis Guide, and if so, how to organize groups to do this.
4. Whether to see several live demonstrations in addition to the demonstration transcript.

COMPONENT III: PLANNING AND PEER TEACHING

1. Allow time for planning; provide feedback.
2. Organize and schedule small groups for peer teaching.
3. Arrange for microteaching. If possible, video-tape or audio-tape the lesson. Obtain the equipment.
4. Analyze the microteaching lesson, alone or with someone. Obtain equipment, either video tape or audio tape.

COMPONENT IV: ADAPTING THE MODEL

1. Whether a group discussion and/or learning activity should be developed around this component.

Figure 7. *A Summary of Organizational Decisions for the Trainee and/or Instructor.*

recommend that you make an audio tape of your microteaching session, so that alone, or with colleagues, you can review the lesson, using the Teaching Analysis Guide.

Component IV: Adapting the Model

The major purpose of this component is to present ways of adapting the model for long-term use in the classroom. We discuss how to incorporate existing curriculum materials by including samples of elementary and secondary texts and showing how the models can provide new approaches to them. We also discuss long-term goals with respect to the development of pupil skills and teacher skills. In addition, we offer a few ideas we may have for "stretching the model" or distilling its essence. In other words, we share our notions about moving away from sequential phases and toward applying elements of the model in a dynamic, ongoing instructional context. The third section in this component covers suggestions for combining the model with other models of teaching.

The major organizational decisions that trainees and/or instructors will need to anticipate during training are summarized in Figure 7.

Tips to the Instructor:
Some Ways to Simplify the Training System

1. Provide more direct instruction and less self-directed reading. For example, in Component I (Describing and Understanding the Model), assign the first reading (Theory and Overview) for the students to read on their own. Plan to teach the ideas in the second reading (Taking Theory into Action) in a lecture-recitation session, using the materials and exercises from the section.
2. Review the syntax of the models at the different stages of instruction.
3. Augment the demonstration transcript with a live demonstration of your own. This will give the students an opportunity to experience the model directly as a learner before planning and peer teaching.

THE MODELS IN THIS BOOK

The social family of models of teaching emphasizes *group process*. The point of view is that the students are a community who need to work together in order to develop themselves as social beings as well as to master academic material. The dynamics of the group enhance the development of the individuals. Knowledge is constructed out of the rubbing together of a variety of minds and emotions around any given situation. Thus, in the study of science, the social models of teaching postulate that students work together to thrash out their different perceptions of problems and generate and test alternative hypotheses; in this way, the process of the group becomes as important as the mastery of the material, but the process is used to enhance the material itself. At the same time, the group learns to work as a unit. Individuals learn to maintain their points of view in the social milieu and to use the viewpoints of others to help clarify their own positions and to carry out solutions to the problems. The teacher's role is at first to lead the group. But increasingly, as the group life takes over, the teacher helps members of the group come to leadership responsibility and take over the roles formerly played by the teacher.

In this volume, we present three group-based models of teaching. One of these is the Role Playing Model, a strategy developed by Fannie and George Shaftel to help students work together, clarify their values, develop human relations skills, and learn to manage problem situations in group and intergroup relations. A second model is the Jurisprudential Model, which is developed for older children and helps them identify the social values underlying important public policy issues in social relations, to develop strategies for clarifying positions on social issues, and to develop policies for their own behavior and that of others in the many kinds of conflict situations that exist in our complex society. The third model, the Simulation Model, brings into the classroom simulations of the social reality that lies outside and helps students play active roles as they approach problems and try to master skills.

Students equipped with the Role Playing Model will increase their ability to approach personal problems by clarifying values, gaining greater understanding of the situation, and developing the skills for negotiating important issues with others. From the Jurisprudential Model they will learn how to manage themselves in a group facing important kinds of conflict, clarify the value stances underlying those conflicts, and learn to approach their own behavior from a social policy point of view. From the Simulation Model they will learn to face problems in the larger world—prejudice, inner-group problems, problems of energy, transportation, communication, economics, and politics.

This family of models should increase the capacity of students to relate to one another effectively, to define and attack problems, to negotiate with one another in school, and in later life to negotiate approaches to the problems that are inherent in any social relation. At the same time, these models help students master subject matter. Simulation is applicable over a wide range of issues. The Role Playing and the Jurisprudential Models are especially effective for the social studies but also deal with the value issues in science, mathematics, literature, and the other important areas of the curriculum.

The Role Playing and Simulation Models may be used with elementary school children, especially at the upper elementary levels. The Jurisprudential Model is reserved for older children. Role Playing and Simulation are both experience-based strategies; that is, the content of learning grows out of a here-and-now situation that is experienced directly in the classroom. Role Playing is useful for teaching concepts and other academic material, as well as for exploring values and feelings. The Jurisprudential Model, in helping students develop stances on public policy issues, also helps them clarify their social values. Simulation is especially suitable to teach content and at the same time to explore the participants' reactions.

As we approach these models, it is important to remember that the teacher's role changes to that of group leader. He or she uses these models to help develop the community of students into an effective organization. At the same time, the teacher gradually withdraws from a leadership role and the students assume increasing leadership in the conduct of activities. This is not to say that the teacher does not continue to feed problems into the process or expose the students to important substantive areas. However, the purpose of the social models is to teach students to work together as a group and to increasingly control their activities. The teacher's task is thus to teach the students how to carry out the models themselves—how to approach problems, develop hypotheses and work together to check them out, thereby building an effective *esprit de corps*.

ROLE PLAYING
MODEL

SCENARIO FOR ROLE PLAYING

We are in a classroom in East Los Angeles, California. The students have returned to the classroom from a recess period. They are complaining excitedly to one another. Mr. Williams, the teacher, asks what the matter is and they all start in at once, discussing a series of difficulties that apparently started at the beginning of the recess period and continued to its end. Apparently, two of the students began to squabble about who was to take the sports equipment outside. Then all of the students squabbled about what game to play. Next, there was an argument about choosing sides for the games. This included a dispute over whether the girls should be included with the boys, or whether they should play separately. The class finally began to play volleyball, but very shortly there was a dispute over a line call and the game never took place.

At first, Mr. Williams displayed his displeasure toward the class. He was angry, not simply over the incident, but because these arguments were a repetition of ones that had been going on from the beginning of the year. At last he said, "OK, we really have to face this problem. You must be as tired of it as I am, and we really are not acting maturely. So we are going to use a technique that we have been using to discuss family problems to approach our own problems right here in this classroom. That is, we're going to use role playing. What I want you to do is to divide into groups now, and try to identify the types of problems that we've been having. Just take today, for example, and outline the kind of problem situations that got us into the fix we're in."

The students began with the argument over taking the sports equipment outside, and then outlined other arguments. Each of these was a typical situation that people face all the time and must learn to take a stand on. After the separate groups of students had made their lists of problems, Mr. Williams appointed one of the students to lead a discussion in which each group reported the kinds of problem situations that had come up; the groups agreed on a half-dozen problems that had consistently bothered the class.

The students then grouped the problems according to type. One type concerned the division of labor. A second problem was deciding principles for selecting teams. A third problem was resolving disputes over the particulars of games such as whether balls had been hit out of bounds, whether players were out or safe, and so on. Mr. Williams then assigned one type of problem to each group and asked them to describe situations in which the problems came up. When they had done this, the class voted on which type of problem to start with. The first problem they selected was disputes over rules, and the actual problem situation they selected was the volleyball game in which the dispute over a line call had occurred.

Together, the class talked about how the problem situation develops. It begins when a ball is hit close to the boundary line; one team believes it is in and the other believes it is out of bounds. The students then argue with one another, and the argument develops until the game cannot continue.

Several students were selected to enact the situation. Others gathered around and were assigned to observe particular aspects of the role playing that followed. Some students were to look for the particulars of how the argument developed. Some were to study one role player and others another, to determine how they handled the situation.

The enactment was spirited. The students selected as role players those who had been on opposite sides during the game, and they became as involved in the argument during the role playing as they had during the actual situation. Finally, they were standing in the middle of the room shouting at one another. At this point, Mr. Williams called, "Time!" and asked the students to describe what had gone on.

Everyone was anxious to talk. The discussion gradually focused on the fact that the attitude of the participants prevented any kind of resolution of the problem. No one was listening to the other person. And no one was dealing with the problem of how to resolve honest disputes. Finally, Mr. Williams asked the students to suggest other ways that people could behave in this kind of conflict situation. The students suggested various ways. Some suggested that you should give in gracefully. But other students objected that if you believe you are right, that is not an easy thing to do. Finally, the students identified an important question to focus on: "How can we develop a policy about who should make calls, and how should others feel about those calls? They decided to reenact the scene by having all the participants assume that the defensive team should make calls only when they saw clear evidence that a ball was out and the other team was objecting that they had not seen the evidence.

Once again the enactment took place. This time, the players attempted to follow the policy that the defensive team had the right to make the call but the offensive team had the right to object to a call. Once again, the enactment resulted in a shouting match; however, after it was over, the students who had watched the enactment pointed out that the role players had not behaved as if there was a resolution of the situation. They recognized that if there were to be games, there had to be agreement about who could make calls and a certain amount of trust on both sides.

They decided to try a third enactment, this time with two new role players inserted into the situation whose job it was to referee disputes. The introduction of referees into the situation completely changed the third enactment. The referees insisted that the other players pay attention to them, which they did not want to do. In "debriefing" this enactment, the students pointed out that there had to be some kind of system that would ensure reasonable order and the resolution of disputes. The students also agreed that as things stood, they probably were unable to resolve disputes without including a referee of some sort, but that no referee would be effective unless the students agreed to listen to the referees and let their decisions be final. They finally decided that in future games, two students would be referees. Those students would not be chosen by any side prior to the game; their function would be to arbitrate and to make all the calls relevant to the rules of the game and their decisions would be final. The students agreed that they would try that system and see how it worked.

The next day Mr. Williams opened up the next issue, and the students repeated this process. The exploration of other areas of dispute continued over the next few weeks. At first, many of the notions that were clarified were simply practical ones about how to solve specific problems. Gradually, however, Mr. Williams directed the discussion to a consideration of the basic values to be considered in order for the group to make decisions on governing individual behavior. The students began to see the problems of communal living, and they developed policies for governing their own behavior, as individuals and as a group. They also began to develop skills in negotiating. The students who were locked in conflict gradually learned that if they behaved in a slightly different way, this often helped others to also behave in a different way, and problems became easier to solve.

The students were practicing Role Playing, a model of teaching developed by Fannie and George Shaftel. Although Mr. Williams's class was having difficulties in one area, they had learned the Role Playing strategy and how to use it, not only to solve specific problems but as a general strategy that they could use to approach a variety of human relations conflict- situations, clarify their social values, and develop general skills for coping with the problems of living together in a complex society.

OUTLINE OF ACTIVITIES FOR THE ROLE PLAYING MODEL

Objectives	Materials	Activity
COMPONENT I: DESCRIBING AND UNDERSTANDING THE MODEL		
1. To recognize the goals, assumptions, and procedures of the Role Playing Model.	Theory and Overview	Reading
2. To gain a sense of the model in action.	Theory in Practice	Reading
3. To identify and develop alternative focuses for Role Playing sessions.	Taking Theory Into Action	Reading/Writing
4. To evaluate your understanding of the Role Playing Model.	Theory Checkup	Writing
COMPONENT II: VIEWING THE MODEL		
1. To become familiar with the Teaching Analysis Guide and identify items you do not understand.	Teaching Analysis Guide	Reading
2. To identify phases of the model and comment on the lesson.	Demonstration Transcript	Reading/Writing/ Discussion
3. **Option:** To apply the Teaching Analysis Guide to other demonstration lessons.	Live demonstration or video-tape/Teaching Analysis Guide	Viewing/Group or Individual Analysis
COMPONENT III: PLANNING AND PEER TEACHING		
1. To select the problem situation.	Selecting the Problem Situation	Reading/Writing
2. To develop and organize materials for the lesson.	Organizing the Materials for Role Playing	Reading/Writing
3. To select a focus for the problem situation and identify its themes and alternative solutions.	Analyzing the Problem and Identifying the Focus	Reading/Writing
4. To construct behavioral objectives for the peer teaching and micro-teaching lesson(s).	Determining Educational Objectives	Reading/Writing
5. To complete the Planning Guide for the Role Playing Model.	Planning Guide	Writing
6. To peer teach the Role Playing Model.	5 or 6 peers, problem situation	Teaching
7. To analyze the Role Playing lesson using the Teaching Analysis Guide.	Teaching Analysis Guide	Writing/Group Discussion/Individual Analysis

OUTLINE OF ACTIVITIES FOR THE ROLE PLAYING MODEL

8. To phrase questions and moves that initiate Role Playing activities.	Initiating the Activities in the Role Playing Model	Reading
9. **Optional:** To teach the Role Playing Model to a small group of students.	Small group of students; problem-statement; audio-cassette recorder; cassette	Teaching/Taping
10. To analyze the microteaching lesson.	Teaching Analysis Guide	Listening to audio recording and analyzing the lesson (by self or in group)

COMPONENT IV: ADAPTING THE MODEL

1. Adapting Role Playing in the classroom.	Combining Role Playing with Other Models of Teaching	Reading

Component I

DESCRIBING
AND UNDERSTANDING
THE MODEL

THEORY AND OVERVIEW

In Role Playing, students explore human relations problems by enacting problem situations and then discussing the enactments. The discussions and enactments can focus on several aspects of human behavior. Together, students can explore feelings, attitudes, values, and problem-solving strategies. Several individuals have experimented with role playing; their treatments of the strategy are remarkably similar. The version we will explore here was formulated by Fannie and George Shaftel.[1] We have also incorporated ideas from the work of Mark Chesler and Robert Fox.[2]

Role Playing as a model of teaching has roots in both the personal and social dimensions of education. It belongs in the personal dimension because it attempts to help individuals find personal meaning within their social world and resolve personal dilemmas with the assistance of the social group. It also belongs in the social dimension because it allows groups of individuals to work together to analyze

[1] Fannie Shaftel and George Shaftel, *Role-Playing for Social Values: Decision-Making in the Social Studies* (Englewood Cliffs, N J.: Prentice-Hall, 1967).
[2] Mark Chesler and Robert Fox, *Role-Playing Methods in the Classroom* (Chicago: Science Research Associates, 1966).

social situations, especially interpersonal problem situations, and to develop decent and democratic ways of coping with these situations. We have chosen to place Role Playing in the social family of models because the social group plays such an indispensable role in human development and because of the unique opportunity that Role Playing offers for resolving interpersonal and social dilemmas.

Goals and Assumptions

On its simplest level, role playing is a general process in which problems are dealt with through action; a problem is delineated, acted out, and discussed. Some students are role players and some are observers. At another level, group members become deeply involved and experience many of the same emotional reactions that they have in similar true-life situations. In a sense, well-done role playing becomes a part of life. A person puts himself or herself in the position of another person and then tries to interact with others who are playing roles. Empathy, sympathy, anger, and affection are all generated during the interaction. The emotional content as well as the words and the actions become part of the later analysis. When the situation is finished, even the observers are involved enough to want to know why the one person reached one decision and the other another, what the sources of resistance were, and whether there were other ways this kind of situation could have been approached.

The essence of role playing is the involvement of participants and observers in a real problem situation and the desire for resolution and understanding that this involvement engenders. The role playing process provides a live sample of human behavior that serves as a vehicle for students to: (1) explore their feelings, (2) gain insights into their attitudes, values, and perceptions, (3) develop their problem-solving skills and attitudes, and (4) explore subject matter in varied ways.

These educational goals reflect several assumptions about the learning process in role playing. First, role playing implicitly advocates an experience-based learning situation in which the "here and now" becomes the content of instruction. The model assumes that it is possible to create authentic analogies to real-life problem situations and that through these re-creations students can "sample" life. Thus, the here and now that is created in the enactment draws out genuine emotional responses and behaviors that the students typically experience and engage in.

A related assumption is that role playing can bring feelings to the surface, feelings that students can perhaps release and certainly recognize. The release of feeling is sometimes called *catharsis*. It is an especially important goal when role playing is used in therapeutic settings in a variation known as psychodrama. Educational uses of role playing, in contrast with therapeutic uses, are oriented to the generation and recognition of feelings. In part, this is because the Shaftels' version of role playing places as much emphasis on the intellectual as on the emotional content; analysis and discussion of the enactment are as important as the enactment itself. Thus, the ability to recognize and talk about feelings is an important goal of role playing. We are concerned that students recognize and understand their feelings and see how their feelings influence their behavior. In psychodrama, the enactment and its emotional and behavioral confrontations are the central activity; discussion and analysis are minimal.

Another assumption, not unlike an assumption of the Synectics models, is that emotions and ideas can be brought to consciousness and enhanced by the group. Problem solving is not stifled by the activity of an overt, public situation.

Furthermore, an expert is not necessary to solve dilemmas or to teach everything. Instead, the collective reactions of the peer group can bring out new ideas and provide directions for growth and change. The model deemphasizes the traditional role of teacher and encourages listening and learning from one's colleagues.

A final assumption is that covert psychological processes involving our own attitudes, values, and belief system can be brought to consciousness by combining spontaneous enactment with analysis. Furthermore, we can gain some measure of control over our belief system if we recognize our values and attitudes and test them against the reality and views of others and against the consequences of our beliefs (what beliefs imply for our lives and those of others.) After we have done this, we are in a position to evaluate our attitudes and values and either hold on to or revise them.

The Concept of Role

Each of us has a unique manner of relating to people, situations, and objects. We may feel that most people are dishonest and cannot be trusted. Or we may feel that everyone is interesting, and we eagerly look forward to all interpersonal situations where we can meet new people. We also evaluate and behave in consistent ways toward ourselves. We may see ourself as powerful and smart, or perhaps afraid and stupid. These feelings about people and situations and about ourselves influence our behavior and determine how we will respond in various situations. Some of us respond with aggressive and hostile behavior, playing the part of a bully. Others withdraw and remain alone, playing the part of a shy or sulking person.

These parts we play are called *roles*. A role is "a patterned sequence of feelings, words and actions. . . .it is a unique and accustomed manner of relating to others."[3] Unless we are looking for them, it is sometimes hard to perceive consistencies and patterns in behavior. But they are usually there. Terms such as friendly, bully, snotty, know-it-all, and grouch are convenient handles for describing characteristic responses or roles.

The roles we play are determined over many years and by several factors. The kinds of people we happen to meet determine our general feelings about people. How those people act toward us and how we perceive their feelings toward us influence the feelings we have about ourselves. The rules of our particular culture and institutions are part of determining which roles we assume and how we play them.

Some of the roles we have assumed do not make us happy. We don't feel good about them. We also misperceive the attitudes and feelings of others because we do not recognize *their* role and *why* they play that role the way they do. Two people can behave in very different ways but share the same feelings. They can desire the same goals, but if their behaviors are misperceived by others, they may not attain those goals.

For a clear understanding of ourselves and of others, it is extremely important that we be conscious of our own and other roles and aware of how they are played. To do this, we must be able to put ourselves in another's place, and to experience as much as possible that person's thoughts and feelings. If we are able to perceive another's role, we can accurately interpret social events and interactions. Role playing is a vehicle that forces us to take the role of others.

[3] *Ibid.,* pp. 8, 5.

The concept of role is one of the central theoretical underpinnings of the Role Playing Model. It is also a major goal. We must teach students how to use the concept of role, how to recognize different roles, and how to think of their own and other's behavior in terms of roles. At the same time, there are many other aspects to this model and many levels of analysis. To some extent, they compete with one another. For example the content of the problem, the solutions to the problem, the feelings of the role players, and the acting itself all serve to involve students in the role play. Therefore, in order to be a salient part of the role playing experience, the concept of role must be interwoven with and kept in the fore throughout all the role playing activities. It also helps if prior to using the model, students have been taught this concept directly.

Role Playing and the Curriculum

There are two basic reasons why a teacher might decide to use role playing with a group of children. One is to begin a program of social education in which a role playing situation forms much of the material to be discussed and analyzed; for this purpose, a particular kind of problem story might be selected. The second reason is to help a group of children deal with an immediate human relations problem; role playing can open up a problem area to the students' inquiry and help them solve the problem. The first situation is a systematic, curricular use of role playing in a program of social education, whereas the second is an incidental use of role playing for counseling and management purposes.

Several types of social problems are amenable to exploration with the aid of this model, including:

1. *Interpersonal conflicts.* A major use of role playing is to reveal conflicts between people so that students can discover techniques for overcoming them.

2. *Intergroup relations.* Interpersonal problems arising from ethnic and racial stereotyping or from heavy-handed, authoritarian beliefs can also be explored through role playing. These problems involve conflict, but the conflict may not be apparent. Role playing situations of this type might be used to uncover stereotypes and prejudices or to encourage acceptance of the deviant.

3. *Individual dilemmas.* These arise when a person is caught between two contrasting values or between his or her own interests and the interests of others. This kind of problem is particularly difficult for young children to deal with, since their moral judgment is still relatively egocentric. Some of the most delicate and difficult uses of role playing make this dilemma accessible to the child and help her understand why it occurs and what she can do about it. Individual dilemmas that might be explored are ones in which a person is caught between the demands of her peer group and those of her parents, or between the pressures of the group and her own preferences.

4. *Historical or contemporary problems.* These include critical situations, past or present, in which policy makers, judges, political leaders, or statesmen had to confront a problem or person and make a decision.

Regardless of the particular type of social problem, student discussion will focus naturally on the aspects of the situation that seem important to them. The students may concentrate on the feelings that are being expressed, the attitudes and values of the role players as seen through their words and actions, the problem solution, or the consequences of behavior. It is possible for the teacher to emphasize any or all of these areas in the enactments and discussions. In-depth curriculum sequences can be based on or built around each of the following focuses:

exploration of feelings
exploration of attitudes, values, and perceptions
development of problem-solving attitudes and skills
subject-matter exploration

We prefer to view these as alternative focuses around which clusters of educational objectives are developed. For example, the development of problem-solving attitudes and skills may include openness to solution, ability to identify the problem, ability to generate alternative solutions, acquisition of new behaviors, making of decisions, and other objectives. It is our experience that when teacher and student discussion tries to touch upon all possible areas, the yield from the learning experience is minimized. Consequently, we advocate selecting one major focus, or possibly two, for a single role playing session. An important function of the teacher, then, is to select and maintain the focus throughout the role playing activities.

Role Playing as a Model of Teaching

The benefits of role playing depend on the quality of the enactment and especially on the analysis of it that follows. They depend also on the students' perception of the role play as similar to a real-life situation. A sincere involvement in the roles is essential if the experience is to be meaningful. Children do not necessarily engage effectively in role playing or role analysis the first time they try it. Many have to learn to engage in role playing in a sincere way so that the content generated can be analyzed seriously. Chesler and Fox suggest pantomimic exercises as a way of freeing inexperienced students.[4] Role playing is not likely to be successful if the teacher simply suggests it to the students, tosses out a problem situation, persuades a few children to act it out, and then conducts a discussion about the enactment.

The Shaftels suggest that the role playing activity consist of nine steps:

1. Warm up the group.
2. Select participants.
3. Prepare observers.
4. Set the stage.
5. Enact.
6. Discuss and evaluate.
7. Reenact.
8. Discuss and evaluate.
9. Share experiences and generalize.

[4] *Ibid.*, pp. 64-66.

Each of these steps or phases has a specific purpose that contributes to the richness and focus of the learning activity. Together, they ensure that a line of thinking is pursued throughout the complex of activities, that students are prepared in their roles, that goals for the role play are identified, and that the discussion afterwards is not simply a collection of diffuse reactions, though these are important too. Figure 1 summarizes the phases and activities of the model, which are then discussed and illustrated in the remainder of this section.

Phases	Activity
1. Warm up the group.	Identify or introduce problem. Make problem explicit. Interpret problem story, explore issues. Explain role playing.
2. Select participants.	Analyze roles. Choose role players.
3. Set the stage.	Set line of action. Restate roles. Get inside problem situation.
4. Prepare the observers.	Decide what to look for. Assign observation tasks.
5. Enact.	Begin role play. Maintain role play. Break role play.
6. Discuss and evaluate.	Review action of role play (events, positions, realism). Discuss major focus. Develop next enactment.
7. Reenact.	Play revised roles, suggest next steps or behavioral alternatives.
8. Discuss and evaluate.	As in Phase Six.
9. Share experiences and generalize.	Relate problem situation to real experience and current problems. Explore general principles of behavior.

Figure 1. *Phases and Activities in Role Playing. (Based on Fannie and George Shaftel's* Role Playing for Social Values, *Englewood Cliffs: Prentice-Hall, Inc., 1967.)*

Phase One: Warm Up the Group

The first step involves introducing students to a problem so that they recognize it as a problem that everyone needs to learn to deal with. The warm up can begin, for example, by identifying a problem within the group:

Teacher: Do you remember the other day we had a discussion about Janey's lunch money? Because she had put her money in her pocket and had not given it to me when she came into the room, it was lost.

We had quite a talk about finding money: whether to keep it or turn it in. Sometimes it's not easy to decide what to do. Do you ever have times when you just don't know what to do?

The teacher sensitizes the group to a problem and creates a climate of acceptance, so that students feel that all views, feelings, and behaviors can be explored without retribution.

The second part of the warm-up is to express the problem vividly through examples. These may come from student descriptions of imaginary or real situations that express the problem, or from situations selected by the teacher and illustrated by a film, television show, problem story, or some other means.

In *Role-Playing for Social Values*, the Shaftels provide a large selection of problem stories to be read to the class. Each story stops when a dilemma has become apparent. The Shaftels feel that problem stories have several advantages. They focus on a particular problem and yet ensure that the children will be able to disassociate themselves from the problem enough to face it. Incidents that students have experienced in their lives or that the group has experienced as a whole, though visually and emotionally involving, can cause considerable stress and therefore be very difficult to analyze. Another advantage of problem stories is that they are dramatic and make role playing relatively easy to initiate. The burden of involving the children in the activity is lightened.

The last part of the warm-up is to ask questions that make the children think about and predict the outcome of the story: "How might the story end?" "What is Sam's problem and what can he do about it?" The teacher in the illustration above handled this step like this:

Teacher: I would like to read you a story this afternoon about a boy who found himself in just such a spot. His parents wanted him to do one thing, but his gang insisted he do something else. Trying to please everybody, he got himself into difficulty. This will be one of those problem stories which stop, but are not finished.

Pupil: Like the one we did last week?

Teacher: Yes.

Pupil: Oh! But can't you give us one with an ending?

Teacher: When you get into a jam, does someone always come along and tell you how your problems will end?

Pupil: Oh, no! Not very often.

Teacher: In life, we usually have to make our own endings—we have to solve our problems ourselves. That's why I'm reading you these problem stories—so that we can *practice* endings, trying out many different ones to see which works the best for us. As I read this story, you might be thinking of what you would do if you were in Tommy Haines's place.

The story is about a boy caught between his father's views and those of his club. He has committed himself financially to a club project his father does not approve of and would not support. Tommy does not have the money and resorts to somewhat devious means of getting it. The problem centers on Tommy's opportunity to clear the debt with his gang. He delivers a package for the druggist and is overpaid five dollars—enough to clear the debt. Tommy stands outside the customer's door, trying to decide whether to return or keep the money. After reading the story, the teacher focuses the discussion on what might happen next, thus preparing for different enactments of the situation:

Teacher: What do you think Tommy will do?

Pupil: I think he'll keep the money.

Teacher: Yes?. . .

Pupil: Because he needs to pay the club.

Pupil: Oh no he won't. He'll get found out, and he knows it.

Phase Two: Select Participants

The children and the teacher describe the various characters—what they are like, how they feel, and what kind of things they might do. The children are then asked to volunteer to role play, or they may ask for a particular role. The Shaftels caution teachers not to assign a role to a child who has been suggested for it, because the person making the suggestion may be stereotyping the child or putting him in an awkward situation. A person must want to play a role or should be the one to suggest himself for it. Although she takes into account the children's preferences, the teacher should exercise some control in the situation.

The teacher can use several criteria for selecting a child for a role. Roles can be assigned to those children who appear to be involved in the problem so that they identify with a specific role, those who express an attitude that needs to be explored, those who will best typify the problem, or those who should learn to identify with the role or place themselves in another person's position. The Shaftels caution the teacher to avoid selecting children who would give "adult-oriented, socially acceptable" interpretations to the role, because such a quick and superficial resolution of the problem dampens discussion and the exploration of the basic issues.[5]

In our illustration, the teacher asks a student to be Tommy and then asks the student what roles need to be filled. He answers that he'll need someone to be the customer and some students to be the gang. The teacher asks several children to fill these roles.

Phase Three: Set the Stage

In this step, the role players plan what they are going to do but do not prepare any specific dialogue. They simply sketch the setting and perhaps one person's line of action. The teacher may help set the stage by asking the students a few simple questions about where the enactment is taking place, what it is like, and so on. It is necessary only that a simple line of action be identified and a general

[5] Shaftel and Shaftel, *Role-Playing for Social Values*, p. 67.

setting clarified so that participants feel enough security in the roles to begin to act.

In our illustration, the setting is arranged so that one corner of the classroom becomes the school where the gang is waiting for Tommy to bring the money; in another corner, a chair is used to represent the door of the customer's house. The teacher asks the boy playing Tommy where in the action he wants to begin, and the boy decides to start with the scene where he is delivering the packages.

Phase Four: Prepare the Observers

It is important that the observers become actively involved so that the entire group experiences the enactment and can later analyze the play. The Shaftels suggest that the teacher involve observers in the role play by assigning them tasks, such as evaluating the reality of the role playing, commenting on the effectiveness and the sequences of the role players' behavior, and defining the feelings and ways of thinking of the persons being portrayed. The observers should determine what the role players are trying to accomplish, what actions the role players took that were helpful or not helpful, and what alternative experiences might have been enacted. Or they can watch one particular role in order to define the feelings of that person. The observers should understand that there will be more than one enactment in most cases and that, therefore, if they would have acted out a certain role in a different way, they may get a chance to do so.

In our illustration, the teacher prepares the observers as follows:

Teacher: Now, you people, as you watch, consider whether you think Jerry's way of ending the story could really happen. How will people feel? You may want to think of what will happen next. Perhaps you'll have different ideas about it; and when Jerry's finished, and we've talked about it, we can try your ideas.[6]

Phase Five: Enact

At this point, the role players enact the situation. They assume the roles and "live" the situation spontaneously, responding realistically to one another. The role playing is not expected to be a smooth dramatization, however. Nor is it expected that each role player will always know how to respond. This is part of life, as well as part of feeling the role. A person may have a general idea of what to say or do but not be able to enact it when the time comes. The action now depends on the children and emerges according to what happens in the situation. This is why the previous steps are so important.

The Shaftels suggest that enactments be short. The teacher should allow the enactment to run only until the proposed behavior is clear, a character has developed, a behavioral skill has been practiced, an impasse is reached, or the action has expressed its viewpoint or idea. She can then ask for a reenactment of this scene if the follow-up discussion reveals a lack of understanding on the part of the students about the events or roles.

The purpose of the first enactment is simply to establish events and roles, which in later enactments can be probed, analyzed, and reworked. During the initial enactment, the players of the major role can be changed in order to demon-

---

[6] *Ibid.*, p. 69.

strate variety of the role and to generate more data for discussion. In our illustration, the boy playing Tommy chooses not to tell the customer that he has overpaid.

Phase Six: Discuss and Evaluate

If the problem was an important one and the participants and the observers were involved, then the discussion will probably begin spontaneously. At first, the discussion may focus on different interpretations of the portrayal and on disagreements over how the roles should have been carried out. Some people may think that individuals would not act the way they were portrayed. More important than these interpretations, however, are the consequences of the action and the motivations of an actor. To prepare for the next step, a teacher should focus the discussion on both of these aspects.

To help the observer think with the role players, the teacher can ask questions such as, "How do you suppose John felt when he said that?" The discussion will probably turn to alternatives, both within the roles and within the total pattern of the situation. When it does, the stage is set for further enactments, in which role players change their roles and interpretations, or play the roles in a different way.

In our illustration, the discussion of the first enactment went like this:

Teacher: Well, Jerry has given us one solution. What do you think of it?

Pupil: Uh-uh! It won't work!

Jerry: Why not?

Pupil: That man is going to remember how much money he had. He'll phone the druggist about it.

Jerry: So what? He can't prove anything on me. I'll just say he didn't overpay me.

Pupil: You'll lose your job.

Jerry: When they can't prove it?

Pupil: Yes, even if they can't prove it!

Teacher: Why do you think so, John?

Pupil: Because the druggist has to be on the side of his customer. He can fire Tommy and hire another boy. But he doesn't want his customers mad at him.

Pupil: He's going to feel pretty sick inside, if he keeps the money.

Teacher: What do you mean?

Pupil: Well, it bothers you when you know you've done something wrong.

Teacher: Do you have any other way to solve this problem?

Pupil: Yes. Tommy should knock on the door and tell the customer about being overpaid. Maybe the man'll let Tommy keep the money.

Teacher: All right, let's try it your way, Dick.[7]

[7]*Ibid.,* p. 71.

Phase Seven: Reenact

The reenactment may take place many times. The students and the teacher can share new interpretations of roles and decide whether new individuals should play them. The activity alternates between discussion and acting. As much as possible, the new enactments should explore new possibilities for causes and effects. For example, one role may be changed so that everyone can observe how that change causes another role player to behave. Or at the critical point in the enactment, the participants may try to behave in a different way and see what the consequences are. In this way, the role playing becomes a dramatic conceptual activity.

In our illustration, a second enactment produces the solution in which Tommy alerts the man to his overpayment and gets to keep the money for being so honest.

Phase Eight: Discuss and Evaluate

In the discussion that follows, the students are willing to accept the solution, but the teacher pushes for a realistic solution by asking whether they think this ending could really happen. One student has had a similar experience but was overpaid only $1.25, which he was allowed to keep. The teacher asks the class whether they think it might be different with five dollars. She asks for another solution, and it is suggested that Tommy consult his mother. There follows some discussion of Tommy's father, concepts about family, and parental roles. The teacher suggests that this third solution be enacted. Here's what happens in the third enactment:

Tommy: Mom, I'm in an awful jam!

Mother: What's the trouble, Tommy?

Tommy: (tells his mother the whole story)

Mother: Why, Tommy, you should have told me sooner. Here, you pay the money (opens purse) and we'll talk this over with Dad when he comes home.

During the discussion of this enactment, the teacher asks what will happen next, and someone suggests that Tommy will get a licking. The students feel that his punishment will relieve Tommy's mind.

Phase Nine: Share Experiences and Generalize

This phase should not be expected to result immediately in generalizations about the human relations situation itself. Such generalizations require much experience. The teacher should, however, attempt to shape the discussion so that the children, perhaps after long experience with the role playing strategy, begin to form general ideas about approaches to problem situations and about the consequences of those approaches. The more adequately the shaping of the discussion is done, the more general will be the conclusions that are reached, and the closer the children will come to hypothetical principles of action they can use in their own lives.

The initial goal, however, is to relate the problem situation to the children's experience in a nonthreatening way. This goal can be accomplished by asking the class if they know someone who has had the experience in question. In our illustration with Tommy and the money, the teacher asks if anyone in the class knows of an instance in which a boy or girl was in a situation like Tommy's. One student describes an experience with his father. The teacher then asks about parental attitudes and the role of fathers with respect to their children's money.

From such discussions emerge principles that all students can articulate and use. These principles can be applied to the particular kind of problem situation, or they can be used by the children as a springboard for the exploration of other kinds of problems. Ideally, the children will gradually master the strategy so that when a problem comes up, either within their group or from a topic they have studied, they will be able to use role playing to gain insight into the problem or at least to achieve clarity about it. Students might, for example, systematically use role playing to improve the quality of classroom democracy.

The Teacher's Role

The teachers' questions and comments should encourage free and honest expression of ideas and feelings. Teachers must establish equality and trust between themselves and their students. They can do this by accepting all suggestions as legitimate and making no value judgments. In this way, they simply reflect the children's feelings or attitudes. For example, if a child reveals anger during the role play, the teacher might point out that he is angry. Or the teacher might summarize a child's views: "You are saying that it is better not to offer to help than to risk hurting someone's feelings."

Though the teacher is reflective and supportive, he is not nondirective. He often selects the problem to be explored, leads the discussion, chooses the actors, makes decisions about when the enactments are to be done, helps design the enactments, and, most significant, decides what to probe for and what suggestions to explore. In essence, the teacher shapes the exploration of behavior by the types of questions he asks, and, through questioning, establishes the focus.

Principles of Reaction

We have identified five principles of reaction we feel are important to this model. First, teachers should accept student responses and suggestions, especially their opinions and feelings, in a nonevaluative manner. Second, teachers should respond in such a way that they help the students explore various sides of the problem situation and recognize and contrast alternative points of view. Third, by reflecting, paraphrasing, and summarizing responses the teacher increases students' awareness of their own views and feelings. Fourth, the teacher should emphasize that there are different ways to play the same role and that different consequences result as they are explored. Fifth, there are alternative ways to resolve a problem; no one way is correct. It is important to look at the consequences in order to evaluate a solution.

The Social System

The social system in this model is moderately structured. The teacher is responsible, at least initially, for initiating the phases and guiding students through the activities within each phase. The particular content of the discussions and enactments is determined largely by the students.

The Support System

Role Playing is an experienced-based model and requires minimal material support outside of the initial problem situation.

Getting Into Role Playing

It takes time for students to get into the activities involved in role playing. There are many new skills for them to acquire. In the early stages of role playing, it is probably not possible or desirable to go through all the phases in one session. At first, the teacher might stop to teach new concepts, such as character or attitude, or to train the students in new skills that are important to help someone get into the role. Gradually, as students become skilled and comfortable in role playing, the activities will probably go faster and the teacher will play a decreasing role, especially in the discussion.

SUMMARY CHART: THE ROLE PLAYING MODEL

Syntax

    Phase One: Warm-up
        A. Present problem.
        B. Discuss problem.
        C. Interpret problem story, explore issues.
        D. Explain role playing.

    Phase Two: Selecting Participants
        A. Analyze roles.
        B. Select players.

    Phase Three: Setting the Stage
        A. Set line of action.
        B. Restate roles.
        C. Get inside problem situation.

    Phase Four: Preparing the Observers
        A. Decide what to look for.
        B. Assign observation tasks.

    Phase Five: Enactment

Phase Six: Discussion
   A. Review action of role play (events, positions, realism).
   B. Discuss major focus.
   C. Develop next enactment.

Phase Seven: Reenactment

Phase Eight: Discussion and Evaluation

Phase Nine: Sharing Experiences and Generalizing
   A. Relate problem situation to real experience and current problems.
   B. Explore general principles of behavior.

Principles of Reaction

1. Accept all student responses in a nonevaluative manner.
2. Help students explore various sides of the problem situation and compare and contrast alternative views.
3. Increase students' awareness of their own views and feelings by reflecting, summarizing, and paraphrasing their responses.
4. Use the concept of role, and emphasize that there are different ways to play a role.
5. Emphasize that there are alternative ways to resolve a problem.

THEORY IN PRACTICE

No amount of description can convey a sense of a model of teaching as well as an example of the model in practice. In fact, reading too much theory before gaining a rough "image" of the practice can be confusing and, for some people, frustrating and discouraging. So we encourage you, at this point of your study of the Role Playing Model, to read the following abbreviated transcript of an actual classroom session. We suggest that you first read only the teacher-student dialogue and then go back to note the annotations. Remember, the goal at this point in your training is to gain a sense of the model—its flow and feeling—not to master the techniques of implementation.

This is a transcript of a Role Playing lesson. The teacher is working with a small group of fifth-grade students who are experiencing the Role Playing Model for the first time. They are exploring a problem involving cheating. The teacher's main focus for this session is on generating alternative solutions for the main character, Mike. Prior to the session, the teacher discussed with the students the idea that there are always alternative ways to handle any problem situation. In doing so, she introduced them to the term "alternatives."

Unfortunately, time does not permit the students to enact more than one solution, but the teacher has done a nice job in the early phases of the model in eliciting alternative suggestions from the students and having them get into the role and feelings of the character. As often happens in the first enactments, there is a stalemate in the problem situation. Stalemates occur because the problem is a real one and the students genuinely do not know how to solve it.

Notice how the teacher establishes and maintains the focus by paraphrasing and summarizing.

T: THE STORY IS ABOUT A PAPER DRIVE. WE ARE GOING TO FOCUS OUR THOUGHTS ON MIKE'S PROBLEM. TRY TO PUT YOURSELVES IN HIS

Teacher sets the students up to focus on the dilemma.

PLACE. (reads) MISS HENRY'S FOURTH-GRADE STUDENTS WERE EXCITED TO WIN THE SCHOOL PAPER DRIVE, BECAUSE THE CLASSROOM BRINGING IN THE MOST PAPER DURING THE WEEK OF THE CONTEST WAS TO BE GIVEN A PICNIC AT THE PINK HORSE RANCH WITH FREE HOT DOGS AND ICE CREAM. SWIMMING AND MOVIES AND RIDES ON THE ROLLER COASTER AND BOATS AND PONIES WOULD BE FREE. EACH DAY AFTER SCHOOL, MISS HENRY'S CLASS BUSILY GATHERED PAPERS, TIED THEM INTO NEAT BUNDLES, AND DELIVERED THEM TO THE BIG TRAILER WAITING AT THE REAR OF THE SCHOOL YARD.

MISS WILSON'S FOURTH-GRADE CLASS WAS ALSO COLLECTING PAPER. EVERYONE KNEW ONE OF THE FOURTH-GRADE CLASSES IN THE SCHOOL WOULD HAVE TO WIN, BECAUSE THEY WERE WORKING SO HARD.

THE DAY BEFORE THE END OF THE PAPER DRIVE, THE KIDS FROM MISS HENRY'S CLASS HEARD THAT SOME OF MISS WILSON'S KIDS HAD CHEATED. THEY HAD TAKEN GARDEN HOSES AND SPRAYED THE BUNDLES OF PAPER SO THAT THEY WEIGHED MORE THAN THEY REALLY WERE. NOW, REMEMBER, THEY ONLY HEARD THAT.

ONE OF THE KIDS IN MISS HENRY'S CLASS SUGGESTED TO HIS CLASSMATES THAT THAT WASN'T FAIR, THAT IF THEY WERE GOING TO WIN THEY WOULD HAVE TO STUFF OLD PIECES OF IRON INTO THEIR BUNDLES TO MAKE THEM HEAVIER. IT WASN'T FAIR TO LET MISS WILSON'S CLASS GET AWAY WITH IT, AND THERE WAS NO WAY TO PROVE IT.

SOME OF THE KIDS AGREED THAT IT WOULD BE A GOOD IDEA TO STUFF IRON PIECES BETWEEN THE PAPER TO MAKE IT HEAVIER. SOME THOUGHT, "UH-UH, THAT'S CHEATING," BUT MARY (A LEADER IN THE CLASS WHOM EVERYONE LISTENED TO) SAID, "IF WE WANT TO WIN WE HAVE TO DO IT." MIKE SAID, "WHAT IF WE GET CAUGHT?" BUT NO ONE WANTED TO LET THE OTHER CLASS WIN, SO THE CLASS DECIDED TO GO ALONG WITH WHAT MARY SAID.

MIKE FELT IT WAS WRONG. HOW COULD THEY BE SURE THE OTHER CLASS HAD REALLY CHEATED? SHOULD HE TELL MISS HENRY WHAT MARY AND THE OTHERS WERE PLANNING TO DO? BUT HE DIDN'T WANT HIS FRIENDS TO GET ANGRY WITH HIM. HE DIDN'T WANT THEM TO CALL HIM A COWARD. WHAT WOULD HIS FRIENDS SAY? AND WHAT WOULD HAPPEN IF THEY GOT CAUGHT? HE SURE WANTED HIS CLASS TO GO TO THE PINK HORSE RANCH. AND ALL THAT FREE ICE CREAM! WHAT SHOULD HE DO? WHAT IS MIKE'S PROBLEM?"

Teacher reads the story.

S: HE REALLY WANTS TO GO TO THE PINK HORSE RANCH, AND HE THINKS IT'S LIKE CHEATING—TO DO THAT. HE DOESN'T WANT HIS FRIENDS TO THINK THAT HE'S A COWARD.

S: I THINK HE SHOULD TELL BECAUSE. . .

T: TELL ME. . .NOT EXACTLY WHAT HE SHOULD DO. LET'S JUST TALK NOW ABOUT WHAT EXACTLY IS HIS PROBLEM.

S: SOME OF THE KIDS IN THE CLASS THINK THAT THE OTHER CLASS WAS CHEATING BY WETTING IT. SO THEY WANT TO CHEAT TOO—TO GET EVEN WITH THEM.

T: OKAY, NOW WHAT DOES MIKE FEEL ABOUT THAT?

S: HE DOESN'T WANT TO DO IT, BECAUSE IT WOULDN'T BE—IF THEY DID DO THAT THEY WOULD BOTH BE CHEATING.

S: SO THEN HE'S FEELING THAT HE WANTS TO WIN, BUT HE DOESN'T WANT TO CHEAT.

T: OK, LET'S NARROW DOWN THE CONCEPT THAT YOU'VE ALL BEEN TALKING ABOUT HERE. WHAT ARE HIS CONFLICTS? WHAT IS HIS PROBLEM?

S: ONE IS THAT THE OTHER CLASS IS CHEATING. HE DIDN'T WANT TO LOSE ANY FRIENDS BY TELLING. THEY WERE GOING TO WEIGHT THE PAPERS DOWN AND HE DIDN'T WANT TO BECAUSE HE DIDN'T WANT TO GET CAUGHT.

T: THAT WAS THE REASON—HE DIDN'T WANT TO CAUGHT? DO YOU THINK THERE'S ANOTHER REASON WHY HE MIGHT NOT HAVE WANTED THEM TO WEIGHT THE PAPERS DOWN? BOBBIE?

S: BECAUSE THAT WOULD BE CHEATING.

T: WHAT KIND OF FEELINGS MIGHT YOU HAVE GOTTEN FROM KNOWING THAT?

S: SORT OF GUILTY.

T: LET'S GET INTO MIKE'S FEELING. HOW DO YOU THINK MIKE IS FEELING AT THIS POINT WHEN HE'S IN THE CLASSROOM?

S: I THINK HE'D FEEL QUITE DISAPPOINTED IN HIS FRIENDS, AND PUZZLED—WHAT COULD HE DO?

T: HOW DO YOU THINK YOU MIGHT FEEL IN THAT POSITION IN THIS CONFLICT?

S: MAD—THAT THE OTHER KIDS HAVE DONE IT.

T: THAT THEY HAVEN'T DONE IT YET, BUT ARE THINKING ABOUT DOING IT.

S: I REALLY THINK MAD—HE DOESN'T KNOW WHAT TO DO. HE'S DISAPPOINTED IN HIS FRIENDS—HE WOULD PROBABLY THINK THEY WOULDN'T DO THINGS LIKE THAT. AND HE DOESN'T KNOW THE ANSWER—DOESN'T KNOW WHAT TO DO.

T: PUZZLED AND DISAPPOINTED—THAT WAS A GOOD WAY TO BRING IT OUT. OKAY, NOW WE'VE

Phase One: Warm-up

Some students immediately offer a solution.

Characterizing the problem

Teacher refocuses on the description of the problem.

Part of the dilemma.

Teacher asks the students to move from the general situation to the specific dilemma for the character.

Statement of the "inner conflict."

Teacher asks for a summary of the problem.

Student offers a summary.

Teacher asks students to speculate on the dynamics of the character.

Getting into the character

Teacher tries to get students to identify with the story.

Teacher now moves to the focus she has chosen for the session—alternatives to cheating.

TALKED ABOUT THE PROBLEM AND HOW HE FEELS ABOUT IT. REMEMBERING THOSE, WHAT CAN HE DO ABOUT HIS PROBLEM? LET'S TRY TO THINK ABOUT A SOLUTION. DIFFERENT POSSIBLE SOLUTIONS. WHAT WAS THE WORD WE TALKED ABOUT BEFORE?

S: ALTERNATIVES.

T: YES—ALTERNATIVES. LET'S TRY TO WORK OUT SOME ALTERNATIVES.

Teacher had introduced concept of alternatives prior to the lesson.

S: HE MIGHT BE ABLE TO GO OVER TO THE OTHER FOURTH-GRADE CLASS TO SEE IF THEY REALLY HAVE WATERED THEIR PAPERS. AND IF THEY HAVE, HE CAN BRING THE PART OF THE CLASS WHO WANTED TO CHEAT OVER AND MAKE THEM SEE THAT. IF THEY HADN'T, HE COULD PROVE TO THEM THAT THEY DIDN'T.

T: IN OTHER WORDS, ARE YOU SAYING THAT HE SHOULD GO AND CONFRONT—GO RIGHT UP TO THEM AND SAY, "DID YOU CHEAT?" IS THAT WHAT YOU'RE SAYING?

Paraphrasing student's idea.

S: NO, I THINK HE SHOULD JUST CHECK.

T: ALL RIGHT—CHECK. WHO WOULD HE CHECK WITH NOW?

S: HE'D PROBABLY JUST LOOK OVER THE PAPERS.

T: YOU WANT HIM TO LOOK OVER TO SEE IF IT REALLY HAPPENED. BUT WOULD THAT HAVE ANYTHING TO DO WITH HOW HE'S FACING THE KIDS RIGHT NOW? REMEMBER, HE'S IN THE SITUATION FACING THOSE KIDS. WHAT'S HE GOING TO DO?

Teacher reminds students of the realities of the problem situation.

S: WELL, IF I WAS IN HIS POSITION I WOULD PROBABLY GO OVER TO THE OTHER CLASS' TEACHER AND TELL HER ABOUT THE PROBLEM—AND TELL THEIR TEACHER ABOUT WHAT THEY THINK'S GOING ON TOO.

Another solution.

T: ALL RIGHT, TELL HIS TEACHER, AND THE OTHER TEACHER, AND YOU WOULDN'T SAY ANYTHING TO THE KIDS THEN?

Teacher clarifies.

S: NO. BECAUSE THEY MIGHT GET...

T: THAT'S ANOTHER WAY. ONE IS TO CHECK UP THE PAPERS AND ANOTHER IS TO TELL THE TEACHERS. WHAT'S ANOTHER SOLUTION THAT HE MIGHT HAVE?

Summary.

S: JUST LET THEM DO IT.

T: JUST TO BE QUIET THEN?

Paraphrases student's idea.

S: YEAH.

T: NOT SAY ANYTHING. LET THEM GO AHEAD AND CHEAT—NOT SAY ANYTHING AND IF THEY WIN, GO TO THE PONY RANCH.

S: OH, NO, THAT MIGHT NOT BE THE BEST WAY TO DO IT. IT IS JUST ANOTHER WAY TO DO IT.

T: THAT'S A VERY GOOD POINT. WE HAVE A LOT OF DIFFERENT ALTERNATIVES, BUT SOME OF THEM MAY BE BETTER THAN OTHERS.

S: I THINK THEY SHOULD NOT DO IT—JUST BE FAIR. I THINK THE OTHER CLASS THAT WET THE PAPERS SHOULD JUST. . .PLAY FAIR.

T: WHAT WOULD YOU TELL MIKE TO DO ABOUT IT? CONFRONT MARY AND THE CLASS AND SAY, "BE FAIR"? YOU WOULD SAY DISCUSS IT RIGHT THEN AND THERE—DISCUSS IT?   Probes student's suggestion.

S: YES.

S: TELL THE TEACHER THAT THEY'RE CHEATING.

T: THAT WAS WHAT BRIAN SAID TOO—TELL THE TEACHER THAT THEY'RE CHEATING. BUT YOU'RE ALSO SAYING TO TELL HIS OWN TEACHER, AREN'T YOU?

S: THEN TELL THE OTHER TEACHER.

T: BUT YOU HAVE TO REMEMBER ONE THING NOW —THAT THE WHOLE CLASS IS BEHIND MARY—AND THAT SO FAR HE'S THE ONLY ONE WHO IS THINKING ABOUT THAT. NOW HE MIGHT—IT DEPENDS ON HOW HE FEELS—REMEMBER THAT. OKAY. LET'S GO OVER NOW WHAT THE ALTERNATIVES WERE. ONE SAID GO OVER AND LOOK AT THE PAPERS; ANOTHER SOLUTION YOU GAVE WAS TELL THE OTHER CLASS'S TEACHER AND YOUR TEACHER AT THE SAME TIME; ANOTHER ONE WAS JUST DON'T SAY ANYTHING—DON'T DO ANYTHING ABOUT IT; THEN SOMEONE SAID TO CONFRONT MARY AND THE CLASS AND SAY WHAT YOU THINK ABOUT IT; ANOTHER ONE IS TELL HIS TEACHER TO ASK THE OTHER TEACHER, BUT GO ALONG WITH THE CLASS—NOT SAY ANYTHING— DO IT SO NOBODY KNOWS YOU'RE TELLING THE TEACHER.

Teacher again reminds students of the reality of the situation.

Teacher summarizes alternatives.

ALL RIGHT, FOR THE FIRST ROLE PLAY, LET'S CHOOSE THE ONE WHERE MIKE CONFRONTS MARY; HE GOES RIGHT UP TO MARY AND TELLS HER WHAT HE THINKS. WE'LL TRY THAT ONE FIRST, AND THEN WE'LL TRY SOME OF THE OTHERS. WHO ARE THE PEOPLE?

Teacher selects the role play.

Phase Two: Selecting Participants

S: MIKE. . .MARY. . .THE REST OF THE CLASS. . .THE TEACHERS. . .AND THE OTHER CLASS.

T: NOW WHAT IS MIKE LIKE—WHAT KIND OF A PERSON DO YOU THINK HE IS? BOBBY?   Role Analysis

S: HE'S A NICE PERSON.

S: A GOOD GUY.

S: SOMEONE WHO NEVER GETS INTO ANY TROUBLE. LIKE IF SOMEBODY TELLS HIM NOT TO DO SOMETHING, SAY HIS MOTHER TELLS HIM NOT TO GO TO HIS FRIEND'S HOUSE, LIKE HE WOULDN'T DO IT. HE WOULD OBEY EVERYBODY AND DO WHAT THEY SAY.

T: WHAT ABOUT MARY? WHAT KIND OF PERSON DO YOU THINK MARY IS?   Analysis of the other character.

S: STUBBORN.

T: WHY DO YOU THINK SHE'S STUBBORN?   Teacher probes student's thinking.

S: BECAUSE SHE WON'T EVEN TAKE IN THE OTHER

IDEAS. BEFORE SHE EVEN THINKS ABOUT IT, SHE WON'T EVEN LISTEN TO MIKE.

S: THE KIND OF PERSON WHO WILL GO ALONG WITH EVERYONE ELSE. SHE WON'T EVEN HAVE HER OWN THOUGHTS; SHE'LL JUST DO WHAT EVERYBODY ELSE IS DOING.

S: SHE WOULDN'T LISTEN TO ANYBODY. SHE HAS TO HAVE SOME OF HER OWN WAY. SHE JUST THINKS HER WAY.

T: IS SHE THE TYPE OF PERSON THAT THE OTHER KIDS WOULD FOLLOW, DO YOU THINK?

Teacher presses for a realistic picture of Mary in view of the original situation.

S: YES.

T: WHY DO THEY FOLLOW HER?

S: SHE SEEMS LIKE THE HEAD GIRL OF THE CLASS.

S: THE BIG SHOT.

T: WHO THINKS THAT THEY CAN PLAY THE ROLE OF MIKE? OKAY, BOBBY, TRY IT. WE'LL TALK ABOUT IT WHEN YOU'RE UP ON THE STAGE HERE AND WE'LL SET THE STAGE. WHAT ABOUT MARY? REMEMBER, WE TALKED ABOUT WHAT KIND OF PERSON MARY IS. LET'S TRY ONE OTHER PERSON WITH MARY TO REPRESENT THE OTHER PEOPLE IN THE CLASS. DO YOU WANT TO TRY IT THIS TIME? YOU'RE ONE OF THOSE WHO GO ALONG WITH—DO YOU WANT TO JUST USE YOUR NAME, MATTHEW?

Selection of Players

S: I WANT TO TAKE A NAME—JEFF.

Phase Three: Setting The Stage

T: WE'VE GOT MARY AND JEFF. AND MIKE, YOU'VE GOT TO FACE THEM. LET'S COME UP INTO OUR STAGE AREA. OKAY, NOW THERE'S TWO THINGS TO THINK ABOUT WHEN YOU TAKE YOUR PARTS. FIRST, YOU'RE NO LONGER REPRESENTING YOURSELVES. MIKE—WHERE'S MIKE, AND MARY AND JEFF? SECOND, WE TALKED ABOUT WHAT KIND OF PERSON THEY ARE. MIKE, WHAT ARE YOU FEELING FACING YOUR CLASSMATES?

Getting into the role.

Setting the stage and getting into the character.

S: I'M NOT SURE OF MYSELF.

T: YOU ALSO SAID HE'S NOT TOO SURE OF HIMSELF BECAUSE HE'S FACING THOSE WHO DON'T THINK LIKE HE DOES. WHAT ARE YOU GOING TO DO, THEN? YOU'RE GOING TO JUST TALK TO THEM AND TELL THEM WHAT YOU FEEL ABOUT IT THIS TIME. OK. MARY, HOW ARE YOU GOING TO REACT? WHAT ARE YOU GOING TO BE DOING, FIRST OF ALL?

Reiterating the time of action.

S: WELL, IN THE FIRST PLACE, JEFF AND I ARE PROBABLY GOING TO BE SEEING IF MARY CAN GET THE IRON AND STUFF. I'M GOING TO SAY WE'RE NOT TOO HAPPY ABOUT THE IDEA.

T: TELL ME A LITTLE BIT ABOUT WHAT YOU'RE GOING TO BE FEELING LIKE—WHAT KIND OF A PERSON YOU'RE GOING TO BE THERE.

S: I THINK I'M GOING TO BE ANNOYED.

T: OK, WHAT'S HAPPENING NOW? THIS IS YOUR CLASS DISCUSSION—YOU'RE TALKING ABOUT IT RIGHT NOW. WHERE ARE WE? WHERE IS THIS TAKING PLACE?

Setting the stage.

S: I THINK IT SHOULD BE AFTER SCHOOL.

S: ABOUT 3:15—IT'S AFTER SCHOOL IN THE AFTER-NOON.

T: OBSERVERS, WE'VE GOT A BIG RESPONSIBILITY HERE. WE'VE GOT TO LISTEN CLOSELY TO WHAT THEY'RE SAYING AND THINK HOW THEY ARE FEELING AS THEIR CHARACTERS. DOES IT SEEM REAL TO YOU—LIKE IT'S A REAL POSSIBILITY? AND MAYBE WHILE THEY'RE UP THERE, SOME OTHER SOLUTIONS MIGHT COME TO MIND. OK, GO TO IT.

Phase Four: Preparing the Observers

Phase Five: Enactment

S: WHERE ARE WE GOING TO GET THE IRON IN THE FIRST PLACE?

S: YOU SHOULDN'T GET THE IRON AT ALL.

S: FUNNY.

S: MAYBE THEY'RE NOT CHEATING AT ALL; MAYBE YOU JUST THINK THEY'RE CHEATING.

S: HOW DO YOU KNOW THEY'RE NOT?

S: HOW DO YOU KNOW THEY ARE?

S: WELL LOOK, WE ALREADY KNOW THE PLACE TO GET THE IRON—RIGHT? TELL THEM WHERE IT IS.

S: GO DOWN TO THE JUNKYARD—DOWN BY MY STREET.

S: BUT WHY DO YOU WANT TO CHEAT?

S: SO WE CAN WIN.

S: BUT YOU DON'T HAVE TO WIN BY CHEATING.

S: HOW DO YOU KNOW THEY'RE CHEATING?

S: CAUSE EVERYBODY SAYS.

S: WELL, HOW DO YOU KNOW THAT EVERYBODY IS RIGHT?

S: WELL, LISTEN, IF THE MAJORITY OF THE CLASS SAY THEY ARE CHEATING, WHAT DO YOU THINK ABOUT IT? LISTEN, THERE ARE AT LEAST TEN KIDS THERE SAYING THE KIDS ARE CHEATING.

S: YEAH, BUT HOW DO YOU KNOW SOMEONE DIDN'T JUST MAKE IT UP? JUST BECAUSE THEY KNOW THAT THEY HAVE MORE PAPERS THAN WE DO—WELL, WE BETTER LEARN IF YOU. . .

S: WELL, ANYWAY, WHICH WOULD YOU RATHER DO—SIT AROUND IN SCHOOL DOING ALL THIS STUPID WORK OR GOING THERE?

S: WELL, IF WE'RE CHEATING I WOULD RATHER STAY HERE, BECAUSE IF WE DO CHEAT, THEN MAYBE IF THEY AREN'T CHEATING, WE CAN'T GIVE THEM ANY FAIR CHANCE.

S: I THINK I'D RATHER GO—THE EASIEST WAY WE COULD.

S: BUT STILL YOU'RE CHEATING.

S: I THINK YOU SHOULD CHEAT.

S: BUT I DON'T THINK YOU SHOULD. THE WHOLE CLASS IS MAYBE SAYING YOU SHOULD CHEAT, BUT STILL IT'S NOT FAIR.

S: HEY, LISTEN, EVERYBODY SAYS TWO WRONGS DON'T MAKE A RIGHT. GUESS WHAT? THE CLASS HAS SAID THAT IT'S RIGHT—THAT WAY, ONE DOESN'T CHEAT—WE DO IT AND IT'S RIGHT.

S: BUT STILL, YOU DON'T KNOW IF THEY'RE CHEAT- ING YET.

S: BUT WE TOLD YOU, WE DO KNOW.

S: BUT YOU HAVE NO PROOF; NO ONE'S SEEN THEM. IT'S JUST SOMEONE SAYS THEY'RE CHEATING.

T: LET'S STOP RIGHT HERE. THINK OF SOMETHING YOU CAN TELL THEM THAT THEY SHOULD DO INSTEAD. TRY THAT.   Teacher breaks into the enactment and offers a suggestion to get the action moving.

S: I THINK YOU SHOULD JUST LEAVE IT ALONE IF THEY ARE CHEATING. SOMEBODY WILL CATCH THEM.

S: WHO IS GOING TO CATCH THEM? ANYWAY, HOW DO YOU KNOW THAT THEY AREN'T CHEATING?

S: BUT STILL YOU DON'T KNOW IF THEY ARE. IF THEY ARE CHEATING, LET THEM CHEAT.   The stalemate continues.

T: OKAY, LET'S STOP RIGHT HERE. YOU'RE AT AN IMPASSE. YOU CAN'T MOVE FARTHER. WHAT'S HAPPENING?   Teacher breaks enactment.

S: HE'S STANDING UP TO HIS RIGHTS.   **Phase Six: Discussion**

T: OKAY, GOOD. LET'S CONTINUE WHAT YOU'RE SAYING AND LET'S BRING IT BACK TO OUR SEATS NOW. OBSERVERS, NOW—TELL US WHAT YOU THINK WAS HAPPENING IN THAT ROLE PLAY.

S: MIKE JUST WOULDN'T TAKE THEIR WORD THAT THEY WERE CHEATING, AND JEFF AND MARY WOULDN'T TAKE HIS WORD, BECAUSE THEY JUST DIDN'T. THEY BOTH HAD DIFFERENT THOUGHTS ABOUT IT.

T: SO, IN OTHER WORDS, THEY HAD A CONFLICT AMONG EACH OTHER. OBSERVERS, OTHER THOUGHTS. WHAT DO YOU THINK ABOUT THAT?   Teacher paraphrases student's ideas.

S: I THOUGHT THEY WERE ALL—THEY SHOULDN'T HAVE ARGUED ABOUT THE WHOLE THING.

S: THAT'S WHAT WE'D NORMALLY DO.

T: IF YOU THINK THAT'S WHAT YOU WOULD NOR- MALLY DO, DID IT FEEL REAL TO YOU?

S: I WAS GOING TO START ARGUING WITH MIKE.

T: WHAT DO YOU THINK ABOUT ONE LITTLE GUY STANDING UP FOR WHAT HE BELIEVES AGAINST THE TOUGH GUYS OF THE CLASS?

S: I THINK IT'S HARD TO DO THAT ALL THE TIME.

S: I WAS ABOUT TO SAY, "BUG OUT."

T: YOU WANTED TO SAY, "BUG OUT," AND YOU SAID YOU DO IT ALL THE TIME. HOW DO YOU FEEL, RELATED TO HOW MIKE FEELS? HOW DID YOU FEEL, THEN, DOING THAT ALL THE TIME?

Probes characters' feelings.

S: YOU JUST DON'T FEEL GOOD BECAUSE ALL MY FRIENDS—THEY SAY THEY WANT TO DO ONE THING, AND I SAY IT'S NOT A GOOD IDEA, BUT THEY JUST GO AHEAD. THEY NEVER EVEN ARGUE OR ANYTHING.

T: BUT YOU FIND IT NECESSARY TO TELL THEM WHAT YOU THINK?

S: YES.

T: WHAT DID YOU OBSERVE AS YOU WERE WATCHING?

S: I THINK THAT MIKE WAS JUST TRYING TO TELL THEM THAT IT'S NOT FAIR—THAT THEY'RE CHEATING. AND THOSE KIDS, THEY THOUGHT CHEATING WAS REALLY NOT—

T: HOW DID YOU FEEL ABOUT THE ROLE THAT MARY PLAYED, AND THAT JEFF PLAYED—AGAINST MIKE? DID YOU GET ANY FEELINGS THAT MIKE MIGHT HAVE AS HE FACES THESE TWO PEOPLE?

S: I THINK MIKE WAS RIGHT—THAT THEY SHOULDN'T DO THAT—BUT HE SHOULD REALLY ASK THE OTHER LEVEL IF THEY DID—THE TEACHER.

Student evaluates the solution.

S: WOULD LEVEL ONE TELL? THE TEACHER WOULDN'T—

T: LET'S STICK WITH THIS SOLUTION NOW—THE ONE WE'RE TRYING TO WORK OUT. MIKE, TELL US—THEY SAW YOU STANDING UP TO THESE TOUGH PEOPLE. HOW DID YOU FEEL STANDING UP TO THE LEADERS OF THE CLASS?

Maintains focus.

S: I WOULD HAVE FELT PRETTY SCARED 'CAUSE ALL THE OTHER KIDS WOULD BE ON THEIR SIDE AND I'D BE ONLY ON MY—THE ONLY PERSON ON MY SIDE, AND THEY MIGHT GET REAL MAD AT ME.

T: WOULD YOU THINK THAT THIS WOULD BE REAL—FOR YOU TO STAND UP IN REAL LIFE?

S: YEAH, MAYBE. I WOULDN'T WANT TO CHEAT OR SOMETHING LIKE THAT.

T: LET'S PUT IT THIS WAY. IF WE HAD MORE TIME, HOW WOULD YOU COMPARE THE SOLUTION OF GOING TO THE TEACHER, WHICH A COUPLE OF YOU SUGGESTED, AND NOT LETTING THE KIDS KNOW AND NOT SAYING TO THE KIDS THAT YOU WERE TOLD THAT THEY WERE CHEATING AND WOULD THE TEACHER PLEASE CHECK—HOW DO YOU COMPARE THAT SOLUTION TO GOING TO THE OTHER KIDS IN THE CLASS, AS WE JUST ROLE PLAYED?

Time has run out. Teacher asks students to hypothesize about their reactions to other solutions.

S: FOR MIKE, PROBABLY GOING TO THE TEACHER WOULD BE BETTER, BUT THE OTHERS—THE CLASS—THEY WOULD PROBABLY WANT TO GO TO THE OTHER CLASS, BECAUSE MIKE HAS MENTIONED THAT THEY SHOULD GO OVER TO THE OTHER CLASS AND CHECK. THE CLASS PROBABLY WOULD HAVE GONE AND CHECKED WITH HIM—WHICH WOULD HAVE BEEN A GOOD IDEA AND WOULD HAVE PROVED IF THEY WERE RIGHT OR WRONG.

T: LET'S TAKE IT AWAY FROM THE PAPER DRIVE NOW AND TALK ABOUT THE SITUATION IN REAL LIFE. WHERE YOU HAVE A PROBLEM, DO YOU CONFRONT YOUR FRIENDS—DO YOU GO AND TELL THEM WHAT YOU THINK—OR DO YOU HAVE TO GO TO A TEACHER? HOW DO YOU DECIDE WHICH TO DO?

Phase Nine: Sharing Experiences And Generalizing

S: I'D GO TO MY FRIENDS IF IT WAS IN REAL LIFE. I'D TELL MY BEST FRIEND AND WE'D WORK IT OUT.

(Discussion of feelings and consequences continues.)

TAKING THEORY INTO ACTION

Role Playing is an extremely versatile model, applicable to several important educational objectives. Through role playing students can increase their ability to recognize their own and other people's feelings; they can acquire new behaviors for handling previously difficult situations, and they can improve their problem-solving skills.

In addition to its many uses, the Role Playing Model carries with it an appealing set of activities. Students like both the action and the acting. Because of this, it is easy to forget that the role play itself (the enactment) is only a vehicle for other educational goals. That is, the various stages of activity and the various processes in this model serve primarily to develop the content of the instruction. They are not ends in themselves, but they help expose students' values, feelings, attitudes, and/or solutions to problems, which the teacher must then explore.

We have found that a single role playing session is usually extremely rich. Discussion can go in many directions—toward an analysis of feelings, a discussion of consequences, the roles themselves and ways to play them, alternative solutions, and so forth. After several years of working with this model, we have come to believe that if any one of these ideas, or objectives, is to be developed adequately, the teacher must make a concerted effort to explore that particular emphasis. Because all these aspects tend to emerge in the role playing process, it is easy to consider them only superficially. One difficulty we are faced with, then, is that an in-depth treatment of any one focus requires time. Trying to touch all possible focuses in any one session is probably not helpful. We feel that it is important to select one major focus, or perhaps two, for any one session. However, this is probably more true at the beginning, when students are getting accustomed to the model and to the exploration of their behavior and feelings. Selecting one major emphasis for the session does not mean that other aspects have no place in the development of ideas. For example, the feelings of the characters will be discussed even when the teacher is trying to get the students to concentrate on alternative solutions to the problem, but in this case the feelings will tie in to a consideration and evaluation of the solutions.

By choosing one or perhaps two emphases for the role play, carefully questioning and responding to students' ideas, and building upon the ideas in the previous phases, the teacher gradually develops each phase so that it supports the particular objectives that have been selected for that session. This is what we mean by developing a focus.

The skill of developing a focus, then, lies in deciding what to emphasize when you use the Role Playing Model. Your decision about the focus will govern the nature of your questions when you teach and will help you maintain one or two consistent themes throughout the many phases and activities of the model. The possible focuses discussed in the Theory and Overview section are organized into four major categories: (1) exploration of feelings; (2) exploration of attitudes, values, and perceptions; (3) development of problem-solving skills and attitudes; and (4) subject-matter exploration. Within each of these categories there are several possibilities, any one of which could be the major focus of a role playing session. Study the list of possible focuses in Figure 2.

Beside selecting and maintaining a focus, another point to keep in mind is that there is usually a key concept related to the focus that students may or may not be familiar with. For example, the notion of inner (or emotional) conflict is central to the purpose of exploring feelings in a problem situation. Usually,

---

I. Role Playing as a vehicle for exploring feelings
    A. exploring one's own feelings
    B. exploring others' feelings
    C. acting out or releasing feelings
    D. experiencing higher-status roles in order to change the perceptions of others and one's own perceptions

II. Role Playing as a vehicle for exploring attitudes, values, and perceptions
    A. identifying values of culture or subculture
    B. clarifying and evaluating one's own values and value conflicts

III. Role Playing as a means of developing problem-solving attitudes and skills
    A. openness to possible solutions
    B. ability to identify a problem
    C. ability to generate alternative solutions
    D. ability to evaluate the consequences to oneself and others of alternative solutions to problems
    E. experiencing consequences and making final decisions in light of experienced consequences
    F. analyzing criteria and assumptions behind alternatives
    G. acquiring new behaviors

IV. Subject-matter exploration
    A. feelings of participants
    B. historical realities: historical crises, dilemmas, and decisions

---

Figure 2. *Possible Focuses of a Role Playing Session.*

dilemmas arise because of conflicting feelings. We suggest that you introduce students to the concept of *inner conflict* in a discussion before beginning a role playing session with that focus. Then, during the lesson you maintain this focus by having the students examine the problem and their feelings in terms of this concept, using the term *conflict*. Other central concepts related to each focus are presented in Figure 3. Reflect on these, and others you may think of, as you prepare for the Role Playing Model. Ask yourself what it is in general you want the students to understand about feelings, values, problem solving, and roles, and how this understanding applies in this situation.

I. Role Playing as a vehicle for exploring feelings
   A. Concept of inner conflict.
   B. Recognizing and naming feelings.
   C. Concept of role.
   D. Feelings can determine behavior.

II. Role Playing as a vehicle for exploring attitudes and values
   A. Concept of value.
   B. Values determine behavior.
   C. Concept of attitude.

III. Role Playing as a means of developing problem-solving attitudes and skills
   A. Concept of behavioral alternatives.
   B. Concept of problem solving and decision making.
   C. Concept of behavioral consequences.
   D. Concept of a problem-solving style.
   E. Concept of criteria for decisions (as ethical criteria).
   F. Concept of risk.

Figure 3. *Sample Concepts Underlying Different Focuses.*

Once you have determined your purposes in using the Role Playing Model, you can consider each phase in terms of the questions you will ask and the themes you will emphasize. For example, rather than asking an open-ended question in the warm-up, such as "What's this story about?" or "What's the problem here?" you might be more specific: "What was John feeling?" or "What values were most important to each of the people in the story?" No one question alone will produce as much exploration as you need. The idea is to design a sequence of questions that probe the events and ideas in the story in terms of the focus or concept you are emphasizing. If students shift the focus to, say, how they might solve the problem, refocus them on John's feelings.

During role playing activities, the teacher can maintain or highlight the focus in her responses to the students' comments and discussion. For example, in addition to the themes you initiate through your questions, you can reiterate the focus by paraphrasing the students' ideas. In this case, you might restate the students' ideas in the context of the focus, or perhaps the context of a broader concept. Often students, especially younger ones, will deal with specifics and you can restate and interpret these on a more general level.

Another way of developing the focus is to encourage students, as they contribute their opinions and analyses of the problem situation, to expand upon their ideas, especially in terms of the focus. If, for example, the focus is on feelings, the student may explain the problem in terms of the actual choices of the person in the situation. The teacher may develop the focus further by asking, "OK, so what's Mike feeling?"

Finally, role playing enables students to compare their perceptions of reality and their ways of solving problems with those of other people. As a result, there will and should be many diverse ideas. One of the ways of tracking all the ideas and of helping the students listen to one another is summarizing—soliciting or supplying a review or list of what has just occurred. This summarizing can embrace the activities of the role play or the solutions that have been offered. These summaries help bring focus to the session.

EXERCISE 1

Two problem situations follow. Read them and then identify two possible focuses for each. Briefly describe each focus in terms of the problem situation, using the list in Figure 2.

The first story, a selection from *A Child in Prison Camp* by Shizuye Takashima, describes a young girl's experience in a concentration camp for the Japanese during World War II. The second story presents the predicament of a Chicano family during the California grape strike. These two stories appear in James A. Banks, *Teaching Strategies for Ethnic Studies*, a very useful source for problem situations related to contemporary social issues.

Spring 1944

The war with Japan is getting very bad. I can feel my parents growing anxious. There is a lot of tension in the camp; rumors of being moved again, of everyone having to return to Japan. Kazuo and his family leave for Japan. Many are angry they have left us. Some call them cowards, others call them brave! I only feel sad, for I like Kazuo so much, so very much.

Father shouts at mother, "We return to Japan!"

"But what are we going to do? You have brothers and sisters there. I have no one. Besides, the children. . . ."

"Never mind the children," father answers. "They'll adjust. I'm tired of being treated as a spy, a prisoner. Do what you like: I'm returning!"

I can see Mrs. Kono looks confused.

"My husband is talking of returning to Japan, too. I think it's the best thing. All our relatives are still there. We have nothing here."

Yuki stares at her. "It's all right for you, Mrs. Kono, you were born there, but we weren't. I am not going. That's all!"

And she walks out of the house.

Mother gets very upset. I know she wants to cry.

"I don't want to go to Japan, either," I say. "They're short of food and clothing there. They haven't enough for their own people. They won't want us back."[8]

---

[8] Excerpt from *A Child in Prison Camp*, © 1971 Shizuye Takashima, published in the United States by William Morrow & Co., Inc. and elsewhere in the world by Tundra Books Inc.

The Sánchez Family and the Grape Strike

Mr. and Mrs. Sánchez and their seven children came from Mexico to live in California one year ago. Mr. Sánchez had been told by relatives who had been to the United States that he could make a lot of money very quickly if he came to California. When Mr. Sánchez arrived in California, he found that it was very hard to make a living working in the fields. Since the Sánchez family has been living in California, it has had to move many times in order to follow the crops and find work. The family has traveled as far as Texas and Michigan to work in the fields.

The work in the fields is very hard. Everyone in the family, except little Carlos, works in the fields so that the family can make enough money to get by with. Even Mrs. Sánchez, who used to stay at home and take care of the home when they lived in Mexico, now must work in the fields. The pay for the work is very low. Mr. and Mrs. Sánchez find that they get further and further into debt each year.

The Sánchez family is now living in the San Joaquin Valley in California. The family went to live there to work in the grape fields. For a while everything there was okay. Recently, a lot of things have been happening in the valley that Mr. and Mrs. Sánchez do not fully understand. Most of the field workers have said that they will not go to work next week because the Mexican American Union, led by Juan Gonzalez, who is very popular with the workers, has called a strike. The union is demanding that the owners of the grape fields pay the workers more money and give them better worker benefits. The workers who belong to the Union are threatening to attack any worker who tries to go to work while the strike is on.

Mr. Sánchez is not a member of the union. He wants very much to go to work next week. He has a lot of bills to pay and needs money for food and clothing. The family simply cannot get by with the small amount of money that the union has promised to give Mr. Sánchez if he joins it and refuses to work next week. Mr. Sánchez also realizes that if the grapes are not picked within the next two weeks, they will rot. He has heard that these strikes sometime last for months. His boss told him that if he wants to go to work next Monday morning—the day the strike is to begin—he will give him protection from the unionized workers. Mrs. Sánchez thinks that Mr. Sánchez should support the strike so that he can make higher wages in the future.[9]

EXERCISE 2

Pick one of the problem situations, and in the table that follows develop a line of questioning for each of the two focuses you selected. Write these questions beside the different phases and activities. Your questions will initiate the activities in the model. You can also develop questions in response to the students (as you imagine their conversation and enactment). As you go through each of the phases, notice the subtle differences between the questioning for the first focus and the questioning for the second. The purpose of this exercise is to call your attention in a vivid way to the cumulative development of a focus through questions and responses, and to the differences in them from one focus to the other.

[9] James Banks, *Teaching Strategies for Ethnic Studies* (Boston: Allyn & Bacon, Inc., 1975), pp. 305-6. Used with permission.

In the space below, identify the focus you have selected:

Focus One:

Focus Two:

Phase/Activity	Focus One	Focus Two

WARM-UP
  Identify or introduce problem.
  Make problem explicit.
  Interpret problem story,
    explore issues.
 	
SELECTING PARTICIPANTS
  Describe roles.
  Choose role players.
 	
SETTING THE STAGE
  Set the line of action.
  Restate the roles.
  Get inside problem situation.
 	
PREPARING THE OBSERVERS
  Assign observation tasks.
 	
ENACTMENT
  Begin role play.
  Maintain role play.
  Break role play.
 	
DISCUSSION AND EVALUATION
  Review action of role play (events,
    positions, realism).
  Discuss major focus.
  Develop next enactment.
  (Skip Phases Seven and Eight)
 	
SHARING EXPERIENCES AND
GENERALIZING
  Relate problem situation to
    real experiences and current
    problems.
  Explore general principles of
    behavior.		

THEORY CHECKUP FOR THE ROLE PLAYING MODEL

Instructions: Circle the response that best answers the question or completes the statement. Check your answers with the key that follows.

1. Which of the following elements is not part of the Role Playing Model?
   a. emotional content
   b. rules
   c. discussion
   d. enactment

2. List the phases of the Role Playing Model.

3. Two boys in Mr. Davis's class were fighting over something that happened between them. Mr. Davis asked the boys to re-create the problem situation in a role play, hoping they could generate an alternative to fighting. In this case, the Role Playing Model was used primarily:
   a. to explore feelings.
   b. to explore attitudes, values, and perceptions.
   c. as a historical re-creation.
   d. to develop problem-solving attitudes and skills.

4. The major planning skill in the Role Playing Model is:
   a. paraphrasing.
   b. choosing a focus.
   c. probing.
   d. summarizing.

5. Every day, an old man in torn clothes sits on a bench near the school and feeds the birds. During recess, the students make fun of the old man and tease him. Ms. Munvy decided to use the Role Playing Model. Which of the following best describes her purpose?
   a. exploring feelings
   b. historical re-creation
   c. developing problem-solving attitudes and skills
   d. exploring values

6. The students are discussing the similarities between the role play problem and their own experiences. They are probably in what phase of the model?
   a. Phase One
   b. Phase Six
   c. Phase Nine
   d. Phase Three

7. A skill in which a speaker restates in new words the ideas of someone else is called:
   a. summarizing.
   b. cuing.

THEORY CHECKUP FOR THE ROLE PLAYING MODEL

    c. paraphrasing.
    d. clarifying.

8. For which of the following educational goals would role playing *not* be appropriate?
    a. exploring social issues
    b. understanding the methods of the disciplines
    c. resolving behavior problems
    d. understanding value conflicts

Theory Checkup Key

1. b

2. Phase One: Warm up the group.
   Phase Two: Select participants.
   Phase Three: Set the stage.
   Phase Four: Prepare the observers.
   Phase Five: Enact.
   Phase Six: Discuss and evaluate.
   Phase Seven: Reenact.
   Phase Eight: Discuss and evaluate.
   Phase Nine: Share experiences and generalize.

3. d
4. a
5. b
6. c
7. c
8. b

Component II

VIEWING
THE MODEL

One of the purposes of Component II is to provide examples of actual sessions in which the Role Playing Model is the strategy being used. Reading the demonstration transcript that follows, hearing a tape of a teacher and students, or viewing a videotape of class activity are alternate means of illustrating the "model in action."

As you study any of these alternatives, you will be introduced to the Teaching Analysis Guide for analyzing the model. This same Guide will also be used in Component III to analyze the peer teaching and microteaching lessons. We want you to become familiar with the Guide now, however, as it will sharpen your perception of the demonstration lesson.

The two activities in this component are (1) reading the Teaching Analysis Guide and (2) viewing (reading) the lesson. Before going on to them, you may wish to reread the material in the Introduction to this book that discusses the purposes and philosophy of the Teaching Analysis Guide.

Analyzing the Teaching: Activity 1

Read through the questions in the Teaching Analysis Guide that follows and identify items that you do not understand. Discuss any difficulties you may have with your instructor or your colleagues.

TEACHING ANALYSIS GUIDE FOR THE ROLE PLAYING MODEL

This Guide is designed to help you analyze the process of teaching as you practice the Role Playing Model. The analysis focuses on aspects of teaching that are important to the syntax of the model, the teacher's role, and specific teaching skills.

The Guide consists of a series of questions and phrases. As you observe a practice session (whether peer teaching or microteaching), analyze the teaching using the rating scale that appears opposite each question and statement. This scale uses the following items:

Thoroughly. This item signifies that the teacher engaged in the behavior to the point where students were responding comfortably and fluently. Appropriateness varies from situation to situation. For example, if the students have been introduced to the concept of role playing in previous role plays and are fluent in its application, it need not be presented again.

Partially. This item signifies that the teacher engaged in appropriate behavior, but not as thoroughly as possible. There is some doubt about whether the students are responding fully.

Missing. The teacher did not engage in the behavior; there appears to be a loss in student response or probably will be one.

Not Needed. The teacher did not explicitly manifest the behavior, but there is no loss. Either the behavior was included in others or the students began to respond appropriately without being led to.

For each question or statement in the Guide, circle the term that best describes the teacher's behavior.

Phase One: Warm Up the Group

Problem Presentation

1. Was the problem introduced and identified?   Thoroughly   Partially   Missing   Not Needed

Discussion of Problem

2. Did the students speculate on or interpret the problem?   Thoroughly   Partially   Missing   Not Needed

3. Did the students identify the general category of the problem situation—for example, peer pressure, or prejudice? (This could also take place in Phase Nine.)   Thoroughly   Partially   Missing   Not Needed

4. Were both sides of the problem discussed?   Thoroughly   Partially   Missing   Not Needed

5. Did the teacher involve the students in setting goals or purposes in terms of the role play?   Thoroughly   Partially   Missing   Not Needed

6. Were all the students involved?   Thoroughly   Partially   Missing   Not Needed

Knowledge of Role Playing

7. Were the students aware of the function and procedures of role playing? If not, were these explained?   Thoroughly   Partially   Missing   Not Needed

62

TEACHING ANALYSIS GUIDE FOR THE ROLE PLAYING MODEL

Phase Two: Selecting Participants (Role Players)

Role Analysis

8. Were the roles identified and described? (This item can also be done in Phases One or Three.) Thoroughly Partially Missing Not Needed

9. Did the role analysis reflect the ideas of the initial discussion of the problem? Thoroughly Partially Missing Not Needed

Selection of Role Players

10. Were the role players chosen? Thoroughly Partially Missing Not Needed

Phase Three: Setting the Stage

Line of Action

11. Was the line of action decided upon before the role playing? Thoroughly Partially Missing Not Needed

12. Did the line of action that was decided upon reflect the ideas in the initial discussion of the problem In Phase One? Thoroughly Partially Missing Not Needed

13. Was the setting described? Thoroughly Partially Missing Not Needed

Phase Four: Preparing the Observers

14. Was there a discussion to prepare observers to: Thoroughly Partially Missing Not Needed
    a. evaluate the realism of the role playing?

    b. analyze the consequences of the role playing behavior? Thoroughly Partially Missing Not Needed

    c. define the feelings of the role players? Thoroughly Partially Missing Not Needed

15. Were specific observation tasks assigned? Thoroughly Partially Missing Not Needed

Phase Five: Enactment

Role Play

16. Did the role play take place? Thoroughly Partially Missing Not Needed

Teacher Role

17. Did the teacher break the role play at an appropriate time? Thoroughly Partially Missing Not Needed

63

TEACHING ANALYSIS GUIDE FOR THE ROLE PLAYING MODEL

Phase Six: Discussion

Focus

18. Was the enactment reviewed in terms of:

    a. the realism of the role play? — Thoroughly Partially Missing Not Needed

    b. a summary of the events and the consequences of different actions for the participants in the role play? — Thoroughly Partially Missing Not Needed

    c. a summary of the arguments that each role player presented? — Thoroughly Partially Missing Not Needed

19. Did a discussion centering on the primary focus take place? — Thoroughly Partially Missing Not Needed

20. During the discussion, did the teacher exhibit the following teacher skills? — Thoroughly Partially Missing Not Needed

    a. summarizing students' ideas
    b. paraphrasing or reflecting students' ideas — Thoroughly Partially Missing Not Needed

Preparing the Reenactment

21. Did the students reflect on the previous role play and consider it in planning the reenactment? — Thoroughly Partially Missing Not Needed

22. In the preparation for the reenactment, which of the following steps were carried out?

    a. role analysis — Thoroughly Partially Missing Not Needed

    b. selection of players — Thoroughly Partially Missing Not Needed

    c. development of the line of action — Thoroughly Partially Missing Not Needed

Teacher Role

23. Was the teacher nonevaluative in her responses? That is, did she primarily reflect and summarize the students' ideas? — Thoroughly Partially Missing Not Needed

Phase Seven: Reenactment

Role Play

24. Did a reenactment take place? — Thoroughly Partially Missing Not Needed

Phase Eight: Discussion and Evaluation

TEACHING ANALYSIS GUIDE FOR THE ROLE PLAYING MODEL

Discussion

25. Did a discussion take place?	Thoroughly	Partially	Missing	Not Needed

Focus

26. Was the enactment reviewed in terms of:

a. the realism of the role play?	Thoroughly	Partially	Missing	Not Needed
b. a summary of the events and the consequences of different actions for the participants in the role play?	Thoroughly	Partially	Missing	Not Needed
c. a summary of the arguments that each role player presented?	Thoroughly	Partially	Missing	Not Needed
d. a comparing and contrasting of the two enactments?	Thoroughly	Partially	Missing	Not Needed
27. Did a discussion centering on the primary focus take place?	Thoroughly	Partially	Missing	Not Needed

Teacher Role

28. Was the teacher nonevaluative in her responses?	Thoroughly	Partially	Missing	Not Needed

Phase Nine: Sharing and Generalizing

Discussion

29. Were similar experiences explored?	Thoroughly	Partially	Missing	Not Needed
30. Did the students reflect on how the role play applied to their own problems?	Thoroughly	Partially	Missing	Not Needed
31. Were the students able to generalize the issues involved in the role play?	Thoroughly	Partially	Missing	Not Needed
32. Were general principles of behavior explored?	Thoroughly	Partially	Missing	Not Needed

Viewing the Lesson: Activity 2

In this section you are asked to read the demonstration transcript that follows, identifying the phases of the model and commenting on the lesson as an illustration of the model. On your own or with a group of your peers, record the occurrence of the phases and comment on the model as it is presented here. You may want to focus on the adequacy of each phase, the quality of the enactments, the nature of the problem situation, or skillful moves that the teacher made (or did not make).

Phase One	Adequate	Minimal	Not at All
Phase Two	Adequate	Minimal	Not at All
Phase Three	Adequate	Minimal	Not at All
Phase Four	Adequate	Minimal	Not at All
Phase Five	Adequate	Minimal	Not at All
Phase Six	Adequate	Minimal	Not at All
Phase Seven	Adequate	Minimal	Not at All
Phase Eight	Adequate	Minimal	Not at All
Phase Nine	Adequate	Minimal	Not at All

Analyzing the Lesson: Activity 3 (Optional)

View a live, taped, or filmed demonstration and analyze the lesson using the Teaching Analysis Guide. You can do this in two ways: either complete the guide as the tape is viewed, or complete it afterward.

If you are viewing the lesson in a group, you may want to divide the task of analysis, with one or more of your colleagues taking a particular phase or aspect of analysis. Duplicate as many copies of the Guide as are needed.

DEMONSTRATION TRANSCRIPT: ROLE PLAYING MODEL

This is a lesson with junior high school students carried out by Michael McKibbin at the Rogers School in Alum Rock, California.

T: WHAT WE'RE GOING TO DO THIS MORNING IS A ROLE PLAYING SITUATION. THE PURPOSE OF ROLE PLAYING IS TO TRY TO GET AT WHAT YOU FEEL, WHAT YOU VALUE, AND THE KINDS OF THINGS THAT YOU DO IN DIFFERENT PROBLEM SITUATIONS. WE'RE GOING TO TALK ABOUT A PROBLEM AND SPECULATE ABOUT THE SITUATION, AND THEN WE'RE GOING TO TALK ABOUT THE CHARACTERS A LITTLE BIT. AFTER WE'VE TALKED ABOUT THE CHARACTERS, WE'LL GET READY TO ENACT THE SITUATION. WHEN WE ENACT THE SITUATION, WE KIND OF WANT TO TALK TO EACH OTHER NATURALLY. ONE OF THE THINGS THAT WE'LL BE DOING WHEN WE ENACT IS THAT THE REST OF US THAT AREN'T BEING THE ACTORS WILL BE OBSERVERS. WE'LL HAVE SPECIFIC TASKS TO LOOK AT IN TERMS OF THE ROLE PLAY, AND THEN AFTER WE'RE DONE WITH THE ENACTMENT, WE'LL KIND OF TALK ABOUT IT AND DISCUSS IT. THEN WE'LL PLAY IT AGAIN A LITTLE LATER AND WE'LL TALK ABOUT IT AGAIN. OK?

S: IS ROLE PLAYING LIKE IMPROVISATION?

T: YES, WELL, THAT'S PART OF IT. THAT'S PART OF IT, BUT THE MOST IMPORTANT PART OF ROLE

Phase I: Warm-Up

Introduction to this concept of Role Playing

Teacher describes the model to the students in very general terms.

Teacher clarifies purpose of role playing.

PLAYING IS THE DISCUSSION OF VALUES AND FEELINGS. YOU KNOW, WHEN WE LOOK AT DIFFERENT PEOPLE'S FEELINGS. OK?

T: HERE'S OUR PROBLEM SITUATION. IT'S ABOUT A CHICANO FAMILY DURING THE CALIFORNIA GRAPE STRIKE, AND I'M GOING TO READ THE STORY TO YOU, AND THEN WE'RE GOING TO SEE IF YOU UNDERSTAND THE STORY. IT'S CALLED "THE SANCHEZ FAMILY AND THE GRAPE STRIKE."

Problem Presentation

Teacher reads the problem.

(reads) MR. AND MRS. SANCHEZ AND THEIR SEVEN CHILDREN CAME FROM MEXICO TO LIVE IN CALIFORNIA ONE YEAR AGO. MR. SANCHEZ HAD BEEN TOLD BY RELATIVES WHO HAD BEEN TO THE UNITED STATES THAT HE COULD MAKE A LOT OF MONEY VERY QUICKLY IF HE CAME TO CALIFORNIA. WHEN MR. SANCHEZ ARRIVED IN CALIFORNIA, HE FOUND THAT IT WAS VERY HARD TO MAKE A LIVING WORKING IN THE FIELDS. SINCE THE SANCHEZ FAMILY HAS BEEN LIVING IN CALIFORNIA, IT HAS HAD TO MOVE MANY TIMES IN ORDER TO FOLLOW THE CROPS AND FIND WORK. THE FAMILY HAS TRAVELED AS FAR AS TEXAS AND MICHIGAN TO WORK IN THE FIELDS. THE WORK IN THE FIELDS IS VERY HARD. EVERYONE IN THE FAMILY EXCEPT LITTLE CARLOS WORKS IN THE FIELDS SO THAT THE FAMILY CAN MAKE ENOUGH MONEY TO GET BY WITH. EVEN MRS. SANCHEZ, WHO USED TO STAY AT HOME AND TAKE CARE OF THE HOME WHEN THEY LIVED IN MEXICO, NOW MUST WORK IN THE FIELDS. THE PAY FOR THE WORK IS VERY LOW. MR. AND MRS. SANCHEZ FIND THAT THEY GET FURTHER AND FURTHER IN DEBT EACH YEAR.

THE SANCHEZ FAMILY IS NOW LIVING IN THE SAN JOAQUIN VALLEY OF CALIFORNIA. THE FAMILY WENT TO LIVE THERE TO WORK IN THE GRAPE FIELDS. FOR A WHILE EVERYTHING THERE WAS OK. RECENTLY A LOT OF THINGS HAVE BEEN HAPPENING IN THE VALLEY THAT MR. AND MRS. SANCHEZ DO NOT FULLY UNDERSTAND. MOST OF THE FIELD WORKERS HAVE SAID THAT THEY WILL NOT GO TO WORK NEXT WEEK BECAUSE THE MEXICAN-AMERICAN UNION LED BY JUAN GONZALES, WHO WAS VERY POPULAR WITH THE WORKERS, HAS CALLED A STRIKE. THE UNION IS DEMANDING THAT THE OWNERS OF THE GRAPE FIELDS PAY THE WORKERS MORE MONEY AND GIVE THEM BETTER WORKER BENEFITS. THE WORKERS WHO BELONG TO THE UNION ARE THREATENING TO ATTACK ANY WORKER WHO TRIES TO GO TO WORK WHILE THE STRIKE IS ON.

MR. SANCHEZ IS NOT A MEMBER OF THE UNION. HE WANTS VERY MUCH TO GO TO WORK NEXT WEEK. HE HAS A LOT OF BILLS TO PAY AND NEEDS MONEY FOR FOOD AND CLOTHING. THE

FAMILY SIMPLY CANNOT GET BY ON THE SMALL AMOUNT OF MONEY THAT THE UNION HAS PROMISED MR. SANCHEZ IF HE JOINS IT AND REFUSES TO WORK NEXT WEEK. MR. SANCHEZ ALSO REALIZES THAT IF THE GRAPES ARE NOT PICKED WITHIN THE NEXT TWO WEEKS, THEY WILL ROT. HE HAS HEARD THAT THESE STRIKES SOMETIMES LAST FOR MONTHS. HIS BOSS TOLD HIM THAT IF HE WANTS TO GO TO WORK NEXT MONDAY MORNING, THE DAY THE STRIKE IS TO BEGIN, HE WILL GIVE HIM PROTECTION FROM THE UNIONIZED WORKERS. MRS. SANCHEZ THINKS MR. SANCHEZ SHOULD SUPPORT THE STRIKE SO THAT HE CAN MAKE HIGHER WAGES IN THE FUTURE. OK. WHAT'S THE PROBLEM?

S: IT'S ABOUT THIS GUY, ABOUT THE PLANTS OR SOMETHING?

S: IT'S ABOUT A CHICANO GROUP THAT CAME FROM MEXICO, AND THEY WANTED TO FIND A WAY TO EARN A LIVING IN THE UNITED STATES. SO HE HEARD FROM HIS RELATIVES THAT CALIFORNIA, WORK IN CALIFORNIA, WOULD BE THE BEST PLACE, AND SO THEY WENT TO CALIFORNIA AND THEY WORKED IN THE CROPS, BUT THEY FOUND IT WAS HARD TO DO THAT, IT WAS REALLY HARD. EVERYBODY BUT THE LITTLEST SON WORKED. EVEN THE WIFE WORKED AND THEY WENT TO TEXAS AND NEW MEXICO AND SOME OTHER PLACES.

T: MICHIGAN, RIGHT?

S: YEAH.

T: ANYBODY ELSE?

S: THE PROBLEM IS WHETHER OR NOT TO STRIKE, 'CAUSE IF THEY DO DECIDE NOT TO STRIKE, THEY'D BE GOING AGAINST FELLOW WORKERS EVEN THOUGH THEY WANT TO STRIKE. BUT IF THEY DON'T STRIKE, THE GRAPES WON'T, YOU KNOW, ROT 'CAUSE THAT'S THE PROBLEM, WHETHER TO LET THE GRAPES ROT OR NOT.

T: OK. WHAT'S THE MOTHER'S POSITION IN THIS?

S: SHE WANTS HIM TO WORK.

T: UH-HUH.

S: TO MAKE THE STRIKE.

T: OK. CAN YOU THINK OF ANY REASONS WHY SHE MIGHT WANT HIM TO WORK?

S: TO PAY OFF THE BILLS AND STUFF.

S: YEAH.

T: OK. ALL RIGHT. WHAT SORTS OF THINGS MIGHT HAPPEN, MIGHT HAPPEN IF HE DOES CHOOSE TO WORK?

S: THE GRAPES WON'T ROT.

T: WHAT ELSE, WHAT OTHER THINGS MIGHT HAPPEN IF HE CHOOSES TO WORK?

Discussion of Problem: Students do not formulate problem immediately. Teacher continues to probe until story is interpreted in terms of the underlying issue.

Interpretation of problem and issues

S: GET BEAT UP.

S: YEAH.

S: BUT IF HE DOESN'T WORK, HE WON'T BE ABLE TO PAY HIS BILLS.

T: YES. YOU'VE TALKED A LITTLE BIT ABOUT WHAT OTHER THINGS MIGHT HAPPEN IF HE CHOOSES NOT TO WORK.

S: WELL, IF THE STRIKE, YOU KNOW, PREVAILS, THEN HE'D GET HIGHER WAGES.

T: ANY OTHER THINGS? WHAT ABOUT HIS RELATIONSHIP WITH HIS FRIENDS AND THAT SORT OF THING?

S: HE'D BE CONSIDERED A TRAITOR.

S: HE WOULD BE A PROBLEM TO THE STRIKERS.

T: YEAH, THERE'S GOING TO BE A LOT OF PRESSURE ON HIM EITHER WAY. ALL RIGHT. WHAT DIFFERENT KINDS OF POSSIBILITIES ARE THERE IN . . . WHAT THINGS MIGHT HE DO?

Getting inside problem situation

S: HE COULD CALL A MEETING OF ALL THE WORKERS.

S: AND HAVE A VOTE OR SOMETHING AND SEE HOW THEY FEEL.

T: OK. WHAT ELSE, WHAT OTHER THINGS MIGHT HE DO? JUST THE SIMPLE ONES. WHAT ARE THE TWO MOST LOGICAL THINGS THAT HE MIGHT DO?

S: WORK.

T: RIGHT. EXACTLY. ONE OF THEM IS WORK, AND WHAT'S THE OTHER ONE?

S: NOT WORK.

T: NOT WORK. THAT'S RIGHT. OK. THOSE SEEM TO BE THREE ALTERNATIVES. LET'S TALK A LITTLE BIT ABOUT OUR CHARACTERS. WHAT SORT OF A PERSON DO YOU THINK MR. SANCHEZ IS?

Phase II: Selecting Participants

Role Analysis

S: HE SEEMS TO BE AN HONEST PERSON AND A HARD WORKER WHO WANTS TO WORK FOR HIS PAY, BUT HE HAS THIS PROBLEM—WHETHER OR NOT TO LET THE GRAPES ROT OR TO GET HIS, YOU KNOW, OR TO GET HIS BILLS PAID OFF, OR TO GO WITH THE STRIKE AND GET HIGHER WAGES IF THE STRIKE PREVAILS.

T: THAT'S RIGHT. ANYBODY ELSE WANT TO ADD ANYTHING TO MR. SANCHEZ? THE KIND OF PERSON HE IS? HE'S IN A REAL SPOT, ISN'T HE? WHAT ABOUT MRS. SANCHEZ? WHAT SORT OF A PERSON DO YOU THINK SHE IS?

S: JUST LIKE AN ORDINARY MOTHER, WORRYING ABOUT HER KIDS.

S: FOOD AND STUFF LIKE THAT. SHE WANTS HIGHER WAGES, IF POSSIBLE.

T: RIGHT.

S: IT WOULD BE EASIER ON THEM.

T: YEAH. SHE'S KIND OF TAKEN A STAND. WHY DO YOU THINK THAT SHE'S TAKEN A STAND?

S: TO TRY TO INFLUENCE HIM.

T: UH-HUH. WHY DO YOU THINK SHE TOOK THAT STAND RATHER THAN ANOTHER ONE? REMEMBER WHAT HER STAND WAS.

S: NOT TO WORK.

T: NOT TO WORK. RIGHT. NOT TO WORK. YEAH. ANY IDEAS?

S: HE'LL GET MORE WAGES.

S: SHE'S PROBABLY WORRYING ABOUT HIS WELL-BEING TOO.

S: YEAH. SHE'S WORRIED ABOUT HER HUSBAND.

T: OK. DO WE NEED ANYBODY ELSE? DO WE NEED, LIKE, FOR EXAMPLE, THEY HAVE WHAT, SEVEN CHILDREN? WAS THAT THE NUMBER THEY HAD?

S: YEAH.

T: DO WE NEED ONE OF THE KIDS? ARE WE GOING TO HAVE THIS BE A FAMILY DISCUSSION OF WHETHER TO WORK OR WHETHER NOT TO WORK?

S: WELL, MAYBE WE COULD BE THE STRIKERS OR FELLOW WORKERS.

T: A FELLOW WORKER? DO YOU WANT TO HAVE ONE FELLOW WORKER WHO'S NOT GOING TO WORK AND ONE FELLOW WORKER WHO IS GOING TO WORK?

Selection of players

S: YEAH.

T: TALKING TO THE MOTHER AND FATHER.

S: UH-HUH.

S: DIFFERENT OPINIONS, HUH?

T: YEAH. IS THAT ALL RIGHT? SO WE HAVE OUR OTHER TWO CHARACTERS—ONE PERSON THAT'S GOING TO SUPPORT THE STRIKE AND ONE PERSON WHO'S GOING TO GO TO WORK ON MONDAY.

I GUESS WE'RE DUE TO SELECT THOSE PEOPLE. WHO WOULD LIKE TO PLAY MR. SANCHEZ? WOMEN CAN PLAY MEN'S ROLES; MEN CAN PLAY WOMEN'S ROLES. THERE'S NO HANG-UP ON THAT. YOU WANT TO PLAY MR. SANCHEZ?

Selecting participants

S: RIGHT.

T: WHO WOULD LIKE TO PLAY MRS. SANCHEZ? (laughter) PATTY, YOU WANT TO TRY IT? IF YOU DON'T WANT TO, YOU DON'T HAVE TO.

S: COME ON.

T: WHO WOULD LIKE TO PLAY THE WORKER? REMEMBER, BOTH MEN AND WOMEN GO TO THE FIELDS. WHO WOULD LIKE TO PLAY THE WORKER WHO IS GOING TO STRIKE? OK.

S: I'M TRYING TO THINK OF ANYTHING TO DO.

T: OK. YOU'RE GOING TO BE THE WORKER THAT'S GOING TO GO TO WORK. YOU CAN BE CONVINCING, HUH?

S: I'VE GOT TO THINK OF SOME GOOD REASONS.

T: NOW, I WANT YOU FOUR TO THINK ABOUT YOUR ROLES AND ABOUT THE KIND OF PERSON YOU ARE AND THE KIND OF FEELINGS YOU HAVE AND THAT SORT OF THING WHILE I TALK TO THE OTHER THREE OF US. OK? YOUR JOB IS TO HELP ME IN THE DISCUSSION. YOUR JOB IS REALLY A VERY IMPORTANT ONE, BECAUSE REMEMBER WHAT I SAID IN THE BEGINNING. DISCUSSION IS REALLY THE MOST IMPORTANT PART. WHAT I WANT YOU TO DO IS, I WANT YOU TO LOOK AT THE REALITY OF THE SITUATION. WOULD PEOPLE REALLY PLAY IT THIS WAY, OR ARE THEY KIND OF JUST ACTING? DO THEY REALLY GET INTO THE ROLES, YOU KNOW, REALLY, THE REALITY OF IT. YOU GOT THAT? WHAT I WANT YOU TO DO IS, I WANT YOU TO LOOK AT PEOPLE'S FEELINGS. YOU KNOW, TO SEE WHETHER PEOPLE WERE REALLY HURTING EACH OTHER'S FEELINGS, OR WERE THEY KIND OF TENDING TO EACH OTHER AND THAT SORT OF THING, OR WERE THEY REALLY KIND OF GETTING AT EACH OTHER? THE FEELINGS THAT MR. SANCHEZ HAS FOR HIS WIFE AND THE REVERSE. OK? GOT THOSE? OK. WHAT I WANT YOU TO DO, I WANT YOU TO THINK ABOUT THE SORTS OF ALTERNATIVES. WE'RE GOING TO PLAY THIS AGAIN, AND I WANT YOU TO PLAY ONE OF THE CHARACTERS WHEN WE PLAY IT THE SECOND TIME. OK? AND I WANT YOU TO THINK ABOUT DIFFERENT WAYS THAT WE MIGHT PLAY THE SAME SITUATION.

S: HOW YOU DO IT?

T: YEAH. RIGHT. HOW YOU MIGHT DO IT DIF-FERENTLY THAN THEY DID IT. IN OTHER WORDS, THINK ABOUT IT. HERE'S ANOTHER WAY WE MIGHT PLAY THE SAME SITUATION.

S: OH, OK, YEAH. I UNDERSTAND.

T: NOW, ARE OUR FOUR ACTORS READY? WHY DON'T WE SIT YOU ON THIS SIDE, MOST OF YOU ARE ON THIS SIDE OF THE TABLE. AND THEN YOU JUST KIND OF ACT OUT YOUR PARTS. OK? REMEMBER, OBSERVERS, WHAT WE'RE LOOKING FOR?

S: YEAH.

S: YEAH.

T: OK. WHENEVER YOU'RE READY. LET'S GO. WHO SHALL WE HAVE START? MR. SANCHEZ, SHALL YOU START?

S: I AM FACED WITH THE DECISION OF WHETHER OR NOT TO STRIKE OR TO WORK, AND I WANT TO KNOW YOUR DIFFERENT VIEWS ON WHY YOU'RE STRIKING OR WHY YOU'RE NOT STRIKING.

S: I AM FULLY CONVINCED THAT WE SHOULD STRIKE. WE'VE BEEN WORKING LIKE THIS FOR TWENTY YEARS. I'VE BEEN OUT THERE IN THOSE FIELDS AND ALL WE GET IS NOTHING—PAY,

Phase IV: Preparing the Observers

Observer: Checking for reality.

Observer: Examining participants' feelings.

Observer: Considering alternatives.

Phase V: Enactment Begins

JUNIOR COLLEGE LIBRARY

PEANUTS, NOTHING! THEY'VE JUST BEEN THROWING RAGS AT US. I THINK WE DESERVE MORE PAY, AND THE ONLY WAY WE'RE GOING TO GET IT IS IF WE STRIKE.

S: I THINK WE SHOULD GO TO WORK BECAUSE THEY'RE GOING TO BE PROTECTING US FROM, LIKE THE STRIKERS, AND WE WILL BE GETTING MORE PROTECTION, SO I THINK WE'D BE OK IF WE WENT TO WORK.

S: OK? IS THAT ALL YOU CAN SAY IS OK? I THINK THAT WE WOULD BE UTTERLY STUPID IF WE WENT TO WORK. I THINK THAT THE ONLY WAY THE PEOPLE ARE GOING TO GIVE US MORE MONEY—AND THAT'S WHAT WE NEED AND YOU KNOW IT AND SO DO I; WE NEED MORE MONEY— AND THE ONLY WAY WE'RE GOING TO GET IT IS IF WE STRIKE. STRIKE IS ALL THE ANSWER.

S: BUT IF WE GO ON STRIKE . . .

S: IF WE GO ON STRIKE?

S: WE WON'T, THE GRAPES WILL ROT ANY WAY, SO WE WON'T BE GETTING PAID THE HIGH WAGES.

S: THE GRAPES WILL GROW AGAIN.

S: NEXT YEAR.

S: YES, THAT'S WHEN WE NEED THE MONEY.

S: WHAT ARE YOU GOING TO DO IN THE MEANTIME? HOW'RE YOU GOING TO PUT FOOD ON THE TABLE? THERE'S A LOT OF DIFFERENT WAYS TO DO THIS. THERE'S A LOT OF PROS AND CONS. I REALLY DON'T KNOW WHICH IS THE BEST WAY TO DO IT OR WHAT'S THE BEST ANSWER, BUT IT WILL BE A HARD DECISION.

T: OK, LET'S STOP THERE. IT SEEMS LIKE WE'VE COME TO AN IMPASSE. (laughter) OK. WE'LL TALK ABOUT IT A LITTLE BIT. THEN WE'LL GO BACK AND THINK ABOUT IT. LET'S LOOK TO OUR OBSERVERS FIRST AND THEN WE'LL COME BACK AND TALK A LITTLE BIT TO EACH OF YOU ABOUT THE SORTS OF THINGS THAT YOU'RE DOING. REALITY! OK? LET'S TALK A LITTLE BIT ABOUT THE REALITY OF THE SITUATION. DO YOU THINK THEY WERE REAL?

Teacher breaks in when discussion bogs down or has reached a good stopping point.

Phase VI: Discussion

S: KIND OF.

T: WHAT SORTS OF, WHAT WERE THE KIND OF PARTS OF IT?

Teacher elicits main focus of discussion.

S: WELL, SHE WOULD HAVE BEEN BEGGING HIM NOT TO WORK SINCE SHE DIDN'T WANT HIM TO WORK OR ANYTHING.

Review of action of role play.

T: OK, YOU THOUGHT SHE WOULD HAVE BEEN MORE ACTIVE AND MORE A PART OF THE CONVERSATION.

S: YEAH.

T: OK. YOU KIND OF AGREE WITH THAT, DO YOU THINK? WHAT WERE YOU FEELING LIKE? WHEN

VERNON REGIONAL
JUNIOR COLLEGE LIBRARY

YOU WERE DOING . . . YOU REALLY DIDN'T QUITE KNOW WHAT TO SAY?

S: NO.

T: OK, BUT YOU KIND OF, YOU WERE THINKING ABOUT THE WHOLE THING. DO YOU THINK A REAL MRS. SANCHEZ WOULD HAVE KIND OF STAYED SILENT NOT KNOWING WHAT TO SAY?

S: NO.

S: SHE WOULD.

T: YOU THINK SHE WOULD HAVE? YOU SAID SHE HAD ALREADY TAKEN A STAND. OK. THAT'S POSSIBLE, BUT IT'S NOT OUT OF THE ORDINARY THAT SHE MIGHT HAVE BEEN QUIET TOO, YOU KNOW. VERY OFTEN, A LOT OF WOMEN, YOU KNOW, LET THE MEN TALK.

S: RIGHT. ESPECIALLY.

T: RIGHT. HOW ABOUT THE REST OF THE REALITY? HAVE YOU ANYTHING ELSE YOU WANT TO SAY?

S: NO, THEY'RE ALL RIGHT.

T: OK. DOES ANYBODY ELSE WANT TO TALK ABOUT IT BEING A REAL SITUATION? DID YOU FEEL COMFORTABLE IN EACH OF YOUR ROLES?

S: AFTER I STARTED TALKING, YES.

S: IT'S JUST THAT I COULDN'T FIND ENOUGH REASONS TO SUPPORT WHY TO STRIKE.

T: IT'S TOUGH, ISN'T IT?

S: YES.

T: IT'S A TOUGH SITUATION.

S: THAT'S THE WAY IT IS. PEOPLE DON'T HAVE ENOUGH REASONS. JUST THAT THE MAJORITY OF PEOPLE ARE GOING ONE WAY.

T: RIGHT, AND IT'S KIND OF A HERD INSTINCT THAT YOU FOLLOW ALONG.

S: I WAS JUST TRYING TO BE A STUBBORN OLD MULE, YOU KNOW.

T: LINDA, LET'S SEE, YOU WERE LOOKING AT THE FEELINGS. WHAT DO YOU THINK ABOUT . . . ANYTHING THAT REALLY CAUGHT YOUR ATTENTION?

S: WELL, HE WAS REALLY GETTING INTO THE ROLE, AND IT SHOWED PHYSICALLY IN THE WAY HE FELT.

T: EDWIN KIND OF LASHED OUT AT PAUL, DIDN'T HE, A LITTLE BIT? WHAT DID YOU THINK ABOUT THAT? DID YOU THINK THAT WAS REALLY, YOU KNOW, THE KIND OF FEELINGS? OK. WE'LL COME BACK TO THAT ONE.

S: REALLY, IT IS, BECAUSE WHEN YOU STRONGLY BELIEVE IN SOMETHING, YOU'RE GONNA REALLY SUPPORT YOURSELF; YOU'RE GOING TO LASH OUT AT ANYBODY THAT COMES UP AGAINST YOU.

Discussion of major focus

Examination of feelings

Teacher picks up a particular incident from enactment and uses it as a focus of feelings.

S: ESPECIALLY IN DISCUSSION, THAT HAPPENS.

S: YEAH.

T: OK. LET'S COME BACK TO YOU IN A LITTLE BIT, IN TERMS OF ALTERNATIVES, 'CAUSE I WANT TO TALK ABOUT, A LITTLE BIT MORE ABOUT THE FEELINGS. IMA, YOU WERE KIND OF COMING OUT, IT SEEMED TO ME, A LITTLE BIT MORE AGAINST GOING TO WORK THAN FOR GOING TO WORK. WAS THERE SOME REASON FOR THAT?

S: YES. IF I GET HURT OR, SAY, YOU KNOW, KILLED OR SOMETHING, IF I GO TO WORK, WHAT'S GOING TO HAPPEN TO MY FAMILY? THERE'S GOING TO BE, YOU KNOW, ROUGHER TIMES ON THEM. I GOTTA THINK OF THEM INSTEAD OF MYSELF.

T: UH-HMMM.

S: AND THAT BROUGHT ME TO MY DECISION.

T: ALL RIGHT. WHAT DIFFERENT SORTS OF WAYS MIGHT YOU PLAY THE SAME THING? OUR FOUR CHARACTERS WILL STAY THE SAME, MR. AND MRS. SANCHEZ AND THE FARM WORKERS—ONE IS FOR AND ONE AGAINST. WHAT DIFFERENT SORTS OF THINGS MIGHT THE PERSON THAT IS FOR GOING TO WORK SAY? PAUL? WHAT OTHER THINGS BESIDES THE ONES THAT YOU SAID?

S: I DON'T KNOW.

T: ANY IDEAS? WHAT OTHER THINGS, WHAT OTHER, YOU KNOW, POSITIONS MIGHT YOU TAKE IN TERMS OF, TRY . . . THE FIRST TIME WE DIDN'T REALLY COME TO ANY KIND OF CONCLUSIONS AT ALL IN TERMS OF WHAT DIFFERENT SORTS OF THINGS MIGHT WE DO. IT'S TOUGH, ISN'T IT? REALLY.

S: YEAH.

S: NONE OF US TALK AT ALL (laughter).

T: YEAH, RIGHT. IT'S A TOUGH, IT'S A HARD SITUATION. ONE OF THE THINGS WE MIGHT DO IS HAVE THE MOTHER HAVE A MORE ACTIVE ROLE.

S: YES.

S: RIGHT.

S: SHE SHOULD TRY TO STAND UP, YOU KNOW, FOR HER HUSBAND'S SAFETY OR SOMETHING, FOR HER HUSBAND'S SAFETY.

T: UH-HMMM. STANDING UP MORE, TALKING MORE ABOUT THE CHILDREN AND THE FAMILY . . .

S: YEAH.

T: AND THINGS LIKE THAT, YOU KNOW, BRINGING IN, YOU KNOW, THE THINGS ABOUT THE DEBTS AND SOME THINGS LIKE THAT. SOME OF THE THINGS THAT YOU WERE BRINGING OUT ABOUT, YOU KNOW, IF WE DON'T TAKE A STAND NOW, WHERE'LL WE TAKE A STAND? YOU BROUGHT THAT OUT FAIRLY WELL, DIDN'T YOU? OK.

Developing next enactment

Preparing for second enactment

THOSE ARE SOME IDEAS. HOW ABOUT SOME MORE THINGS THAT MR. SANCHEZ MIGHT SAY?

S: WELL, LIKE WE'LL SAY THE ISSUE.

T: HE REALLY WILL BE ON THE FENCE, YOU MEAN, AND REALLY TALK ABOUT THE DIFFERENT FACTS AND THE VALUES, REALLY KIND OF GET AT THE VALUES, ACT AND TAKE A PART. IT'S ALL RIGHT, BECAUSE THE OBSERVERS HAVE A VERY IMPORTANT PART, TOO, BUT THESE PEOPLE SHOULD HAVE THE FIRST OPTION ON WHETHER THEY WANT TO TAKE A PART OR NOT, SINCE THEY DIDN'T ACT IN THE FIRST ONE. OK? AND THEN THE ONLY THING THAT I ASK YOU IS THAT YOU DON'T PLAY THE SAME ROLE THAT YOU DID THE FIRST TIME. OK? IN TERMS OF THE OTHER PEOPLE. IS THERE ANYBODY THAT WOULD LIKE TO PLAY MRS. SANCHEZ? OK, YOU WANT TO PLAY HER THIS TIME? OK. THINK ABOUT THE SORTS OF THINGS THAT YOU WANT TO TALK ABOUT. I'M GOING TO ASK YOU A LITTLE BIT ABOUT THE KINDS OF THINGS YOU WANT TO DO THIS TIME WITH YOUR ROLE. HOW ABOUT MR. SANCHEZ? ANYBODY?

S: DON'T LOOK AT ME! (laughter)

S: WHO, ME?

S: YEAH, OK.

T: OK?

T: OK. WHO WOULD LIKE TO BE THE PERSON THAT WANTS TO GO ON STRIKE?

S: I GUESS I WOULD BE.

T: OK. ALL RIGHT. WOULD YOU RATHER NOT PLAY THAT ROLE THEN? YOU WOULDN'T? WHO WANTS TO GO ON STRIKE?

S: OH, I GUESS I WILL.

T: OK. AND WHO WANTS TO STAY, AND WHO WANTS TO GO TO WORK?

S: I GUESS I WILL.

T: YOU WANT TO BE THE PERSON THAT WANTS TO GO TO WORK? OK.

(Discussion proceeds to the orientation of observers and role players, followed by second enactment.)

S: ACCORDING TO MY WIFE, SHE'S TOLD ME THAT THE BEST THING TO DO FOR ME IS TO STRIKE, BUT I FEEL MAYBE IT MIGHT BE BETTER FOR THE GRAPES, TO BRING THE GRAPES IN. REALLY, I DON'T KNOW WHAT TO DO, SO I CALLED THIS MEETING TO FIND OUT WHAT MIGHT BE THE BEST DECISION.

S: STRIKE, AND THEN MAYBE, YOU KNOW, YOU COULD JUST EAT ONE BIG MEAL A DAY AND THEN KEEP THE OTHER MONEY TO PAY OFF YOUR BILLS AND MAYBE WORK IN, MAYBE FIND ANOTHER JOB FOR A WHILE.

Selection of players

Preparing second set of observers

Phase Seven: Reenactment

S: AND WHAT DO YOU HAVE TO SAY ABOUT THAT?

S: WELL, WE'RE GOING TO BE LOSING A LOT OF MONEY. SHE SHOULD HAVE ENOUGH PAY TO DO THAT, A LOT OF WORK.

S: YEAH, WELL I . . .

S: IF YOU WORK, YOU'RE GOING TO GO AGAINST ALL YOUR FRIENDS. YOU DON'T TRUST THEM?

S: I REALLY DON'T KNOW WHAT TO DO. I'D REALLY LIKE HELP; I'D BE HAPPY IF YOU GUYS WOULD HELP ME OUT, YOU KNOW.

S: YOU SHOULD STRIKE. YOU SHOULD DO WHAT EVERYBODY ELSE IS DOING.

S: YEAH, STRIKE.

S: NO, HE SHOULDN'T, BECAUSE HE'LL BE LOSING A LOT OF MONEY.

S: SO?

S: THEY'LL HELP YOU OUT. THEY'RE NOT GOING TO LET YOU STARVE.

S: I GUESS EVERYBODY IN THE COMMUNITY COULD HELP EACH OTHER, RIGHT? IF WE DID STRIKE.

S: BUT WHAT ABOUT THE GRAPES? THEY'LL GO TO ROT.

S: THEY DON'T WORRY ABOUT US, THE GRAPE OWNERS. WHY SHOULD WE CARE ABOUT THEM?

S: IF THEY CARED ABOUT US, THEY'D GIVE US MORE WAGES AND WE WOULDN'T HAVE TO STRIKE. RIGHT!

S: I SEE, SO IF THE GRAPES ROT, THAT'LL JUST BE ANOTHER PUNISHMENT FOR THE PEOPLE.

S: WE WILL, TOO, IN A WAY, BUT THIS IS THE ONLY WAY WE CAN GET HIGHER WAGES.

S: I SEE.

S: WHAT IF WE ALL LOSE OUR JOBS? HOW ARE WE GOING TO FIND ANOTHER JOB FOR THOSE MANY PEOPLE?

S: WELL, IT SEEMS TO ME THAT THE BEST ALTER-NATIVE IS TO STRIKE. THIS IS GOING TO BE HARD WITH ALL OF US. ALL OF US ARE GOING TO HAVE TO CONTRIBUTE TO EACH OTHER AND HELP EACH OTHER OUT IN EVERY WAY. BUT IT SEEMS TO ME THAT'S THE ONLY CONCLUSION I CAN COME TO. I MEAN, YOU KNOW, IT'S THE ONLY WAY OUT.

S: WE HAVE TO STAND TOGETHER.

S: STAND TOGETHER, FOR ALL OF US, FOR EACH OTHER, AND THAT WAY, MAYBE WE CAN LIVE UNTIL THE STRIKE IS OVER AND WE HAVE HIGHER WAGES, AND THEN OUR FAMILIES WILL BE BETTER OFF.

S: NO, BECAUSE IT STILL ISN'T EARNED MONEY.

S: BUT THE STRIKE ISN'T JUST FOR CERTAIN FAMILIES. IT'S FOR EVERYBODY. A STRIKE IS FOR EVERYBODY.

T: OK. GOOD JOB! NOW LET'S TALK A LITTLE BIT ABOUT WHAT YOU'VE JUST DONE IN TERMS OF THE ENACTMENT. I THOUGHT YOU REALLY GOT INTO IT.

Phase VIII: Discussion and Evaluation

S: ARE WE GOING TO DO IT AGAIN?

T: NO, THIS IS IT. THAT'S THE LAST PART. OK. LET'S TALK ABOUT THE REALITY FIRST. PATTY? DO YOU THINK IT WAS REAL THIS TIME?

Using observers to help facilitate the discussion.

S: YEAH, THEY REALLY DIDN'T SAY THAT MUCH.

S: TO THE PART THAT GROWN-UPS KEPT SAYING TO GET MORE FOOD ON THE TABLE. IN OTHER WORDS, HE WASN'T SAYING WHAT PROTECTION THEY WOULD HAVE IF THEY DIDN'T GO ON STRIKE. THEY SHOULD HAVE BEEN TALKING ABOUT PROTECTION. OTHERWISE . . .

Paraphrasing

T: OK. WHAT WERE YOU LOOKING . . . YOU WERE LOOKING AT FEELINGS, WEREN'T YOU? WHO DO YOU THINK REALLY EXPRESSED, WHAT KIND OF FEELINGS DO YOU THINK CAME OUT?

Exploring feelings

S: THE FATHER OF THE FAMILY REALLY DIDN'T ASK TOO MUCH. THE SECOND ONE WAS BETTER THAN THE FIRST ONE.

T: UH-HMMM. HOW SO?

S: 'CAUSE THEY WERE TALKING MORE AND GOT INTO IT MORE.

S: I THINK IT WAS WRONG A LOT MORE.

T: UH-HUH.

S: THERE WASN'T AS MUCH EMPTY SPACES. THERE WAS A LOT OF THINGS COME UP.

T: RIGHT. IDEAS WERE COMING OUT. OK. HOW ABOUT THE SENSE OF WHAT'S GOING TO HAPPEN IF IT WAS PLAYED THIS WAY?

S: THEY CHOSE TO STRIKE. I THINK THAT WAS THE RIGHT DECISION MYSELF. THE UNION, IF YOU GO ON STRIKE, THAT MONEY IS PUT ASIDE TO HELP YOU WHILE YOU ARE ON STRIKE, RIGHT? AND THEY'RE GOING TO BACK YOU, AND IF THE OWNERS TRY SOMETHING, THAT'S WHY THE UNION IS THERE, TO HAVE PROTECTION. THEY'RE GOING TO, THEY'RE, YOU KNOW, THE UNION IS GOING TO UNIFY ALL THE MEMBERS OF THE UNION, AND THEY'RE GOING TO HELP THEM OUT. AND IN THE END THE OWNERS ARE GOING TO HAVE TO BEND BECAUSE, YOU KNOW, THEY HAVE TO COME FORTH BECAUSE THEY'RE LOSING ALL THIS MONEY SINCE THE GRAPES ARE NOT BEING PICKED. THEY'RE GOING TO ROT ANYWAY, WHETHER THEY'RE PICKED OR NOT, YOU KNOW.

Reflection

T: RIGHT.

S: AND I THINK IT WILL BE GOOD. I THINK IT WAS THE RIGHT DECISION.

T: OK. HOW ABOUT THE VALUES? FOR EXAMPLE, WHAT KIND OF, LET'S SEE, CAROL, YOU WERE FOR OR AGAINST?

Teacher focuses on values.

S: I WAS AGAINST THE STRIKE.

T: AGAINST THE STRIKE. WHAT KIND OF VALUES DO YOU THINK CAROL HAD?

S: I'M TRYING TO REMEMBER WHAT SHE SAID.

T: OK. CAROL, MAYBE YOU CAN HELP US BY SAYING WHAT SORTS OF THINGS WERE REALLY IMPORTANT TO YOU.

S: SO THEY'D GO BACK TO THEIR JOBS. SO THEY CAN AFFORD FOOD ON THE TABLE FOR THEIR FAMILY.

T: RIGHT.

S: MOST OF EVERYBODY WILL BE OUT OF WORK AND LIKE, SOME OF THE PEOPLE WHO'VE NEVER BEEN ON A JOB BEFORE . . .

S: IF THEY CAN AFFORD TO PAY THEM, THEN THEY CAN AFFORD TO PAY US THE EXTRA MONEY.

T: WHAT DO YOU THINK ABOUT THAT?

S: BECAUSE IN THE LONG RUN THEY'LL BE LOSING MORE MONEY.

S: I DON'T KNOW.

T: OK. HOW ABOUT, HOW ABOUT THE VALUES THAT, YOU CAME DOWN FINALLY FOR, IN FAVOR OF STRIKING, DIDN'T YOU? WHY? WHY DID YOU DO THAT?

Teacher refocuses on values.

S: OH, FOR MANY REASONS. FIRST OF ALL, I WOULDN'T GET MUGGED (laughter).

T: NOT BAD.

S: I'D BE PROTECTING MY WIFE AND MY FAMILY. I WOULD ALSO BE PROTECTED BY THE UNION, LIKE, WHEN YOU SAID, YOU KNOW, WE'D HAVE MONEY TO SURVIVE AND ALSO THE COMMITTEE COULD CHIP IN FOR EACH FAMILY. WE COULD WORK TOGETHER SO THAT WE COULD, YOU KNOW, LIVE UNTIL THE STRIKE WAS OVER, AND THEN WHEN IT WAS OVER WE WOULD EVEN HAVE MORE MONEY, AFTERWARDS, BECAUSE THE WAGES WOULD BE HIGHER, YOU KNOW, IF IT CAME OUT RIGHT.

Reflection

T: WHAT HAPPENS IF THE STRIKE LASTS THREE MONTHS?

Examining consequences

S: UH, WELL, THAT COULD PRESENT A PROBLEM.

S: IT SEEMS, YOU KNOW, EVERYBODY, IF EVERY-BODY FEELS THIS WAY, YOU'D EACH HAVE SOMEBODY TO GO CRY ON THEIR SHOULDERS. YOU KNOW, YOU HAVE FRIENDS AROUND YOU WHO FEEL THE SAME WAY, SO THEY CAN HELP YOU RELEASE SOME OF THAT PAIN AND THAT WAY, IT WOULDN'T BE—IT WOULD BE BAD—BUT

IT WOULDN'T BE THAT BAD IF EVERYBODY FELT THE SAME WAY.

T: OK. YOU JUST KIND OF HAVE TO HANG TO-GETHER, HUH? OK. SAME QUESTION, WHAT HAPPENS?

S: WELL, FIRST OF ALL, LIKE SHE SAID, YOU KNOW, FRIENDS AND EVERYTHING. BUT SOMETIMES I THINK, IF I WAS ACTUALLY MR. SANCHEZ AND IT WAS GOING ON FOR THREE MONTHS, I WOULD KIND OF BE THINKING MAYBE I MADE THE WRONG DECISION, YOU KNOW. I'D BE THINKING MAYBE I SHOULD HAVE GONE THE OTHER WAY, YOU KNOW. AM I A GOOD FATHER? DID I DO THE RIGHT THING, YOU KNOW?

T: IT ALWAYS COMES UP, DOES IT?

S: YEAH.

T: SAME QUESTION. WHAT HAPPENS IF IT LASTS A LONG TIME?

S: YOU START GETTING DIFFERENT THOUGHTS; YOU START PANICKING.

T: WHAT KIND OF THINGS MIGHT YOU BE ABLE TO DO?

S: EXPLAIN TO THEM AGAIN. THREE-FOURTHS OF THEM FEEL, YOU KNOW, WHAT THEY'RE DOING IS FOR A GOOD CAUSE AND IT'S REALLY GOING TO HELP THEM OUT IN THE LONG RUN.

S: IT HAS TO BE THIS WAY 'CAUSE THEY'RE ON STRIKE, RIGHT? SO, YOU KNOW, IT'S HARD, BUT IF THEY STAY TOGETHER IT'LL BE ALL RIGHT.

S: SOONER OR LATER, THEY'RE GONNA FIND OUT THAT THE JOB THEY WANTED, THEY'RE GONNA LOSE IT, AND THEN THEY'RE NOT GOING TO HAVE NOTHING.

S: AND NO ONE'S GOING TO HELP US?

S: PROBABLY IF THEY CAN'T PAY THAT MUCH. PROBABLY IF THEY, THEY'D PROBABLY BE GETTING MORE MONEY FROM THE JOB THAN THEY NEEDED.

S: BUT IF IT LASTS, LIKE, FOR THREE MONTHS, MAYBE THEY AREN'T WORKING, BUT THEN THE GROWERS AREN'T GETTING ANY MONEY EITHER.

S: RIGHT.

S: SO THEY'LL BE HURTING TOO.

T: WHICH ONE WILL BE HURTING MORE THOUGH, INCIDENTALLY? THE GROWERS OR THE PICKERS?

S: THE PICKERS.

S: THE GRAPES THAT WERE ROTTING, YOU KNOW, THAT WAS ALSO AN ADVANTAGE. BECAUSE THE GRAPE OWNERS, YOU KNOW, THAT WOULD BE A DISADVANTAGE TO THEM, BECAUSE THEN THEY WOULDN'T HAVE ANY GRAPES.

Integration and reflection

S: IT'D PUT PRESSURE ON THEM.

S: MORE THAN ON US.

T: OK. LET'S THINK ABOUT THE SITUATION. IF YOU WERE IN THE SAME SORT OF SITUATION AND IT WAS YOUR FAMILY, DO YOU THINK THAT YOU WOULD PROBABLY GO OUT ON STRIKE OR DO YOU THINK YOU WOULD BREAK DOWN AND WORK?

S: I'D GO FOR THE PROTECT ME, YOU KNOW.

T: YOU PROBABLY WOULD WORK, HUH?

S: NO, OUT ON STRIKE.

T: WHAT WOULD YOU DO?

S: STRIKE.

T: YOU THINK YOU WOULD?

S: YOU WOULD, WOULDN'T YOU?

S: NO, BECAUSE YOU DON'T KNOW WHAT WOULD HAPPEN. YOU DON'T KNOW, YOU DON'T KNOW WHAT'S GOING TO HAPPEN IF, LIKE SAY, YOU WENT ON THE STRIKE, THEN AFTER THREE MONTHS YOU, YOU KNOW, LOSE.

T: THAT'S RIGHT. YOU MAY HAVE THAT HOUSE AND THAT MORTGAGE TO PAY AND ALL THOSE SORTS OF THINGS.

S: YEAH.

T: LOTS AND LOTS OF PROBLEMS.

S: IT COSTS SO MUCH AND YOU DON'T HAVE THAT MUCH, AND THE UNION ONLY PAYS SO MUCH, AND THEN THEY . . .

T: YEAH. LINDA? WHAT WOULD YOU DO IN THE CIRCUM . . .

S: I DON'T KNOW.

T: YOU'RE NOT TALKING ABOUT YOUR CHARACTER ANY MORE; YOU'RE TALKING ABOUT YOURSELF.

S: I STILL THINK I'D STRIKE. BECAUSE, I MEAN, YOU'RE MORE LIABLE TO GET HURT IF YOU WORKED.

T: RIGHT.

S: YOU'D LOSE, WELL, IN A WAY, TO ME, YOU'D LOSE A LOT MORE, BECAUSE YOU'D BE LOSING YOUR FRIENDS, YOUR CLOSE ONES, 'CAUSE THEY'D PROBABLY STRIKE. WITH ME, THAT'S BEFORE . . .

T: THAT'S REALLY OF VALUE TO YOU.

S: UH-HUH.

T: YEAH, THAT'S NEAT.

S: UH-HUH, FRIENDS.

S: I REALLY THINK I WOULD STRIKE.

T: BECAUSE OF YOUR PROTECTION, OR BECAUSE YOUR FRIENDS, OR BECAUSE, YOU KNOW, THE

Phase IX: Sharing and Generalizing

Relating problem situation to real experience and current problems

HERD INSTINCT THAT YOU MENTIONED A LITTLE EARLIER? WHAT WOULD BE THE REASON THAT YOU WOULD?

S: I WOULD PROBABLY STRIKE FOR TWO REASONS— FOR MY OWN LIFE, YOU KNOW, AND LIKE, YOU KNOW, HEALTH, AND THE REST OF MY FAMILY.

S: YEAH, SAY IF YOU LOSE FRIENDS, BUT YOU CAN STILL KEEP YOUR JOB, REALLY.

S: YOU GOT TO WORRY ABOUT YOUR FAMILY. THEY'RE CLOSER THAN YOUR FRIENDS.

T: OK. ANYBODY ELSE WANT TO SAY ANYTHING ABOUT THE FAMILY SANCHEZ?

S: NO.

T: OK. THANKS, YOU DID A GOOD JOB ON THIS.

Exploring general principles of behavior

PLANNING
AND
PEER TEACHING

In this component you will plan a lesson based upon the Role Playing Model and then teach this lesson to a small group of peers, evaluating the lesson using the Teaching Analysis Guide.

Five steps in planning and organizing Role Playing lessons have been identified. Short discussions of the considerations involved in each of these steps are provided to guide you through planning a Role Playing lesson. The five planning steps are:

1. selecting the problem situation
2. organizing the materials for role playing
3. analyzing the problem and identifying the focus
4. determining educational objectives
5. completing the Planning Guide

The sections on these planning steps should be read in conjunction with your preparation of the peer teaching lesson and the completion of the Planning Guide at the end of this section. Steps 1 and 2 correspond to Part I of the Planning Guide (Problem Situation), Step 3 to Part II (Focus), Step 4 to Part III (Educational Objectives), and Step 5 to Part IV (Syntax).

Step 1 (Selecting the Problem Situation) discusses some of the factors involved in selecting an appropriate problem situation. It also identifies eight thematic sources, or categories, of problem situations and provides a way of thinking about the relative complexity of different problem situations. Step 2 (Organizing the Materials for Role Playing) identifies curriculum materials that contain problem situations. We also discuss the considerations involved in constructing your own problem stories and introduce supplementary materials such as briefing sheets. Step 3 asks you to analyze the content of the problem story for its major theme(s), values(s), and/or solution(s). At this point you will articulate a major focus. Once you have determined the major focus, you can think more specifically about the behavioral objectives you want to accomplish in this lesson. Step 4 outlines several categories of objectives. Finally, Step 5 asks you to complete the Planning Guide.

After you plan the lesson, you will peer-teach it to a small group of your colleagues. Select a topic (problem situation) that is appropriate for adults, but, if you wish, one that may also be used later when you microteach with a small group of students. We recommend this so that your peer teaching will seem real to you and your colleagues.

After you analyze the peer teaching lesson using the Teaching Analysis Guide, you may want to read the section on some considerations in initiating role playing activities that follows the Teaching Analysis Guide. In that section we review the various activities of the model and consider some of the factors involved in initiating each one. We provide examples of teacher statements or questions. To a certain extent, the impact of the model on the students' thoughts and feelings will depend on the clarity of your directions and on the questions you ask in pursuing one or two themes. However, it is probably best not to dwell on these refinements until *after* you have completed one peer teaching session. No doubt, there will be parts of the lesson that did not develop as you had anticipated. With the aid of the Teaching Analysis Guide and the discussion that follows it, you will probably identify alternative ways to initiate and carry out the activities.

A summary of the parts of this component includes:

A. Planning the lesson
   1. selecting the problem situation
   2. organizing the materials for role playing
   3. analyzing the problem and identifying the focus
   4. determining educational objectives
   5. completing the Planning Guide
B. Peer teaching the lesson
C. Analyzing the peer teaching using the Teaching Analysis Guide
D. Considerations in initiating the activities in the Role Playing Model
E. Microteaching the lesson

SELECTING THE PROBLEM SITUATION

The adequacy of the topic depends on many factors, such as the age of the students, their cultural background, the complexity of the problem situation, the sensitivity of the topic, and the students' experience with role playing. In general, as students gain experience with role playing and develop a high degree of group cohesiveness and acceptance of one another, as well as a close rapport with the teacher, the more sensitive the topic can be. The first few problem situations should be matters of concern to the students but not extremely sensitive issues. It's not a bad idea to ask the students themselves to develop a list of themes or problems they would like to work on. Then, the teacher can locate or develop problem situations that fit the themes.

The age and developmental stage of the students can be a source of topics as well as a guide for unsuitable topics. For example, very young children are concerned with issues of sharing. A problem situation concerning careers, sexual relationships, or certain parent-child relationships would not be appropriate for elementary students. Conversely, high school students are very much concerned with careers and sexual or parental relationships. (But sometimes and with some groups these may be too sensitive!) In general, we feel that the personal and social concerns students experience at different developmental stages are a good source of themes from which to develop problem situations.

The sex of the students and their ethnic and socioeconomic background influence their choice of topic[1] and, according to Chesler and Fox, their expectations for the role play. It goes without saying that different cultural groups experience different sets of problems and concerns. They also solve them differently! Most teachers know this and account for these differences in their curriculums all the time. As with age, we prefer to view culture as a source of problem situations. That is, problems that are typical for a particular ethnic group, sex, or socioeconomic class can become the basis of problem situations.

Problem situations can be built around value (or ethical) themes, such as honesty, integrity, responsibility, achievement, and fairness, or around emotions, such as anger, frustration, competitiveness, rejection, and loneliness. Behaviors in others (or ourselves) that are problematic can also be the basis of problem situations. Aggression, withdrawal, and avoidance are all grist for creating problem situations. Eric Berne and others who have written in the field of transactional analysis describe roles, scripts, or "games people play."[2] Situations and characters that typify the roles or scripts provide a good basis for constructing problem situations. Small situations that are troublesome or uncomfortable to handle also make good problem situations. Examples of these include introducing a new friend to our parents, making a complaint at a store, getting along as a newcomer in class, asking the teacher for an extension on a paper, and interviewing for a job. Finally, problem situations can be built around social issues, such as racism, prejudice, and sexism, or around social issues facing a particular community, such as a teacher strike or a crime increase. James Banks' book, *Teaching Strategies for Ethnic Studies*, is particularly helpful in providing problem situations centering in multi-cultural issues and social problems.[3] These various sources of problem situations are summarized in Figure 1.

[1]Children from upper-middle-class homes tend to be more comfortable expressing themselves verbally, whereas children from lower socioeconomic groups often use more physical modes of expression and assertion.
[2]Eric Berne, *Games People Play* (New York:Grove Press, 1967).
[3] James Banks, *Teaching Strategies for Ethnic Studies* (Boston: Allyn & Bacon, Inc., 1975).

1. issues arising from developmental stages
2. issues arising from sexual, ethnic, or socioeconomic class
3. value (ethical) themes
4. difficult emotions
5. scripts or "games people play"
6. troublesome situations
7. social issues
8. community issues

Figure 1. *Sources of Problem Situations.*

Problem situations can vary in complexity. The simplest problem is what Chesler and Fox call problem situations for one main character.[4] Although there may be more than one role player in the situation, the behavior to be enacted is really only a problem for *one* of the participants, and the situation typically does not involve a decision. Rather, it usually involves something we are not comfortable doing, such as confronting a friend with bad news or approaching a new classmate. These constitute perhaps the least complex, though not necessarily the easiest, type of problem situation. In these situations, one person serves as a "prop" for the talking and action of another. Next in complexity is the situation with two or more active characters and where there are alternative solutions. For example, if you borrow someone's car and it is hit while outside your house, what should you do? The problem here is not just how to discuss the situation with another person (as in the one-main-character situation) but *whether* to discuss it, and if so, *what* to discuss. There is a whole series of issues and decisions to be made here. Still, the facts are pretty straightforward and the situation is relatively simple, though again, not easy. Problem stories with complex plots and several characters are more difficult. (The paper-drive story in the transcript lesson in Component 1 is an example of a more complex plot.) Finally, problem situations dealing with value themes, social issues, or community issues are very complex because, in order to be meaningful, they call for rather extensive background information and personal experience, as in the case of social issues. Or they can be very sensitive, as in the case of sex or race. Finally, they are abstract, requiring rather deeply worked-through commitments, as in the case of values.

There are no hard-and-fast rules about levels of difficulty in problem situations, but intuitively it seems that the sequence just described is a reasonable guide:

1. one main character
2. two characters and alternative solutions
3. complex plots and many characters
4. value themes, social issues, and community issues

[4] Mark Chesler and Robert Fox, *Role-Playing Methods in the Classroom* (Chicago: Science Research Associates, 1966), p. 67.

EXERCISE 1

Identify two themes, topics, or situations for each of the sources of problem situations listed below. We would like you to either base your selections on the particular group of students you teach or arbitrarily select one age or culture group. Before identifying the role play topics, describe the students in terms of age, grade, sex, ethnic identity, and other characteristics that might influence your choice of topics.

Students:

Topics:

    1. Developmental Stages

    2. Sexual, Ethnic, or Socioeconomic Class

    3. Value (Ethical) Themes

    4. Difficult Emotions

    5. Games People Play

    6. Troublesome Situations

    7. Social Issues

    8. Community Issues

ORGANIZING THE MATERIALS FOR ROLE PLAYING

The materials for Role Playing are minimal but important. The major curricular tool is the problem situation. However, it is sometimes helpful to construct briefing sheets for each role. These sheets describe the role or the character's feelings. Occasionally, we also develop forms for the observers that tell them what to look for and give them a place to write it down.

There are many source materials for problem situations. Films, novels, and short stories are excellent sources. More commonly used are problem stories or outlines of problem situations. Problem stories are just what their name implies: the teacher reads (or has the students read) a short narrative that describes the setting, circumstances, actions, and dialogue of a situation. One or more of the characters faces a dilemma in which a choice must be made or an action taken. The story ends unresolved.

In the transcript lesson in Component I about the paper drive, the teacher adapted one of the problem stories from the Shaftels' book. The following problem story, entitled "Squawk Box," is also adapted from the Shaftels' work.

> The boys were choosing up sides for a ball game when Andy came to school that morning early. He stood by as Neil and Jerry took turns naming the fellows each wanted. Neil got five on his side. Jerry had just chosen four. Andy was the only boy not yet chosen.
>
> "I don't want Andy," Jerry said. "He can't play ball."
>
> "You've got to take him. There's nobody else."
>
> Andy blushed. He knew he was clumsy and a slow runner. He wasn't very good at baseball or football, or any of the games that the boys played. He was a year older and bigger than most of the group. They made fun of him.
>
> Jerry said, "I'd rather have four people than have him spoil our team. We'd lose with him on it!"
>
> They all turned away from Andy, leaving him standing alone, ignoring him. Andy made a fist. He was mad enough to fight Neil and Jerry. But then what would the teacher say? He wondered, though, how he could let them get away with that. He had feelings too! He just wanted to be their friend. What should Andy do?[5]

Many resource materials now commercially available include stories or problem stories whose endings can be omitted or changed. The Shaftels' book and Chesler and Fox's book each contain a section of problem stories.

We also want to encourage you to write your own problem story. It's easy to do and enables you to tailor the details of the situation and your description of it to the students' background. You can also add important twists to the dilemmas that will give structure to the problem and push the students' thinking.

Outlines of problem situations are more parsimonious in description than problem stories; they simply sketch the major details and events of a situation:

> You are late for an important meeting, and you want to telephone the group that you will be late. Your brother is talking to a friend and won't get off the telephone. What do you do?

Rewriting the "Squawk Box" story as an outline, you might say:

> The boys in the sixth grade class were choosing up sides for a baseball game. Everyone had been chosen but Andy. Neither side wanted to have Andy on their team because he was not a good player. Both the captains said in front of

[5] Fannie and George Shaftel, *Roleplaying for Social Values: Decision Making in the Social Studies* (Englewood Cliffs, N.J.: Prentice-Hall, Inc., 1967), pp. 343-44.

him that they did not want him. Everyone walked away leaving Andy alone. He felt very angry. What would you do if you were Andy?

It is helpful to analyze your problem situation before you begin the role play. What theme(s) is represented? For example, the "Squawk Box" story contains the themes of fairness, rejection, integrity in friendship, and responsibility of the group to respect and support the individual.

It is also helpful to consider alternative ways to handle the situation. For example, the Chesler and Fox story, "John's Choice," gives us the problem situation and possible solutions:

> John's best friend, Mark, was about to move away from the school. The class liked Mark and had decided to give him a surprise party. John was excited and helped the class set the plans for Friday afternoon. On Thursday evening, John's father came home with tickets for the next afternoon's circus. He knew how much John liked the circus.
>
> John came running home to tell his parents about the party. He was glad to see his father, but then the circus tickets came out of his father's pocket. Now John felt he had to be at the party to say goodbye to Mark. He also wanted to go to the circus. He wanted both things. What do you think John could do?
>
> Possible solutions:—He could explain the conflict to his father and try to get the circus tickets changed for another time.—He could invite Mark over this evening to say goodbye and then go to the circus tomorrow.—He could give up the tickets and go to the party.—He could ask the teacher and the class to change the party to the morning.[6]

Briefing sheets tell a little about the character and his likes and dislikes, strengths and weaknesses, interests, and relationships with other characters, as for example:

Teacher: You are new to this school and not too sure of yourself. Your principal is very strict and believes that students should not be given too much freedom. You believe that after students have completed their work and other responsibilities, they should be permitted to explore the resources of the classroom and school. Sometimes you are timid in expressing your concerns and speak in a soft voice.

Principal: You run a tight ship and are noted for having a well-run school. You are concerned about your teachers' professional growth. You like to visit and talk with each of them. You believe it's important to try new educational ideas, but discipline and order are also important. Your manner of speaking is cheery and sometimes teasing.

These are the types of characterizations that students should develop if briefing sheets are not provided ahead of time. We think it important that students learn to develop characterizations on their own. However, briefing sheets may be useful in early role playing sessions, or in problem situations in which stereotyping might occur. Even if the students construct the role descriptions themselves, it's helpful if

---

[6] Chesler and Fox, *Role-Playing Methods*, p. 74.

they write them down to refer to if they are having difficulty getting into the role. Furthermore, written role descriptions emphasize the concept of role in a concrete manner.

Briefing sheets can also be used for role training. Students often find it difficult in the initial stages of role playing to get into a role; they either play themselves or a stereotype of a role. Prior to enacting the problem situation, the students can practice getting into their roles or practice different roles, using the briefing sheets as a guide.

EXERCISE 2

Take one of the topics or themes that you identified in Exercise 1. Write this up either as a problem story or as an outline of a problem situation. The problem situation should be one that is appropriate for you and that you would enjoy peer teaching. Feel free to use a film, short story, or other source material as the basis for your problem situation. Then develop briefing sheets for two of the characters in your problem situation.

Complete Part I (The Problem Situation) of the Planning Guide at the end of this section.

ANALYZING THE PROBLEM
AND IDENTIFYING THE FOCUS

Once you have developed an actual problem situation, it's important to reflect on its *content*. What are the themes in this situation? What are the values at issue? What are the value conflicts? If you have thought about the content in advance and considered the advantages and disadvantages of various positions, you will probably be able to probe the students' thinking in a richer way.

EXERCISE 3

Analyze your problem situation and determine its themes, possible positions, and values or value conflicts. Write these in the space below.

Theme(s):

Possible Solutions:

Value(s)

Perhaps you had a specific focus in mind before you selected the particular problem situation you did. Maybe that's why you chose it. More likely, you selected the problem because it is a relevant issue, and did so before you determined a specific focus. Remember that each problem situation lends itself to many focuses. Be sure to decide which one you want to emphasize. To some extent, all role plays are concerned with feelings and consequences of behavior, but in addition to these aspects, one focus should be developed in greater depth than the others.

The range of possible focuses was discussed in Component I. A list of these is reproduced in Figure 2. Look over this list and decide on your focus. Then, complete Part II of the Planning Guide.

DETERMINING EDUCATIONAL OBJECTIVES

The range of educational objectives attendant to the Role Playing Model is large. We have organized these objectives into four broad categories and divided each category into several subcategories. Earlier we discussed these categories in terms of establishing a main focus for the role play; however, we can also use them to derive the educational objectives of a Role Playing lesson (see Figure 2).

Our choice of behavioral objectives will come from the original curricular goals as well as from the students' level of role playing skills. At first, we might develop objectives that indicate student mastery of skill in using the model rather than our actual curricular objectives. The Teaching Analysis Guide can serve as a guideline for this. Are the students able to respond to our moves? Do they have difficulty identifying the problem, summarizing the action, and making connections between the problem situation and real-life examples?

  I. Role Playing as a vehicle for exploring feelings
     A. exploring one's own feelings
     B. exploring others' feelings
     C. acting out or releasing feelings
     D. experiencing higher-status roles in order to change the perceptions of others and one's own perceptions
 II. Role Playing as a vehicle for exploring attitudes, values, and perceptions
     A. identifying values of culture or subculture
     B. clarifying and evaluating one's own values and value conflicts
III. Role Playing as a means of developing problem-solving attitudes and skills
     A. openness to possible solutions
     B. ability to identify a problem
     C. ability to generate alternative solutions
     D. ability to evaluate the consequences to oneself and others of solutions to problems
     E. experiencing consequences and making final decisions in light of experienced consequences
     F. analyzing criteria and assumptions behind alternatives
     G. acquiring new behaviors
 IV. Subject-matter exploration
     A. feelings of participants
     B. historical realities: historical crises, dilemmas, and decisions

---

Figure 2. *Possible Focuses and Educational Objectives of a Role Playing Lesson.*

The categories in Figure 2 also serve as guidelines for objectives. Within each of these four categories, you can probably think of additional objectives. However, you will want to be more specific than Figure 2 about the behaviors you are looking for.

EXERCISE 4

Look over the list of objectives in Figure 2 and in the space below, add two others that were not mentioned. For your peer teaching session, select or formulate at least two behavioral objectives. Record these in Part III of the Planning Guide.

1.

2.

Completing the Planning Guide

By now you should have completed Parts I, II, and III of the Planning Guide, that is, the Problem Situation, Focus, and Educational Objectives. The remaining section concerns skills for initiating the phases and responding to the students. Some teachers find it helpful to mentally "walk through" the model by formulating on paper the actual initiating moves for each phase and the key responding moves. Complete Part IV of the Planning Guide now, and then move on to your peer teaching and microteaching.

PLANNING GUIDE FOR THE ROLE PLAYING MODEL

I. The Problem Situation

    A. Provide a brief description of the problem situation you developed in Exercise 1.

    B. What is the source of your problem situation? (Check One.)

        _____ film   _____ outline of a problem situation

        _____ problem story   _____ literature

        _____ other

II. The Focus

    A. Identify the primary goal or focus you have in mind for this Role Playing sequence.

        1. Role Playing as a vehicle for exploring feelings:

_____ a. exploring one's own feelings and motivations

_____ b. exploring others' feelings (empathy) and motivations

_____ c. acting out or releasing feelings

_____ d. experiencing higher-status roles in order to change the perceptions of others and one's own perceptions

2. Role Playing as a vehicle for exploring attitudes, values, and perceptions:

_____ a. identifying values of culture or subculture

_____ b. clarifying and evaluating one's own values and value conflicts

3. Role playing as a means of developing problem-solving attitudes and skills:

_____ a. openness to possible solutions

_____ b. ability to identify a problem

_____ c. ability to generate alternative solutions

_____ d. ability to evaluate the consequences to oneself and others of alternative solution to problems

_____ e. experiencing consequences and making final decisions in light of experienced consequences

_____ f. analyzing criteria and assumptions behind alternatives

_____ g. acquiring new, more productive behaviors

4. Subject-matter exploration

_____ a. feelings of participants

_____ b. historical realities: crises, dilemmas, and decisions

B. Provide a brief analysis of the focus

C. What concept(s) solutions, alternatives, values, attitudes, etc., underlie this focus?

III. Educational Objectives

Formulate at least two educational objectives.

IV. Syntax

Formulate initiating and probing questions for each phase. Use the Summary Chart of Key Questions at the end of this component as a guide.

Phase One: Warm-Up

Phase Two: Selecting Participants

Phase Three: Setting the Stage

Phase Four: Preparing Observers

Phase Five: Enactment

Phase Six: Discussion

Phase Seven: Reenactment

Phase Eight: Discussion and Evaluation

Phase Nine: Sharing Experiences and Generalizing

ANALYZING THE PEER TEACHING LESSON

Usually, five or six people are necessary for peer teaching the Role Playing Model, but this depends on the number of characters in the problem situation. There should be at least two observers. Role Playing takes a little longer than many other models, perhaps forty-five minutes for adults. The first few times you micro-teach with students, however, it's probably best to hasten the activities somewhat.

After you peer teach the lesson, analyze your teaching by completing the Teaching Analysis Guide that follows. Duplicate as many copies of the Guide as you may need to analyze the peer teaching and microteaching of all group members.

Role Playing is a lengthy and somewhat complex model to implement. It takes practice to acquire or recognize all the skills that it entails. We have found it particularly true of this model that teachers need to try the model at least once *before* reading further about the requisite teacher skills. After you have completed your peer teaching and analyzed the lesson using the Teaching Analysis Guide, you may want to read the section titled Some Considerations in Initiating Activities that follows the Guide and use it for ideas to solve problems that emerged during the teaching episode.

TEACHING ANALYSIS GUIDE FOR THE ROLE PLAYING MODEL

Phase One: Warm Up the Group

Problem Presentation

1. Was the problem introduced and identified?	Thoroughly	Partially	Missing	Not Needed

Discussion of Problem

2. Did the students speculate on or interpret the problem?	Thoroughly	Partially	Missing	Not Needed
3. Did the students identify the general category of the problem situation—for example, peer pressure or prejudice? (This could also take place in Phase Nine.)	Thoroughly	Partially	Missing	Not Needed
4. Were both sides of the problem discussed?	Thoroughly	Partially	Missing	Not Needed
5. Did the teacher involve the students in setting goals or purposes in terms of the role play?	Thoroughly	Partially	Missing	Not Needed
6. Were all the students involved?	Thoroughly	Partially	Missing	Not Needed

Knowledge of Role Playing

7. Were the students aware of the function and procedures of role playing? If not, were these explained?	Thoroughly	Partially	Missing	Not Needed

Phase Two: Selecting Participants (Role Players)

Role Analysis

8. Were the roles identified and described? (This item can also be done in Phases One or Three.)	Thoroughly	Partially	Missing	Not Needed
9. Did the role analysis reflect the ideas of the initial discussion of the problem?	Thoroughly	Partially	Missing	Not Needed

Selection of Role Players

10. Were the role players chosen?	Thoroughly	Partially	Missing	Not Needed

Phase Three: Setting the Stage

Line of Action

11. Was the line of action decided upon before the role playing?	Thoroughly	Partially	Missing	Not Needed
12. Did the line of action that was decided upon reflect the ideas in the initial discussion of the problem in Phase One?	Thoroughly	Partially	Missing	Not Needed

TEACHING ANALYSIS GUIDE FOR THE ROLE PLAYING MODEL

13. Was the setting described? Thoroughly Partially Missing Not Needed

Phase Four: Preparing the Observers

14. Was there a discussion to prepare observers to:

   a. evaluate the realism of the role playing? Thoroughly Partially Missing Not Needed

   b. analyze the consequences of the role playing behavior? Thoroughly Partially Missing Not Needed

   c. define the feelings of the role players? Thoroughly Partially Missing Not Needed

15. Were specific observation tasks assigned? Thoroughly Partially Missing Not Needed

Phase Five: Enactment

Role Play

16. Did the role play take place? Thoroughly Partially Missing Not Needed

Teacher Role

17. Did the teacher break the role play at an appropriate time? Thoroughly Partially Missing Not Needed

Phase Six: Discussion

Focus

18. Was the enactment reviewed in terms of:

   a. the realism of the role play? Thoroughly Partially Missing Not Needed

   b. a summary of the events and the consequences of different actions for the participants in the role play? Thoroughly Partially Missing Not Needed

   c. a summary of the arguments that each role player presented? Thoroughly Partially Missing Not Needed

19. Did a discussion centering on the primary focus take place? Thoroughly Partially Missing Not Needed

20. During the discussion, did the teacher exhibit the following teacher skills? Thoroughly Partially Missing Not Needed

   a. summarizing students' ideas Thoroughly Partially Missing Not Needed
   b. paraphrasing or reflecting students' ideas

TEACHING ANALYSIS GUIDE FOR THE ROLE PLAYING MODEL

Preparing the Reenactment

21. Did the students reflect on the previous role play and consider it in planning the reenactment? Thoroughly Partially Missing Not Needed

22. In the preparation for the reenactment, which of the following steps were carried out? Thoroughly Partially Missing Not Needed

    a. role analysis Thoroughly Partially Missing Not Needed

    b. selection of players Thoroughly Partially Missing Not Needed

    c. development of the line of action Thoroughly Partially Missing Not Needed

Teacher Role

23. Was the teacher nonevaluative in her responses? That is, did she primarily reflect and summarize the students' ideas? Thoroughly Partially Missing Not Needed

Phase Seven: Reenactment

Role Play

24. Did a reenactment take place? Thoroughly Partially Missing Not Needed

Phase Eight: Discussion and Evaluation

Discussion

25. Did a discussion take place? Thoroughly Partially Missing Not Needed

Focus

26. Was the enactment reviewed in terms of:

    a. the realism of the role play? Thoroughly Partially Missing Not Needed

    b. a summary of the events and the consequences of different actions for the participants in the role play? Thoroughly Partially Missing Not Needed

    c. a summary of the arguments that each role player presented? Thoroughly Partially Missing Not Needed

    d. a comparing and contrasting of the two enactments? Thoroughly Partially Missing Not Needed

27. Did a discussion centering on the primary focus take place? Thoroughly Partially Missing Not Needed

TEACHING ANALYSIS GUIDE FOR THE ROLE PLAYING MODEL

Teacher Role

28. Was the teacher nonevaluative in her responses?	Thoroughly	Partially	Missing	Not Needed

Phase Nine: Sharing and Generalizing

Discussion

29. Were similar experiences explored?	Thoroughly	Partially	Missing	Not Needed
30. Did the students reflect on how the role play applied to their own problems?	Thoroughly	Partially	Missing	Not Needed
31. Were the students able to generalize the issues involved in the role play?	Thoroughly	Partially	Missing	Not Needed
32. Were general principles of behavior explored?	Thoroughly	Partially	Missing	Not Needed

SOME CONSIDERATIONS IN INITIATING ACTIVITIES

There are many activities in Role Playing that the teacher initiates and must move students through quickly, while maintaining the cumulative development of the problem situation throughout all the phases of the model. The conceptualization of the problem and characters in the first few phases sets the context for the enactment; the data generated from the enactment is used to explore a particular focus. Because the various activities in this model feed into one another, it is important to study each of them carefully and consider their function and their relationship to one another.

In your peer teaching, you may have felt that central issues are not developed and followed through from phase to phase. This is a common experience, especially when teaching students. Generally, it occurs because the initiating moves for one or more of the phases are not adequately structured. In first experiences with Role Playing sessions, it is natural for teachers to concentrate on getting through the stages and not be too concerned about sharpening their execution of them.

In this section we again discuss each of the phases of role playing, this time presenting the rationale and considerations involved in initiating each activity and illustrating alternative ways of initiating them. Recall some of the problems you may have experienced in your peer teaching and see if these comments address themselves to those difficulties.

Phase One: Warm-Up

The warm-up phase has several functions. The first is to present the situations and involve the students in the attendant issues or problems . A second is to increase the students' knowledge of role playing. A third is to increase their comfort with role playing.

Introducing the Problem

In this move, the teacher tries to convey a sympathetic attitude toward the situation and to focus students' attention on the problem. For example:

"We are often caught between what we want to do and what someone else wants us to do. This is a story about such a situation. Try to think of what you might do."

"Sometimes it's hard to tell a good friend something negative—for instance, when he's bothering us or hurting our feelings. Here's a situation like that. How would you handle it?"

Awareness of Role Playing

It is important to have students perceive behaviors and feelings in terms of a total role—not just an isolated behavior or personal characteristic. ("A role is a pattern or sequence of feelings, words, and actions.") Being able to see patterns in human behavior and understand apparently diverse reactions in terms of a common mode of relating reduces the complexity of social behavior. It also makes us better able to gain insight into our role behaviors and those of others. Consequently, it is helpful to speak of the characters and the problem situation in terms of the various role names involved. For example, the teacher and students can identify common roles, such as the bully, the aggressive person, the shy person, the goody goody, the know-it-all, the bragger, and the grouch. Having a neat conceptual handle, the students can then explore the motivations and feelings underlying a role and identify the behaviors that are characteristic of that role.

The second teacher task in the warm-up is thus to acquaint the students with the concept of role and explain the purpose and procedures of role playing. For example:

"You will be stepping into another person's place in order to experience his or her thoughts, feelings, and set of behaviors and to see how you affect others. Some questions you might ask yourselves about a role being played by another are: 'What does he mean by that?' 'What would it mean if I did that?' "

Comfort with Role Playing

A third purpose of the warm-up is to help students who are unfamiliar with role playing become relaxed and comfortable expressing themselves publicly. Chesler and Fox suggest a pantomimic exercise such as smiling or chewing, or activities such as this: "Read aloud from one of your school books, pretending that you have a mouthful:—of marbles,—of straight pins,—of peanut butter."[7] Another possibility is to have students briefly imitate the character in the problem story, or a character in a different situation, or to imitate the character in a way that would *not* be "in role."

These preparatory exercises for learning how to get into a role are helpful for beginning role players. We recommend you try Chesler and Fox's list of suggestions or make up your own.[8]

[7] *Ibid.*, p. 64.
[8] *Ibid.*, pp. 64-66.

Phase Two: Selecting and Preparing the Role Players

Role Analysis

One of the important jobs in this phase is to prepare the role players for their roles. In addition to describing the role, it is important to delineate and generalize about the character—his feelings and ideas. Questions such as, "What kind of person is he?" "What is important to him?" and "What are some of the things he feels?" are helpful. Chesler and Fox also suggest that teachers and students "build a past" for the character—that is, know or imagine something of the person's history, such as his family and his accomplishments.

Selecting the Participants

The roles to be played are developed out of the proposal or design of the situation. Although the problem story or outline may determine the entire situation, often, especially with complex problems, the students will construe the way the situation should be set up initially and who should be involved. They may add characters not in the original story. If one student has suggested a particular "script," you might ask,

"Johnny, why don't you come up here and show us what you mean?"

"Whom will you need to help you, Johnny?"

"Class, whom will we need for this enactment?"

In the first enactments, it's best to call upon those who are comfortable with role playing. It's also desirable to avoid assigning people to play their real-life roles. The students can take turns at the roles, or they can volunteer for them. Those who are reluctant to play a role should not be pressured into doing so.

Phase Three: Setting the Stage

Two activities are important here. Students must be clear on the line of action they will follow in the enactment and on the details of the situation.

Setting the Line of Action

The line of action is not a script, nor does it program the outcome of the problem situation. It simply specifies one approach, and thereby provides a structure for the role playing. To set the line of action, the teacher might say:

"Okay, let's explore your idea of what happens when Tommy keeps the money."

After identifying other possible lines of action, the teacher and/or students should decide on one they will try in the enactment.

Getting Inside the Situation

This move provides additional structure for the role players and reality for the role play. It involves describing the time and place and perhaps one person's activity—who is doing what. The teacher might initiate consideration of these factors with questions such as:

"Where is this taking place?"
"What is it like in this place?"
"How do you happen to be there?"
"What time of day is it?"
"Mary, what are you doing when Sue walks in?"

Phase Four: Preparing the Observers

In this model, the observers must be as actively involved in the situation as the role players. The teacher accomplishes this by assigning specific tasks and/or roles to the observers. There are three major areas that need to be covered by the observers: the actions (or a specific aspect of the action) and their consequences, the feelings and thoughts of the actors, and the realism of the role playing and of the handling of the problem. It is best to assign one task to each observer or to each group of observers. Chesler and Fox describe the observers in terms of *identifiers* and *critics*. Identifiers are instructed to identify with the feelings, thoughts, and actions of an actor so that they can interpret these later for the group. Critics monitor the realism and handling of the problem.[9] Another way to cast the directions to the observer is to describe the motivations and behavior of a particular role—for instance, the bully or the shy person. Observers can also be called upon to suggest next steps of action if the role playing bogs down. Some examples of the kind of instructions you might give to observers are:

"As you watch the actors, decide if that's how they would behave in real life."
"Try to think what will happen after his parents visit the teacher."
"Try to decide what Tony is feeling and why he acts the way he does."

Phase Five: The Enactment

The teacher's function here is to monitor the enactment. If it drags or presents a vague, unclear episode that will be hard to analyze, the teacher must intervene, clarifying and restructuring the situation:

"Okay, let's stop for a minute. Let's clarify what's going on here."
The teacher (or students) may prompt a role play by making suggestions to get the action rolling. If a character gets out of role, the teacher can break the enactment temporarily to remind the student of the role:

"Sue, would a bully just stand there?"
Finally, if the role playing is becoming too uncomfortable emotionally for one of the players, the teacher should break the enactment. Otherwise, the enactment should be broken as soon as the objectives have been met or the original alternative played out. The teacher can intervene to shift to another solution or to set up a similar enactment, perhaps with new role players:

"What is happening?"
"What will happen now?"
"Does anyone want to take the part of Sam?"

Phase Six: Discussion of the Role Playing

The thrust of the discussion should be toward the main focus that was selected for the session. The reports from the observers as to the sequence of action and its consequences, the realism of the role play, and the feelings of the actors can

[9]*Ibid.*, p. 36.

be integrated into the theme of the discussion. It is important to cover three areas in the discussion:

1. Review the actions, organizing the data of the observers and the cause-and-effect sequences.
2. Review the primary issues of the role play: the actors' feelings, what the characters wanted in the situation, and why the characters responded the way they did. The actors can be consulted as to what they were actually feeling, and the observers can offer their interpretations.
3. Consider alternative ways of responding.

Analysis of Feelings (observed)

The goal here is to analyze the feelings of the role players toward themselves and others, changes in their feelings, and the feelings that resulted from others' actions:

"How does Tommy feel?"
"Why does he feel that way?"
"How does he feel toward his father?"
"Who will be affected by Tommy's behavior?"
"How will they feel?"
"Did any of the role players *change* their feelings? If so, why?"
"How did the characters show their feelings?"

Analysis of Behavioral Realism

This move probes the realism of the enacted situation, the role, and proposed solutions and circumstances:

"Did it seem real to you? If so, why?"
"Do you think that could really happen?"
"Would it matter if circumstances were different?"
"Why do you think that would happen?"
"Would he really behave that way with his parents?"

Consequences of the Action

The purpose of this move is to establish the events and analyze the consequences of observed or proposed behavior:

"What happened?"
"What were the results of Nelson's behavior?"
"When he did that, what happened?"
"What will happen if Tommy doesn't give the money back?"
"How did Nelson's action make Tommy feel?"

Behavioral Alternatives

Often, the purpose of the Role Playing session is to focus on decision making and problem solving, especially on the generation of alternative solutions:

"What could you suggest to solve the problem?"
"Do you have another way to handle the situation?"
"What else could he have done?"
"Are there other possibilities for resolving the conflict?"

Phase Seven: Reenactment

The moves here are the same as in Phase Five (the initial enactment).

Phase Eight: Discussion and Evaluation

The emphasis here is on comparing and contrasting the two role plays in terms of feelings and actions, and evaluating the two:
"How are the role plays different from each other?"
"What would be the consequences of each?"
"Which alternative satisfies you the most? Why?"

Phase Nine: Sharing Experiences and Generalizing

It is important here for students to associate the role play problem with real-life problems and to generalize their opinions to other situations:
"Did you ever have a similar problem? Tell us about it."
"How did you solve your problem?"
"How does your problem relate to our story problem?"
"What new ways to work out your problems did you learn from the role play? If none, why?"

A SUMMARY OF KEY QUESTIONS

Phase	Key Questions
Phase One: Warm-up	What is the problem? How did the characters feel about the problem? Why? What can they do about the problem? What are the alternatives?
Phase Two: Select Participants	Who are the people in this story? What are they like? What kind of person is _____ ? Who thinks he/she can be _____ ? What are you doing as _____ ? Why?
Phase Three: Set Stage	What is happening? Where is it happening? When?
Phase Four: Prepare Observers	How did the characters seem to feel? How did they show their feelings? What did _____ want?

How did he/she go about getting it?

Did this seem real to you? Why?

Are there other ways to resolve the conflict?

Phase Six: Discuss and Evaluate

Does everyone agree that the problem can be settled this way?

Did the role players *change* feelings in any way?

Phase Eight: Discuss and Evaluate

How were the two role plays alike? How were they different?

What was _____ feeling in the first role play? in the second role play?

What are the consequences of the first role play? the second?

Which alternative satisfies you the most? Why? Why not?

Phase Nine: Share Experiences and Generalize

Did you ever have a similar problem? Tell us about it.

How did you solve your problem?

How does your problem relate to our story problem?

What new ways did you learn from the role play about working out your problems?

AFTER PEER TEACHING: MICROTEACHING

Peer teaching was an opportunity to "walk through" the pattern of activities of the model you are using. It should have helped you identify areas of understanding or performance that were amiss for you!

Aside from the specifics of the Teaching Analysis Guide, we would like you to reflect intuitively on your peer teaching experience. Did you feel that the essence of the Role Playing Model was incorporated into the learning activity? Were you able to maintain the teacher's role as you had anticipated?

As you prepare your first Role Playing session with a small group of students, identify aspects of the activity that you want to improve upon or include. Usually, these aspects are such things as being more precise in your directions, cuing students, and giving them examples of role playing. We suggest walking yourself mentally through the microteaching before actually engaging in it.

It is natural in microteaching to wonder, "Am I doing this right?" Except for any glaring omissions or commissions that may have emerged in your peer teaching, the pursuit of excellence in a model is more a matter of refinement, style, and personal goals for the teaching situation. If you have been operating in the "Did I get this right?" frame of mind, now is the time to change to "What do *I* want to get across or elicit in this first teaching situation? How will I go about doing that?" If you have internalized the *basic* goals, principles, and procedures of the model, now is the time to shift from an external way of thinking to an internal one. Build the variations that seem appropriate to you.

We suggest audio-taping your first microteaching session so that you can reflect on the lesson afterwards. The students will respond differently from your peers. It is a good idea to use the Teaching Analysis Guide with your microteaching lesson. You may also want to share the experience with your colleagues and receive their comments and suggestions.

The fourth and last component of the Role Playing Model suggests ways to use the model over a long-term curricular sequence and ways to adapt curricular materials to it. The emphasis of your training in this model will gradually shift now from mastering the basic elements of teaching to curriculum design and application.

Component IV

ADAPTING
THE MODEL

In this component, we move from training and teacher performance to curricular application and long-term use of the model. We discuss ways of combining Role Playing with other models of teaching.

COMBINING ROLE PLAYING
WITH OTHER MODELS OF TEACHING

In this component, we consider four ways in which Role Playing can be combined with other models of teaching to build a long-term curricular sequence of activities. These are:

1. to generate data for concept-building activities
2. as a stimulus for further inquiry
3. to bring realism to previously learned material
4. as a means of testing one's values

Generating Data for Concept Building

During the enactments and in the discussions that precede and follow them, a great deal of information about human behavior and emotion is transmitted. Much of it is based on students' immediately experienced feelings and perceptions. Consequently, the data can be quite vivid and meaningful. We believe that the information generated during Role Playing gives the teacher a unique opportunity to help students build more abstract concepts in the emotional and social domains. For example, the behaviors or feelings attendant to particular roles can be specified and categorized, and the roles can be labeled. Types of problem solutions can be identified. Students can identify which behaviors and solutions are aggressive, passive, or assertive, or they can identify the values underlying different solutions. Attitudes and feelings can be grouped together on the basis of similarity. On the one hand, for example, attitudes of superiority, prejudice, equality, or fair-mindedness can be identified. On the other hand, behaviors and feelings reflecting sadism, masochism, or protectiveness can be pointed out. It may be helpful to record students' ideas and reactions during role playing activities so that they can be utilized later in concept building. It is also possible to direct students to record their reactions or thoughts immediately after they complete the activities. The data from role playing is especially suited to the forming of new concepts, using Hilda Taba's Concept Formation Model, but the teacher can also develop Concept Attainment exercises using the Concept Attainment Model(s) discussed in *Information Processing Models of Teaching*, another of the three books in this series.

We believe Role Playing is a particularly effective anchor for building a general program in affective education. It puts students in immediate touch with their feelings and reactions and, combined with other models (such as Concept Formation and Concept Attainment) leads the way to new symbolic "handles" for describing human behavior and emotion and then evaluating these ideas.

Stimulating Further Inquiry

Role Playing makes an excellent stimulus for further inquiry, either into a particular social or community issue or into the nature of human feelings and emotions. Used in this way, Role Playing can be combined with subject areas such as literature (students can read biographies of individuals in similar situations) or with the Inquiry Training or Jurisprudential Model.

Bringing Realism to Previously Learned Material

Role Playing can bring realism to information that was acquired in a more didactic, expository fashion. It is also an informal measure of students' understanding. For example, students may have read about particular events in history (or in literature) and the circumstances surrounding the decisions of the times. Role Playing gives them an opportunity to experience those circumstances and the psychological and social constraints upon historical figures. Similarly, conceptual material from the behavioral sciences can be applied through Role Playing. If, for example, students have studied a unit about the basis for authority and leadership or about various leadership styles (as they do in a fifth-grade curriculum by Lippitt and Fox[1]), the teacher can build this knowledge into the role playing activities. In building the character and role, the teacher can ask students, "What type of leadership style does this person use? What's the basis for such authority?" In general, the more that Role Playing is supplemented by knowledge and concepts from psychology and social psychology, the more powerful the intellectual analyses and the more transferable the learning can be.

Testing One's Values

Finally, it's one thing to clarify our values intellectually through models such as the Jurisprudential Model or through other value-clarification exercises. It's another to see if they hold in our behavior, especially in emotionally charged situations. Role Playing is an effective way to augment a value-oriented curriculum built around other models. Value-oriented curriculums contribute intellectual strength to Role Playing. If students have explored the concept of value and alternative values, they can construct and analyze enactments in accordance with different values and value conflicts.

---

[1] Ronald Lippitt and Robert Fox, *Social Science Laboratory Units* (Chicago: Science Research Associates, 1969).

JURISPRUDENTIAL

MODEL

SCENARIO FOR THE JURISPRUDENTIAL MODEL

The senior class of Mervyn Park High School is planning their traditional spring arts festival. Generally this occurs on an April Friday and Saturday and consists of a variety of events built around the performing and visual arts. Usually the class itself presents a musical play. There is also a chamber music concert, several jazz performances, and art exhibits. The performers and exhibitors are a combination of students and invited professionals. Admission charges usually cover the cost of the professionals plus a handsome senior class gift to the high school. Before the festival, the committee in charge of organizing the event surveys students, faculty members, and the community to identify potential performers and exhibitors.

The tentative program for this year has just been formulated. One of the items arouses considerable controversy. The committee has invited a professional modern dance group to perform a piece called "The Body That Dances Is Yours." This piece includes narration and discussion as well as dancing. It emphasizes the dancers' need to be completely comfortable with their body and their body image. Dancers discuss the problems of overcoming feelings of inhibition and growing to be comfortable with their bodies and their sexuality.

One of the members of the community obtains a copy of the tentative agenda of the festival from a neighbor whose daughter is a member of the committee. This member of the community is upset and approaches the school principal, asking him to remove the item from the program. The principal objects, saying that the students are responsible and that he trusts them to put together a fine program, one whose quality will be attractive to the diverse elements within the student body and community without offending anyone. Another community member, unsatisfied, asks the Board of Education at its next meeting to remove the scheduled dance program from the arts festival agenda. A motion to that effect is made by a member of the board, and the motion is carried. Hearing about this, the student body decides to boycott classes for the remainder of the year.

The adviser to the senior class persuades the students to come to a meeting with her. Everyone in the class is present. She also persuades several members of the Board of Education to come to the meeting, as well as the principal of the school and the community member.

When all are assembled, she presents several members of her senior civics class and says, "I think it's in our interest to work out things so that they are fair to everyone concerned and so that the solutions to this problem are based on an understanding about our most important values. I have asked these students to lead the discussion this afternoon to try to clarify the values that are at stake, help us understand the facts in the situation, and come to an understanding of our real priorities for action."

One of the members of the class begins. He has brought with him a newsprint tablet and a set of felt pens. "I would like us first to clarify as many facts as we can," he says. The large group of students, faculty, school administrators, and the community member sit for a moment, unresponsive. Then someone says, "Well, one fact is that the dance group has been invited." The recorder notes this on the newsprint pad. A Board of Education member says, "I was told that these are dirty dances." Another board member says, "None of us has seen the group perform." One of the students remarks, "The dance group was recommended by Mr. Solway [one of the teachers]."

Gradually, after some discussion and clarification, the facts of the case emerge. After inquiring whether there are any more items that should be clarified, the student who is leading the discussion asks, "Now what are the policy issues that we have to consider here?" "Freedom of speech," says one student. "Speech?" says someone else. "Yes, speech. Dance is a form of expression. It should be regarded as free speech and protected under the Constitution." One of the Board of Education members stands up and argues, "I think it the responsibility of the school to maintain order; and a moral environment is the important issue." "Can we separate those?" asks the student. "Let's put your responsibility to maintain order as one policy question and your responsibility to maintain a moral environment as another one." "Okay."

After a lively discussion, the series of important policy issues are identified and related to the facts. One issue is whether the Board of Education or the administration of the school has the right to interfere with the agenda at all, whether it is the responsibility of the students to govern themselves. A second issue is the responsibility of the Board of Education and the administration to maintain order, a third is their responsibility to maintain a moral environment, a fourth is the responsibility of the students and the administration of the school to create an educational atmosphere.

The student who has led the discussion until this point now turns the meeting over to another student, Susan Markov. Susan begins by saying, "Now that we've identified some of the issues, we want you to feel free to identify others as we go along. Sometimes we are not able at the outset to determine the important issues we have to deal with." Then she says, "Now let's identify the values that underlie each of the issues. Sometimes we find that an issue implies a particular value. For example, if one of the issues is the right to free speech, our value is clearly that of free speech. Other issues present us with values that are opposed to one another."

In the ensuing discussion, a series of underlying values are identified and the conflicting values of the situation are clarified. Next, Susan asks the group to identify the facts that relate to each issue in this case. It is generally agreed that dance is a form of speech, and that there is a particular message in this dance unit. It is also agreed that if the Board of Education or the administration of the school prevents the students from presenting the dance group, their action is a violation of free speech. The issue that remains is whether such action is justified in the interest of order or the moral tone of the school; it is left undecided whether the dance group is in fact immoral. Susan then says, "Let us assume that the dance group indeed does explore sexuality and body awareness in a school setting. Making that assumption, which we will come back to, let's have some people take a position—that is, state what they believe should happen—and then let's try to identify the social values underlying that position and the consequences if the position were approved."

At this point, a number of positions are stated. After they are clarified, Susan leads a discussion to establish whether any values would be violated by any of the positions and what the desirable and undesirable consequences of the positions would be, were the positions to be carried out. As the discussion proceeds, the group gradually develops a series of priorities for the values in question and works toward a policy position with which they can live because of this value basis, the consequences they foresee.

The students who led this discussion had been exposed for several weeks to the jurisprudential approach to the clarification of public issues and the different values that underlie them. These students had been taught a strategy, a bit of which was articulated above as they led the group meeting over the dance group question.

OUTLINE OF ACTIVITIES FOR THE JURISPRUDENTIAL MODEL

Objective	Materials	Activity

COMPONENT I: DESCRIBING AND UNDERSTANDING THE MODEL

Objective	Materials	Activity
1. To recognize the goals, assumptions, and procedures of the Jurisprudential Model.	Theory and Overview	Reading
2. To gain a sense of the model in action.	Theory in Practice	Reading
3. To use the values framework; to recognize three types of problems and four patterns of argumentation.	Taking Theory Into Action	Reading/Writing
4. To evaluate your understandings of the Jurisprudential Model.	Theory Checkup	Writing

COMPONENT II: VIEWING THE MODEL

Objective	Materials	Activity
1. To become familiar with the Teaching Analysis Guide and identify items in it that you do not understand.	Teaching Analysis Guide	Reading
2. To identify phases of the model and comment on the lesson.	Demonstration Transcript	Reading/Writing/Discussion
3. **Option:** To apply the Teaching Analysis Guide to other demonstration lessons.	Live demonstration or videotape/ Teaching Analysis Guide	Viewing/Group or Individual Analysis

COMPONENT III: PLANNING AND PEER TEACHING

Objective	Materials	Activity
1. To understand the features of case materials and develop skill in case material preparation.	Developing the Case	Reading
2. To prepare an analysis of public policy cases.	Analyzing the Case	Reading/Writing
3. To prepare analogies for exploring the students' stance.	Developing Analogies	Reading/Writing
4. To complete the Planning Guide for the Jurisprudential Model.	Planning Guide	Reading/Writing
5. To peer teach the Jurisprudential Model.	4 or 5 peers, case materials	Teaching
6. To analyze the Jurisprudential lesson using the Teaching Analysis Guide.	Teaching Analysis Guide	Writing/Group discussion

OUTLINE OF ACTIVITIES FOR THE JURISPRUDENTIAL MODEL

7. **Option:** To teach the Jurisprudential Model to a small group of students.

Small group of students, case material, audio recorder, audio tape

Teaching/Taping

8. To analyze the microteaching lesson.

Teaching Analysis Guide

Individual or group listening to audio tape/Writing

COMPONENT IV: ADAPTING THE MODEL

1. To become aware of the possibilities of combining the Jurisprudential Model with other models of teaching.

Combining the Model with Others

Reading/Group Discussion

Component I

DESCRIBING
AND UNDERSTANDING
THE MODEL

THEORY AND OVERVIEW

The purpose of the Jurisprudential Model is to help students learn how to formulate defensible stances on public policy issues. Issues such as "Should the United States get out of Vietnam?" and "Should we encourage policies that redress the inequalities suffered by a particular group of people?" are recent policy issues. In this period when our society is undergoing many cultural and social changes, the Jurisprudential Model is especially useful, because we are all rethinking our positions on important legal, ethical, and social questions. As a society, we are reinterpreting our social values and our legal-ethical framework. The Jurisprudential Model will help students participate in this definition and redefinition of social values.

The Jurisprudential Model is somewhat complex, both in its intellectual framework and in the actual teaching process. This section describes the goals, assumptions, and procedures of the model. The second section in this component (Taking Theory Into Action) introduces the idea of legal-ethical concepts (due process, justice, equality) as a means of describing a particular situation or issue in more general terms. It also presents a process by which we can debate our stances on public policy questions.

114

Goals and Assumptions

In creating the Jurisprudential Model, Donald Oliver and James Shaver asked the question: What is the nature of citizenship in a democratic system? Based on their analysis of a democratic society and of the role requirements for individuals who maintain that system, Oliver and Shaver formulated a strategy that would develop in students part of the knowledge and skills they need to perform their functions as citizens.

Oliver and Shaver's model of society and social values is a society in which people differ in their views and priorities and in which social values conflict legitimately with one another. Controversial issues are not simple; there is no one right solution. In order to sustain such a model of society and still have a productive social order, citizens must be able to talk with one another and negotiate their differences. The process of rational consent is one of free and open debate through which differences in values are negotiated. The Jurisprudential Model provides this common process; it consists of a values framework and a method of discussion.

A skillful citizen is one who can intelligently analyze and take a stance on public issues. The stance taken should be the one that best reflects the concepts of justice and human dignity, two values that Oliver and Shaver feel are fundamental to a democratic society. Oliver and Shaver's image of a skillful citizen is very much that of a competent jurist or judge. Their goal is for students to develop policy stances by using a model of jurisprudential (or legalistic) thinking, as judges and jurists do. Imagine for a moment that you are a Supreme Court justice hearing an important case. Your job is to listen to the evidence that is presented, to analyze the legal positions taken by both sides, to weigh these positions and the evidence, to assess the meaning and provisions of the law, and, finally, to make the best possible decision. This is the role students are asked to create as they consider public issues.

Oliver and Shaver identify three areas of competence that a skillful analyzer and discusser of public issues must develop. The first area is familiarity with the values of the American creed, as embedded in the principles of the Constitution and the Declaration of Independence. These principles form the *values framework*—the basis for judging public issues and for making legal decisions. Students must be able to perceive the actual values and value conflicts represented in any controversial situation so that their policy stances are truly derived from ethical considerations. To do this, they must be aware of and understand what the key values of our society are—the core, as it were, of our society's ethical system.

The second area of competence is a set of skills for clarifying and resolving issues. It is not enough simply to identify the value questions in a controversy. Usually, a controversy arises because two important values are legitimately in conflict or because public issues, when examined closely, prove not to adhere truly to the core values of our society. Whenever a conflict of values arises, three kinds of problems are likely to be present.

The first kind of problem (*value problem*) involves clarifying which values or legal principles are in conflict, and choosing among them. The second kind of problem (*factual problem*) involves clarifying the facts around which the conflict has developed. The third kind of problem (*definitional problem*) involves clarifying the meanings or uses of words which describe the controversy.[1]

The process of clarifying and resolving issues by solving these three kinds of problems is called *rational consent*.

The third area of competence is knowledge of contemporary political and public issues. This requires that students be exposed rather systematically to the spectrum of political, social, and economic problems facing American society. Although a broad understanding of the history, nature, and scope of these problems is very important, the Jurisprudential Model is concerned primarily with the student's stance on the policy issues that emerge when a specific situation becomes a legal case. When that happens, the situation is focused upon a defined area of controversy. Thus, the Jurisprudential Model calls for a *case study approach* to curriculum. Students explore policy issues in terms of a specific legal case rather than in terms of a general study of values.

To summarize, the prerequisites for skillful execution of the role of citizen are:

1. an understanding of the values framework of the American creed
2. mastery of the intellectual skills of legal reasoning
3. knowledge of public issues

The goal of the Jurisprudential Model is for students to develop *policy stances* and *dialogue skills* by using these competencies. This goal includes thought-out, substantive policy positions and the acquisition of legal-ethical concepts and skills. The primary aims of discussion are clarification and problem-solving. With respect to the actual policy decision, the goal is to "have students understand the complexity of the problem and be able to make their positions reflect that complexity. Consensus may not be reached and doubts may remain. . ." Oliver and Shaver also point out several attitudinal goals. Among these are "looking at discussion as a process for mutual inquiry and clarification, rather than combat," "rewarding people for conceding and qualifying their positions instead of ridiculing them for 'losing' or 'giving in,'" and "recognizing that each person is entitled to his/her own opinion."[2]

The Jurisprudential Framework as a Model of Teaching: Socratic Dialogue

Oliver and Shaver's work encompasses many complex ideas. They present us with a model of society, a conception of values, a conception of dialogue, as well as curriculum and pedagogical considerations. The variations of this model of teaching that emerge from the richness of their analysis are numerous. However, the teaching strategy that seems most reflective of Oliver and Shaver's educational goals and unique to their theoretical framework is clearly a teaching strategy built around a

[1] Donald Oliver and James P. Shaver, *Teaching Public Issues in the High School* (Boston: Houghton Mifflin, 1966), p. 89. Reprinted with permission of the authors.
[2] A description of goals can be found in Donald Oliver and James P. Shaver, *Cases and Controversy: Guide to Teaching the Public Issues Series* (Middletown, Conn.: American Education Publishers, 1971), p. 7.

Socratic or *confrontational* model of discussion, which places the teacher in an adversary role.

In the Socratic style, the teacher asks the student(s) to take a position on an issue or to make a value judgement, and then challenges the assumptions underlying the students' stand by extending the position to its most extreme implications. The function of the teacher is to probe the students' positions until they become more clear and more complex, reflecting consideration of alternatives. In the course of doing this, the teacher questions the relevance, consistency, specificity, and definitional clarity of the students' ideas. Most characteristic of the Socractic style is the *use of analogies* as a means of contradicting students' general statements and testing the logic and limits of their position. For example, some of us may believe that students should have a greater voice in their education, but would we also support their having complete freedom in choice of curriculum, non-compulsory schooling, or a greater voice in decision-making in other institutions such as the community or home? These are analogous situations that test and define the logic and limits of our position. One of the skills you will develop in this model is planning analogies and using them in dialogue with students. Using a Socratic style, the teacher guides the students through an analysis of the issue in a non-adversial, didactic manner prior to challenging the students' position.

A sample of Socratic dialogue, which is the heart of the model, appears in the transcript below. The students have been discussing the voting rights issue. The policy question is, "Should the Federal Government compel Southern states to give Negroes equal voting rights?" The setting for this session is a ninth-grade public school classroom in Philadelphia. The year is 1962. The teacher has oriented the class to the case and the students have identified the values in conflict as states' rights versus equality of opportunity. One of the students, Steve, has volunteered to state his position and defend it. Steve has taken the position that blacks should have the right to vote. The teacher and students are exploring Steve's stance; and throughout the Socratic dialogue the teacher uses several patterns of reasoning to challenge his position. These patterns are noted in the annotations, as are other principles of reaction.

Notice that in Socratic dialogue, the students take a position and the teacher challenges the position with questions. The teacher's questions are designed to push students' thinking about their stance. Some of the considerations that bear on the strength of a stance are: Does it hold up well against positions reflecting alternative values? Is it consistent across many situations? Are the reasons for maintaining the position relevant to the situation? Are the factual assumptions on which the position is based valid? What about the consequences as a result of this position? Will the student hold on to this stance in spite of the consequences?

T: WHAT DO YOU THINK, STEVE?

S: I THINK THAT THE POLICE POWER OF LOCAL GOVERNMENT CAN GO ONLY SO FAR, THAT THE CONSTITUTIONAL RIGHTS OF VOTING—MAYBE THE NEGROES SHOULD HAVE THEM.

    Steve takes a position.

T: NEGROES SHOULD HAVE THE RIGHT TO VOTE EVEN THOUGH THERE MAY BE ALL KINDS OF VIOLENCE AND RESISTANCE? WE SHOULD SEND TROOPS INTO THE SOUTH AND PROTECT EVERY INDIVIDUAL'S RIGHT TO VOTE?

    Teacher explores the stance by pointing out undesirable consequences of the position (Pattern 3).

S: I'M NOT SAYING THAT. I DON'T THINK THAT WE WOULD HAVE TO SEND DOWN TROOPS.

Steve qualifies his position.

T: BUT WHAT IF IT DID GO THAT FAR?

Teacher continues probing.

S: PROBABLY, YES.

T: SUPPOSE PEOPLE CALLED NEGROES WHO INTENDED TO VOTE ON THE PHONE AND SAID, "IF YOU VOTE TOMORROW, SOMETHING MIGHT VERY WELL HAPPEN TO YOUR KIDS." DO YOU THINK WE SHOULD SEND THE FBI DOWN THERE TO INVESTIGATE THESE INTIMIDATIONS?

Teacher checks to determine the point at which the value is violated (Pattern 1).

S: NO.

T: WHY NOT?

S: IF THE THREAT IS CARRIED OUT, THEN I WOULD SEND DOWN TROOPS OR THE FBI.

Steve establishes the point at which the value is violated.

T: AFTER SOMETHING HAS HAPPENED TO THE COURAGEOUS NEGRO'S FAMILY, THEN YOU WOULD SEND SOMEONE DOWN TO STOP IT? YOU DON'T GO ALONG WITH THE NOTION THAT, IF THERE IS AN ATMOSPHERE OF FEAR AND INTIMIDATION, WE SHOULD DO SOMETHING TO CHANGE THE ATMOSPHERE SO THAT PEOPLE WILL BE FREE TO VOTE? WE SHOULDN'T DO ANYTHING UNTIL THERE IS ACTUAL VIOLENCE?

Teacher checks consistency of Steve's position (Principle of Reaction).

S: IN THE CASE OF NEGROES, YES.

T: WHY?

S: BECAUSE I DON'T WANT TO GIVE THEM COMPLETE POWER TO VOTE. THIS IS TAKING A LITTLE OF IT AWAY.

Steve changes his position.

T: YOU WANT TO DENY SOME NEGROES THE RIGHT TO VOTE, A RIGHT YOU ARE WILLING TO GIVE TO WHITES?

Teacher tests the new position for consistency (Principle of Reaction).

S: YES.

T: WHY?

S: BECAUSE I FEEL THAT NEGROES ARE INFERIOR TO WHITES.

Steve gives underlying assumption for his position.

T: IN WHAT RESPECT?

S: IN INTELLIGENCE, IN HEALTH, IN CRIME RATES.

T: YOU ARE SUGGESTING THAT IF A PERSON IS TUBERCULAR OR SICK, YOU SHOULD DENY HIM THE RIGHT TO VOTE?

Teacher uses an analogy to test Steve's position (Pattern 2).

S: NO.

T: BUT IF A NEGRO IS SICK, WE DON'T LET HIM VOTE?

S: LET HIM VOTE, SURE. IT IS JUST THAT I THINK THEY ARE INFERIOR FOR THESE REASONS. I'M NOT SAYING BECAUSE OF THESE REASONS I'M NOT GOING TO LET HIM VOTE.

T: THEN FOR WHAT REASONS AREN'T YOU GOING TO LET HIM VOTE?

S: BECAUSE I THINK THEY ARE INFERIOR BECAUSE
     OF THESE REASONS. (Student then laughs self-
     consciously, aware of his inconsistency.)[3]

By having to take a stand and defend a position, students become emotionally involved in the analysis. They are literally forced to clarify their values and to come to a complex justification of policy positions. Thus the model, unlike many other teaching strategies, simultaneously integrates the personal and the intellectual.

Syntax

The exploration of students' stances through confrontational dialogue may be the heart of the model, but several equally important activities are involved in first, helping students *formulate* the stance they eventually defend, and then in helping *revise* their position after the argumentation. All of these activities, the analysis as well as the confrontation, are part of jurisprudential thinking. Thus in the Jurisprudential Model of teaching there are six phases of activity:

Phase One: Orientation to the Case
Phase Two: Identifying the Issues
Phase Three: Taking a Position
Phase Four: Exploring the Stances
Phase Five: Refining and Qualifying the Position
Phase Six: Testing the Factual Assumptions

In Phase One the teacher introduces the students to case materials. This may include reading a story or historical narrative out loud or watching a filmed incident depicting a value-controversy. The second step in orienting students to the case is to review the facts. This too can be done in a number of ways; the teacher can ask students to recall the sequence of events, analyzing who did what to whom and why, or accomplish the same review of the facts through an enactment of the controversy.

In Phase Two the teacher leads the students to synthesize the facts of the case into a public policy issue; that is, the students must characterize the case in terms of a decision for action or choice.

A PUBLIC POLICY ISSUE is a question involving a choice or a decision for action by citizens or officials in affairs that concern a government or community.

Policy issues can be phrased as general questions: "Should the United States stay in Vietnam?" "Should capital punishment be abolished?" "Should Government regulate automobile design?"

Public policy issues can also be phrased as choices for personal action: "Should I write my Congressman to protest draft laws?" "Should I petition the Governor to commute a criminal's death sentence?" "Should I write to a candidate asking him to pledge support for auto design regulations?"[4]

[3] Oliver and Shaver, *Teaching Public Issues*, pp. 150-152.
[4] Donald Oliver and Fred Newman, *Taking a Stance: A Clear Guide to Discussion of Public Issues* (Middletown, Conn.: American Education Publishers, 1967), p. 29.

EXERCISE 1

To get the feeling of how public policy issues work in this model, indicate which of the questions below are public issues and then try to formulate a public policy question for the case situation. Remember that a public policy issue involves a choice or decision for action in matters of concern to a government or community.

a) _____ Should nuclear power plants be built near large urban areas?
b) _____ Was President Kennedy's decision to blockade Cuba in 1963 a correct decision?
c) _____ Should the United States continue to sell large amounts of wheat to the Soviet Union?
d) _____ Which method of home heating is more ecologically sound, electricity or natural gas?

Answers: a and c are public policy issues; b is not because it calls for judgment about a historical question (no decision for action is involved); d is not because it is a technical question that can be resolved scientifically, without necessity of a decision for public action.

EXERCISE 2

Read the paragraph below. Then, in your own words, formulate a public policy question that captures the essence of the situation:

In most states, the funds for education come from real estate taxes. School districts with many expensive homes and high property values have more money with which to educate children than do school districts with poor neighborhoods and low property values. Yet it could be argued that the poor districts are precisely where the most money is needed.

Public policy question:

(*Sample answer:* Should the state require that school districts equalize expenditure for each pupil so that the same amount is spent for the education of each student, regardless of where they live?)

After the public policy issue has been identified, the next step is to characterize the legal-ethical issue underlying it. This is the point where teachers and students *abstract the general values from the concrete situation* (freedom of speech versus protecting the general welfare, or local autonomy, or equal opportunity) and *identify conflicts between values* (Can you identify the value or value conflict in the public policy question you just formulated?).

Up to this point in the model, the students have not been asked to express their opinions or take a stand. They have used some legal tools for analyzing the conflict situation in order to develop a position. *Phase Three* (Taking a Position) begins to move into the personal meaning-system of the students. Here they are asked to articulate a position on the issue and state the basis for their position. In the example above, a student might take the position that the state should not legislate how much a school district can spend on each pupil because this would constitute an unacceptable violation of local autonomy.

In Phase Four the stance is explored, either with the teacher or with other students. Up to this point, the model of discussion has been an analytic one. At this point, the teacher shifts to a Socratic or confrontational style as he or she probes the students' position. In enacting the Socratic role, the teacher (or a student) may use one or more of four patterns of argumentation. (These patterns of debate are explained and illustrated in the Theory into Action section.)

1. Establishing the point at which a value is violated

2. Clarifying the value conflict through analogies

3. Proving desirable or undesirable consequences of a position

4. Setting value priorities: asserting priority of one value over another *and* demonstrating lack of gross violation of the second value

Phase Five consists of refining and qualifying the position(s). Sometimes this stage may fall naturally into Phase Four as a result of the dialogue. At other times, the teacher may have to prompt the students to restate their position in light of the discussion in Phase Four. A good way to do this is to ask students to identify the most convincing stance(s).

While Phase Five clarifies the reasoning in a value position, *Phase Six* (Testing the Factual Assumption) further weighs the viability of the position by identifying the factual assumptions behind it and examining them carefully. This final phase is a quick check of the soundness and validity of the final position taken in Phase Five. The teacher helps the students check to see whether their position holds up even under the most extreme conditions and situations imaginable. Eventually, the students should be able to carry out the process unassisted, providing them with maximum control of the process.

The six phases of the Jurisprudential Model can be divided into analysis (Phases One, Two, and Three) and argumentation (Phases Four, Five, and Six). The analyses activities prepare the material for exploration. Ideally, the argumentation produces the strongest possible stance. The exploration of the stance is carried out in a Socratic (confrontational) style of dialogue, whereas the analysis and final testing of stances is more in the style of an analytical discussion. Thus there are actually two styles of teaching in this model. For all the phases except Phase Four, the teacher employs an analytic discussion style. In Phase Four, the teacher uses a Socratic dialogue (or confrontational style).

Social System

The amount of structure in this model ranges from high to moderate. The teacher initiates the phases, but moving from phase to phase is, in some cases, dependent on the student's ability to complete the task required by the phase. The teacher plays several roles in this model. Eventually, the students should be able to carry out the process unassisted, thereby gaining maximum control of the process.

Principles of Reaction

The teacher's reactions, especially in Phases Four and Five are not evaluative— in the sense of approval or disapproval. They probe substance. The teacher reacts to students' comments by questioning relevance, consistency, specificity or generality, and definitional clarity. The teacher also enforces continuity of thought, so that one thought or line of reasoning is pursued to its logical conclusion before other argumentation is raised.

To play this role well, the teacher must anticipate student value-claims and be prepared to challenge and probe those claims. In the Socratic role, the teacher probes one student's opinion at length before challenging other students. Socratic dialogue avoids eliciting random student opinions without getting at the depth of reasoning underlying those opinions; it is a confrontation style of discussion. Sometimes teachers confront students by arguing their own position; however, true Socratic dialogue questions the assumptions, logic, values, and consistency of the *student's* own position.

A Socratic dialogue can easily become a threatening cross-examination or a game of "guess what the teacher's right answer is." You, as teacher, must make it clear that the clarification of issues and the development of the most defensible position in a case are the objectives. The questioning of evidence and assumptions must be tempered with supportiveness. The merits of the case, and not of the students, are the basis for evaluation.

Summary

The purpose of the Jurisprudential Model is to develop a person who can intelligently analyze and take stances on public issues—a skillful citizen. This is accomplished through the use of legal thinking and open dialogue. The three areas of competency necessary to be a skillful citizen are:

1. a value framework based on the key principles of the Constitution and Declaration of Independence
2. a process for clarifying and resolving conflict based on legal reasoning
3. knowledge of contemporary public issues

Many teaching strategies and styles can be developed from Oliver and Shaver's work. We have based this model on the Socratic method, in which students take a position on social issues and the teacher or other students question the assumptions of the position. The flavor is distinctly confrontational.

SUMMARY CHART: THE JURISPRUDENTIAL MODEL

Syntax

Phase One: Orientation to the Case
     A. Introduce materials.
     B. Review facts.

Phase Two: Identifying the Issues
     A. Synthesize facts into a public policy issue(s).
     B. Select one policy issue for discussion.
     C. Identify values and value conflicts.
     D. Recognize underlying factual and definitional questions.

Phase Three: Taking a Position
   A. Articulate a position. State basis of position in terms of the social value or conse-
      quences of the decision.

Phase Four: Exploring the Stance(s): Patterns of Argumentation
   A. Establish the point at which value is violated (factual).
   B. Prove the desirable or undesirable consequences of a position (factual).
   C. Clarify the value conflict with analogies.
   D. Set priorities. Assert priority of one value over another *and* demonstrate lack of gross
      violation of second value.

Phase Five: Refining and Qualifying the Position
   A. State position and reasons for position, and examine a number of similar situations.
   B. Qualify position.

Phase Six: Testing Factual Assumptions Behind Qualified Position
   A. Identify factual assumptions and determine if they are relevant.
   B. Determine the predicted consequences and examine their factual validity (will they
      actually occur?).

Principles of Reaction:

1. Maintain a vigorous intellectual climate where all views are respected; avoid direct evaluation
   of students' opinions.
2. See that issues are thoroughly explored.
3. Probe the substance of students' thinking through questioning relevance, consistency,
   specificity, generality, definitional clarity, and continuity.
4. Maintain dialectical style: use confrontational dialogue, questioning students' assumptions
   and using specific instances (analogies) to contradict more general statements.
5. Avoid advocating a stand.

Social System:

Moderate to high structure, with teacher initiating and controlling the discussion; however,
an atmosphere of openness and intellectual equality prevails.

Support System:

Source documents that focus on a problem situation.

THEORY IN PRACTICE

   No amount of description can convey a sense of a model of teaching as well as an example of
the model in practice. In fact, reading too much theory before gaining a rough "image" of the
practice can be confusing and, for some people, frustrating and discouraging. So we encourage
you, at this point of your study of the Jurisprudential Model, to read the following abbreviated
transcript of an actual classroom session. We suggest that you first read only the teacher-student
dialogue and then go back to note the annotations. Remember, the goal at this point in your

training is to gain a sense of the model—its flow and feeling—not to master the techniques of implementation.

This transcript illustrates the Jurisprudential Model in exploring a case in which the central issue is students' rights to freedom of expression in school. The lesson was taught to high school students by an experienced teacher. This lesson was the students' first exposure to the Jurisprudential Model. As a result, much of the lesson was devoted to analysis (Phase One, Two, and Three), as contrasted with argumentation (Phases Four, Five, and Six).

Phase One: Orientation to the Case

T: WE HAVE THREE THINGS TO DO IN THIS PHASE. I'M GOING TO INTRODUCE YOU TO THE CASE MATERIAL AND THEN WE'RE GOING TO CHAT ABOUT THEM FOR A FEW MINUTES AND JUST REVIEW THE FACTS OF THE CASE, WHICH I'LL PUT UP HERE ON THE BOARD. THEN WHAT WE WANT TO DO IS THINK ABOUT THE CASE AND COME UP WITH ONE OR MORE PUBLIC POLICY ISSUES. I THINK WE'LL PROBABLY FIND THAT THIS IS NOT CUT AND DRIED, THAT WE CAN FORMULATE THE ISSUES IN A NUMBER OF WAYS. (Teacher reads case about high school students who protest involvement in war)

Teacher gives the students a preview of the Jurisprudential process.

Teacher presents the case.

ON A RECENT EVENING, A GROUP OF STUDENTS HAVE GOTTEN TOGETHER AND DECIDED TO SPEAK OUT AGAINST THE WAR BY WEARING BLACK ARMBANDS TO SCHOOL AS A SYMBOL OF MOURNING FOR THOSE WHO HAVE BEEN KILLED IN THE WAR. LEE HIGH SCHOOL HAS 1500 STUDENTS AND, LIKE MOST OTHER HIGH SCHOOLS, THE STUDENTS HAVE DIVERGENT VIEWS ON THE QUESTION OF AMERICAN INVOLVEMENT IN THE WAR.

THE PRINCIPAL OF LEE, ELMER GRANT, LEARNED OF THE PLAN TO WEAR ARMBANDS AHEAD OF TIME AND ADOPTED A POLICY THAT ANYONE WEARING AN ARMBAND WOULD BE ASKED TO REMOVE IT; IF THEY REFUSED TO DO SO, THEY WOULD BE SUSPENDED UNTIL THEY WERE READY TO COME BACK TO SCHOOL WITHOUT THE ARMBAND. YESTERDAY, LOUISE, BENNY, AND ED WERE SUSPENDED FROM SCHOOL FOR WEARING ARMBANDS. IN AN INTERVIEW YESTERDAY AFTERNOON, MR. GRANT EXPLAINED THAT HE HAD ISSUED THE NO-ARMBAND POLICY TO AVOID DISRUPTION OF THE EDUCATION PROCESS AT LEE. HE SAID, "IF WE ALLOW STUDENTS TO WEAR THESE PROTEST ARMBANDS, IT WILL CAUSE HEATED DEBATE ABOUT THE WAR WHICH WILL INTERFERE WITH SCHEDULED CLASSROOM ACTIVITY. I AM ALSO AFRAID THAT IT MIGHT LEAD TO VIOLENCE AMONG THE KIDS AND POLARIZE THE STUDENT BODY."

BEFORE WE GO ANY FURTHER, LET'S JUST THINK ABOUT THE CASE AND REVIEW SOME OF THE IMPORTANT FACTS HERE.

S: DID THE PRINCIPAL PUBLISH THE POLICY ABOUT

THE ARMBANDS BEFORE ANYBODY ACTUALLY WORE THEM?

T: YES. THEY ISSUED A NO-ARMBAND POLICY.

S: THE STUDENTS WHO WORE ARMBANDS WERE PROTESTING THE WAR OR SHOWING MOURNING FOR THE PEOPLE KILLED.

S: I THINK THEY WERE MORE OR LESS PROTESTING THE WAR AND IT ALL CAME OUT OF THE FACT THAT THEY HAD SOME FRIENDS KILLED IN THE WAR. AND THEY DIDN'T BELIEVE IN IT.

T: ARE THERE ANY OTHER FACTS WE WANT TO PUT UP HERE?

S: THE PRINCIPAL'S REASON FOR THE BAN--THAT IT WOULD POLARIZE THE STUDENT BODY AND DISRUPT THE SCHOOL PROCESS.

S: WHAT ABOUT THE HISTORY OF THE WAR? DO WE KNOW ANYTHING ABOUT THAT?

S: IT HAD BEEN GOING ON FOR TEN YEARS, WAS IT? ELEVEN?

S: WHAT TYPE OF INVOLVEMENT—

T: THE TYPE OF INVOLVEMENT HAD CHANGED.

S: FROM MONEY TO MILITARY. WE HAD OUR TROOPS FIGHTING THERE.

T: NOW, LOOKING AT THESE FACTS, CAN WE COME UP WITH A PUBLIC POLICY QUESTION? DO YOU REMEMBER WHAT A PUBLIC POLICY QUESTION IS? LET ME GO OVER THAT AND GIVE YOU AN EXAMPLE. A PUBLIC POLICY QUESTION IS A "SHOULD" QUESTION, FOR ONE THING, AND IT IMPLIES AN ACTION. "SHOULD CAPITAL PUNISHMENT BE ABOLISHED?" "SHOULD GOVERNMENT REGULATE AUTOMOBILE DESIGN?" THOSE ARE VERY GENERAL POLICY QUESTIONS. WE CAN ALSO BE MORE SPECIFIC ABOUT IT; AND WE CAN ALSO BE PERSONAL. "SHOULD I WRITE MY CONGRESSMAN TO PROTEST DRAFT LAWS?" THAT'S STATING A PUBLIC POLICY QUESTION IN TERMS OF A PERSONAL ACTION. LET'S SEE IF WE CAN COME UP WITH A PUBLIC POLICY QUESTION HERE THAT WE WANT TO FOCUS ON. WE MIGHT BE ABLE TO COME UP WITH A NUMBER OF PUBLIC POLICY QUESTIONS, AND THAT'S OK. ULTIMATELY I THINK WE MIGHT HAVE TO TAKE ONE AND FOCUS ON THAT.

Phase Two: Identifying the Issue

S: SHOULD STUDENTS HAVE THE RIGHT TO EXPRESS THEIR FEELINGS ABOUT THE WAR BY WEARING ARMBANDS?

T: OK. WHAT IS ANOTHER PUBLIC POLICY QUESTION?

Note that the teacher does not evaluate or criticize the student's suggestion when it meets the definition of a public policy question.

S: WERE THEY APT TO DISRUPT THE STUDENTS' LEARNING?

T: I THINK THAT'S ONE OF THE FACTUAL QUESTIONS WE MIGHT WANT TO EXPLORE HERE, BUT IT WOULDN'T BE A PUBLIC POLICY QUES-

Teacher reminds student of a criterion for public policy issues.

TION, BECAUSE IT DOESN'T IMPLY AN ACTION.

S: SHOULD THE PRINCIPAL HAVE THE RIGHT TO SUSPEND ANY STUDENT?

T: GOOD. AN EXTENSION TO THAT QUESTION COULD BE, "SHOULD THE PRINCIPAL HAVE THE RIGHT TO SUSPEND ANY STUDENTS FOR EXPRESSING THEIR OPINIONS?"

Teacher expands student suggestion.

S: I HAVE A COUPLE: SHOULD STUDENTS BE PERMITTED TO WEAR ARMBANDS? AND I'LL PUT IT ANOTHER WAY WHICH IS MORE GENERAL: SHOULD STUDENTS BE PERMITTED TO USE THE SCHOOL AS A PLACE TO DEMONSTRATE THEIR POLITICAL VIEWS?

T: ANY OTHER IDEAS?

S: SHOULD STUDENTS BE ALLOWED TO EXPRESS FEELINGS ABOUT THE WAR IN SCHOOL BY WEARING ARMBANDS?

T: THAT LAST ONE SEEMS TO CAPTURE THE ESSENCE OF THE CASE. LET'S CHOOSE IT AS THE PUBLIC POLICY ISSUE THAT WE'LL EXAMINE TODAY. (Teacher writes the issue on the chalkboard.)

Teacher selects one public policy issue for discussion.

WHAT WE WANT TO DO NOW IS TO IDENTIFY THE VALUES IN CONFLICT HERE IN THIS PARTICULAR SITUATION. WHAT VALUES ARE INVOLVED HERE?

Teacher makes transition to identifying values and value conflicts.

S: FREEDOM OF SPEECH?

T: GOOD. ARMBANDS CAN BE A FORM OF SPEECH. NOT EVERYBODY WOULD HAVE RECOGNIZED THAT.

WHAT ARE SOME OF THE OTHER VALUES THAT MIGHT BE INVOLVED HERE?

S: EQUAL PROTECTION UNDER THE LAW.

T: OK. ANY OTHER IDEAS?

S: DUE PROCESS.

T: DUE PROCESS—IN WHAT WAY?

S: WERE THEY GIVEN THE RIGHT TO A HEARING, OR WERE THEY GIVEN NOTICE OF IMPENDING ACTION?

T: VERY GOOD. ANY OTHER? HOW ABOUT FROM THE POINT OF VIEW OF THE PRINCIPAL?

S: PRESERVATION OF PEACE AND ORDER.

T: EXCELLENT.

OK. NOW WE HAVE SEVERAL VALUES IDENTIFIED. LET'S BEGIN TO PAIR THEM UP TO SEE WHICH VALUES ARE IN CONFLICT. DOES ANYONE HAVE A SUGGESTION?

Teacher makes transition to identifying values in conflict.

S: PERSONAL LIBERTY VERSUS GENERAL WELFARE.

S: PERSONAL LIBERTY VERSUS EQUAL PROTECTION.

T: GOOD. HOW ABOUT SOME MORE VALUE CONFLICTS?

S: PERSONAL LIBERTY VERSUS PEACE AND ORDER.

T: OK. LET'S FOCUS ON THAT ONE. PERSONAL LIBERTY VERSUS PEACE AND ORDER. THE NEXT THING WE HAVE TO DO HERE IS LOOK AT WHAT DEFINITIONAL PROBLEMS AND FACTUAL QUESTIONS WE'VE GOT. FOR THIS, WE'VE GOT TO GO BACK TO OUR PUBLIC POLICY QUESTION. WHAT DEFINITIONAL PROBLEMS DO WE HAVE HERE?

Teacher selects a pair of values in conflict.

I COULD ARGUE THAT WHAT THE STUDENTS ARE DOING BY WEARING THE ARMBANDS AND THE QUESTIONS THEY ARE RAISING IN THE SCHOOL ARE EVERY BIT AS MUCH A PART OF EDUCATION AS WHAT THEY WERE AFRAID OF DISRUPTING.

S: WOULD THE ACTUAL QUESTION THEN BE, "DID THE WEARING OF THE ARMBANDS DISRUPT THEM?"

T: NO, THAT'S A FACTUAL QUESTION. THE DEFINITIONAL QUESTION IS, "WHAT IS EDUCATIONAL?"

S: UNDER DEFINITIONAL PROBLEMS WHEN YOU SPEAK OF PERSONAL LIBERTY YOU HAVE TO BE VERY SPECIFIC ABOUT WHAT YOU'RE TALKING ABOUT, AND I THINK IT'S RATHER GENERAL THERE.

T: WHAT IS PERSONAL LIBERTY?

Teacher asks for definition from student.

S: PERSONAL LIBERTY IS A KIND OF CLUSTER OF CONCEPTS THAT ARE SPELLED OUT IN THE CONSTITUTION, LIKE FREEDOM OF SPEECH.

T: SHOULD WE PUT FREEDOM OF SPEECH HERE INSTEAD OF PERSONAL LIBERTY? (Students agree.)

Statement of values in conflict is refined.

T: OK. NOW OUR VALUES IN CONFLICT ARE FREEDOM OF SPEECH VERSUS PEACE AND ORDER.

NOW I'M GOING TO REVIEW WHAT WE'VE DONE. WE HAVE OUR PUBLIC POLICY ISSUE AND WE'VE ANALYZED IT TO SELECT A PAIR OF VALUES IN CONFLICT. WE'VE ALSO IDENTIFIED A SET OF KEY TERMS THAT MAY NEED TO BE DEFINED AND FACTS TO BE ESTABLISHED. BEFORE WE GO ANY FARTHER, I'M GOING TO ASK YOU TO TAKE A POSITION IN THIS CASE. SHOULD STUDENTS BE ALLOWED TO EXPRESS THEIR FEELINGS ABOUT THE WAR IN SCHOOL BY WEARING ARMBANDS? WHERE DO YOU STAND?

Phase Three: Taking a Position

TAKING THEORY INTO ACTION

The Jurisprudential Model, perhaps more than other models, requires intellectual mastery of several ideas before it is possible to guide students through phases of activity. Figure 1 relates the ideas to be discussed in this section to the phases of the model that draw on them. As you study the material, you may want to see how the information or concept fits into the activities of the model.

PHASE ONE: Orientation to the Case
Introduce materials.
Review facts.

PHASE TWO: Identifying the Issues

Synthesize facts into a public policy issue(s).	What is a public policy issue?
Select one policy for discussion.	What is a value?
Identify values and value conflicts.	What are the basic social values?
Recognize underlying factual and definitional questions.	What are factual problems?
	How are they resolved?
	What are definitional questions?
	How are they resolved?

PHASE THREE: Taking a Position

What are the ways to defend or attack a policy stance? (What are the patterns of argumentation?)

PHASE FOUR: Exploring the Stances

PHASE FIVE: Refining and Qualifying the Position

What is the best stance?

PHASE SIX: Testing the Consequences

Figure 1. *Ideas Underlying the Phases of the Model.*

In general, the material in this section describes the legal-ethical framework and the legal reasoning process of rational consent. A legal-ethical framework enables us to describe a particular situation or conflict in more general terms. Once the situation has been characterized, the legal reasoning tools of rational consent assist us in developing the strongest possible stance on the issue.

A Framework of Values

The values that concern Oliver and Shaver in their strategy are political and social values—values such as personal freedom, equality, and justice—which are "the major concepts used by our government and private groups to justify public policies and decision."[5] When we speak of a framework of values for analyzing public issues, we implicitly mean the *legal-ethical* framework that governs American social policies and decisions, which is found in the Declaration of Independence and the Constitution of the United States. These two documents articulate the principles of American government and our societal goals. A partial list of these appears in Figure 2.

Part of the resolution of differences in any specific controversy involves screening the details of the case through this legal-ethical framework in order to identify the values and policies that are in question. Social values help us to analyze controversial situations because they provide a common framework that transcends any one particular controversy. However, in most controversial situations, two general rules of ethical conduct are in conflict with one another. Thus, although

[5] Oliver and Shaver, *Teaching Public Issues*, p. 64.

Rule of Law: Actions carried out by the government have to be authorized by law and apply equally to all people.

Equal Protection Under the Law: Laws must be administered fairly and cannot extend special privileges or penalties to any one person or group.

Due Process: The government cannot deprive individual citizens of life, liberty or property without proper notice of impending actions (right to a fair trial).

Justice: Equal opportunity.

Preservation of Peace and Order: Prevention of disorder and violence (reason as a means of dealing with conflict).

Community Welfare: Progress and welfare of the whole community and nation.

Personal Liberty: Freedom of speech, right to own and control property, freedom of religion, freedom of personal associations, right of privacy.

Separation of Powers: Checks and balances among the three branches of government.

Local Control of Local Problems: Restriction of federal government power and preservation of states' rights.

Figure 2. *The Legal-Ethical Framework: Some Basic Social Values.*

a framework of social values permits us to speak of diverse conflict situations in common terms, it does not tell us how to go about resolving controversies.

The 1960s and 1970s have witnessed many social problems, frequently involving conflicting values. A list of some of these problem areas and their underlying value conflicts appears in Figure 3. As you read over these topics, you will note that although the values are identified, the controversies still remain. Alternative policy stances are possible on any topic, and most issues can be argued on a number of grounds.

Oliver and Shaver emphasize that values can be seen or used on what they call a *dimensional* basis, as contrasted to an *ideal* basis. If social values are construed as ideals, then they have to be dealt with on an either/or basis; either one lives up to a value or one does not. If, for example, you approve of equality of all races before the law in the ideal sense, you feel it either has been achieved or has not. On the other hand, if you see values on a dimensional basis, then you judge degrees of desirable conditions on a continuum. For example, you can accept a compromise that ensures some but not all possible equality. Politically, you might opt for such a position in the hope of getting a little bit more next time around.

Using the example of free speech, Oliver and Shaver suggest that if we see free speech as a total ideal—something to be preserved at all costs and all situations—then we are unable to cope with situations where it might be desirable to abrogate free speech temporarily in deference to public safety. For instance, a speaker might be prevented from continuing a speech before a hostile crowd about to turn on him violently. In such a case, one might restrict his free speech in order to provide for his safety and prevent the crowd from destructive action that might be regretted later on.

In the Jurisprudential Model of teaching, the best stance on an issue is one

Problem Areas	Sample Unit Topics	Conflicting Values[a]
Racial and Ethnic Conflict	School Desegregation Civil Rights for Nonwhites and Ethnic Minorities Housing for Nonwhites and Ethnic Minorities Job Opportunities for Nonwhites and Ethnic Minorities Immigration Policy	Equal Protection Due Process Brotherhood of Man v. Peace and Order Property and Contract Rights Personal Privacy and Association
Religious and Ideological Conflict	Rights of the Communist Party in America Religion and Public Education Control of "Dangerous" or "Immoral" Literature Religion and National Security: Oaths, Conscientious Objectors Taxation of Religious Property	Freedom of Speech and Conscience v. Equal Protection Safety and Security of Democratic Institutions
Security of the Individual	Crime and Delinquency	Standards of Freedom Due Process v. Peace and Order Community Welfare
Conflict Among Economic Groups	Organized Labor Business Competition and Monopoly "Overproduction" of Farm Goods Conservation of Natural Resources	Equal or Fair Bargaining Power and Competition General Welfare and Progress of the Community v. Property and Contract Rights
Health, Education, and Welfare	Adequate Medical Care: for the Aged for the Poor Adequate Educational Opportunity Old-Age Security Job and Income Security	Equal Opportunity Brotherhood of Man v. Property and Contract Rights
Security of the Nation	Federal Loyalty-Security Programs Foreign Policy	Freedom of Speech, Conscience, and Association Due Process Personal Privacy v. Safety and Security of Democratic Institutions

[a]The "v." in the listing of values suggests that the top values conflict with the bottom values. While this is generally true, there are, of course, many exceptions. One can argue, for example, that a minimum wage law was a violation of property and contract rights and that it was also against the general welfare.

Figure 3. *Identification of General Problem Areas* (From Donald Oliver and James Shaver, *Teaching Public Issues in the High School*, Boston: Houghton-Mifflin, 1966, pp. 142-43).

that maintains a *balance of values*—a stance in which each of the values in conflict is compromised or violated only minimally. To achieve such a balance, each party in a controversy should try to understand the reasons and assumptions behind the other's position. Only by way of such rational dialogue can useful compromises be reached.

To gain a better sense of the legal-ethical framework of values and the idea of a values conflict, complete Exercise 1. Ask yourself what policy stance would represent a balance of values in which neither value is sacrificed completely.

EXERCISE 1

Read the descriptions of the two situations below. Then identify the values in conflict in each situation. (The list of conflicting values in Figure 3 will be helpful in this exercise.)

1. Two police officers observe a man "acting suspiciously" in a high crime-rate neighborhood. As they approach him, he turns and runs away, entering a house half a block away. The police follow him into the house and find him trying to flush a large quantity of narcotics down the toilet. The police have no search warrant for entering the house or seizing the drugs.

Values in conflict: _____ v. _____

What policy stance would represent a balance of these values?

2. A newspaper prints a story containing information classified as secret by the federal government. The reporter who wrote the story is summoned to court and asked to reveal the source of the classified information. The reporter refuses to reveal his source, even though he is threatened with imprisonment.

Values in conflict: _____ v. _____

What policy stance would represent a balance of these values?

Rational Consent: A Legal-Reasoning Process

Once situations have been described in terms of their conflicting social values, policy stances are reached through the process of dialogue known as *rational consent*. This process implies commitment to reason and reflection and the right of all parties to express themselves before being bound by a decision. It involves free and open discussion of a controversial issue. Through an understanding of their respective positions, individuals can negotiate their differences in values.[6]

Rational consent is based on the concepts and procedures of legal reason, which we refer to as levels of analysis and patterns of argumentation. This section describes three levels of analysis used to define a controversial situation and four patterns of argumentation used to develop a defensible stance.

The four patterns of argumentation suggest lines of questioning you can use when probing a student's position. The particular strategy to be used depends on the type of conflict involved in the policy issue. Do not try to remember all the

[6] *Ibid.,* p. 61.

details, but when you identify a particular type of conflict in planning to teach, refer back to this material for tools you will use in probing students' positions. Remember that the flavor of the dialogue is Socratic. That is, you continually question students to defend the logic of their conclusions, the consistency of their stance, and the range of alternative values. A different level of analysis is appropriate for each of these three types of questions. In the first, a great deal hinges on the definition of the terms *humane* and *humanity*; the second question is clearly a factual one; the third, however, is again a value question.

Discussions of the death penalty and similar issues raise these important questions but fail to deal with them systematically. People tend to dwell on issues they feel favor their side of the argument and refuse to deal with issues that operate against them. Discussion can be more productive when individuals go beyond the initial statement of issues to the question of an appropriate strategy for resolution. We now examine these three levels of analysis and the ways of approaching each one in the course of discussion.

Definitional Problems

Ambiguous or confusing use of words is a basic problem in discussion of public controversy.[7] Unless we recognize common meaning in the words we use, discussion is very difficult and agreement on issues, policies, or actions is virtually impossible. To resolve definitional disagreements, it is necessary first, to determine whether participants in a discussion are using the same term in a different way or different terms for the same referent, and second, to establish a common meaning.

If participants in a discussion seem to be using the same term to mean different things, they should be asked to give a definition. Two types of definition are possible: (1) definition by example, or (2) definition by criteria—listing the distinguishing characteristics of the term being used.

If it turns out that there is, in fact, a disagreement over definition, then there are several means for clarifying communication. Participants may: (1) appeal to common usage by finding out how most people use a word or by consulting a dictionary; (2) stipulate the meaning of the word for purposes of discussion by listing agreed-upon criteria; (3) obtain more facts about an example to see if it meets agreed-upon criteria for a definition.

Suppose, for example, that one student maintains that, as a person of Irish descent, he is a minority in this country. Another student disagrees, maintaining that only blacks and American Indians are entitled to minority status. Clearly, the two students are not defining minority in the same way. The first student is using the criteria of numbers and ethnicity, whereas the second student is using criteria based on number and racial characteristics. In addition, the second student is overheard to reply to the first, "The Italians have never been discriminated against the way the blacks and Indians have. Look at the Kennedys. They made it and they were Irish." The first student responds, 'Well, the Jews were discriminated against and they made it. You wouldn't consider them for minority student scholarships, would you?"

As this discussion continues, many implicit criteria begin to emerge. The two students, part of a college scholarship committee, have to agree upon criteria

[7]*Ibid.,* p. 92.

that will define the term minority in this situation—eligibility for scholarships. Perhaps popular usage will apply, but it is likely that more specific criteria will need to be outlined. The scholarship committee will also have to deal with economic need, and since that is a relevant criteria for eligibility, they will also have to define the term "economic need."

Value Problems

Valuing means classifying things, actions, or ideas as *good* or *bad*, *right* or *wrong*. If we speak of something as a value (such as honesty), we mean that it is good. As people make choices throughout their lives, they are constantly making value judgments, even if they cannot verbalize their values. The range of items or issues over which each of us makes value judgments is vast—art, music, politics, decoration, clothes, people. Some of these choices seem less important than others, and the degree of importance has something to do with what we mean by a value. Not everything we consider good is a value; some are personal preferences. Nevertheless, many choices of ideas, objects, or actions do become subjects of discussion in our society and communities, such as art or the physical environment. These are value issues involving artistic taste or judgment of beauty.

Value conflicts are usually at the center of most political and social controversies. Because there is usually some validity to each value stance, there is no "correct" solution. As you may remember, Oliver and Shaver suggest that the best solution is one in which there is a balance of values, in which each value is compromised or violated only minimally.

Value judgments imply not only that something is good or bad, but that some action (decision) will or should be taken on the basis of this judgment. Once a decision is made explicit, it is possible to analyze the original value judgment by predicting that on the basis of this decision: (1) certain consequences will occur; (2) other consequences will be avoided; or (3) important social values will be violated if the decision is not made. Disagreements about such predicted consequences can often be resolved by obtaining evidence to support the prediction. This is true both for specific consequences and social value violations. In searching for supporting evidence, a problem of value conflict is reinterpreted into one of factual problems.

Factual Problems

In political issues, controversy usually arises from disagreement over values. But such disagreements are rarely over the goodness of a particular value. Rather, they tend to be concerned with whether a value has been violated or whether adopting a particular policy will lead to undesirable consequences. In both of these instances, a value position is supported by a factual claim. When this occurs, it is necessary to determine the reliability of a factual claim.

The reliability of a factual claim can be established in two ways: (1) by evoking more specific claims, and (2) by relating it to other general facts accepted as true.[8] In both approaches, evidence is used to support the truth of a factual claim.

For example, suppose we make the claim: Lowering the speed limit will

[8] *Ibid.*, pp. 103-4.

reduce accidents and save gas. The first way we might support the statement is to look at more *specific* claims. We might find that:

1. In cities that have adopted the 55 MPH speed, accidents have decreased.
2. Gasoline consumption decreased under the 55 MPH speed limit, while the number of miles driven remained the same.

The greater number of specific claims we can identify to support the conclusion we are trying to prove, the more reliable the conclusion becomes.

A second way to support the claim is to relate it to other general facts that are accepted as true. In this example, we might find that cars traveling at 55 MPH can stop 25 percent faster than cars traveling at 65 MPH.

In general, then, we can back a factual conclusion by giving specific information that supports the general conclusion under dispute and by showing that the conclusion is logically related to other facts.

Supporting evidence used to support a claim may be questioned, however, either because of its quality or quantity. Evidence may be based on intuition, authority, personal observation, or proof by analogy. Each of the sources has possible shortcomings, and one of the ways of proving evidence unreliable is by testing it for the shortcomings inherent in each of these sources. For example, the expert (authority) may prove *not* to be an expert, the personal observation may be biased or questionable. Thus, factual statements alone are not enough. We must look at their reliability and accuracy.

A summary of the three types of problems and ways of analyzing them appears in Figure 4.

Definitional Problems (Two types of definition: criteria and example)
1. Determine how most people use the term (common usage).
2. Agree on a meaning (stipulation).
3. Obtain more information about the example (see if it fits the criteria).

Value Problems
1. Good or bad consequences will follow from the decision.
2. Good or bad consequences will be avoided by the decision.
3. Important social values will be violated if the decision is *not* made.

Factual Problems
1. Support a factual claim with specific evidence.
2. Support a factual claim with related evidence.
3. Question the reliability of the evidence.

Figure 4. *Summary of Three Types of Problems and Ways of Classifying Them.* (Based on Donald Oliver and James P. Shaver, "Selected Analytic Concepts for the Classification of Public Issues," *Teaching Public Issues in the High School*, Boston: Houghton-Mifflin, 1966, pp. 88-113.)

EXERCISE 2

For each of the following examples, identify whether it is a definitional problem (D), a value problem (V), or a factual problem (F).

_____ 1. The citizens of Redwood City are protesting the building of a highway because they feel it will increase the pollution and noise.

_____ 2. All over the world, women are pressing for equality with men.

_____ 3. Sarah, a high-school student, is discussing the topic of responsibility with her parents. Sarah believes she is shouldering her share of responsibility by caring for the family pet and washing the cars. Her mother believes she should also earn her own allowance.

_____ 4. United States participation in Vietnam was an act of imperialism in a civil war of another country.

_____ 5. Poor people in this country are entitled to the same quality of medical care as the middle and upper classes.

_____ 6. If we institute a state income tax, we will discourage businesses from locating here.

Answers

1. F	4. D
2. V	5. V
3. D	0. F

Using the examples above, generate statements that reflect the ways of analyzing them. For instance, the VALUE PROBLEM "Women are pressing for equality with men" can be countered with "Divorce rates will increase if women are given full equality." (Bad consequences will follow from the decision.) Do this for each type of question and each of the ways of analyzing them.

I. DEFINITIONAL PROBLEM: United States participation in Vietnam was an act of imperialism in a civil war of another country.
   1. Determine common usage.
   2. Stipulate a meaning.
   3. Test whether example fits the criteria.

II. VALUE PROBLEM: All over the world, women are pressing for equality with men.
   1. Good or bad consequences will follow.
   2. Good or bad consequences will be avoided.
   3. Important social values will be violated.

III. FACTUAL PROBLEM: The citizens of Redwood City are protesting the building of a highway because they feel it will increase the pollution and noise.
   1. Specific supporting evidence.
   2. Related supporting evidence.
   3. Reliability of evidence.

Patterns of Argumentation

In the course of defending or attacking a policy stance, four patterns of argumentation are commonly used. Two of them argue from a factual standpoint and two of them focus on value issues directly. You may find yourself or your students pursuing one or more of these lines of reasoning in supporting or attacking a policy stance. The four patterns are:

1. Factual emphasis: Establishing the point at which value is violated
2. Factual emphasis: Proving the desirable or undesirable consequences of a position
3. Clarifying the value conflict
4. Setting value priorities: Asserting priority of one value over another and demonstrating lack of gross violation of the second value

To illustrate, the first pattern (Establishing the point at which value is violated) was used to argue the school desegregation issue in 1954. Both sides agreed theoretically on the value of equality of education, but the segregationists argued that black schools were, in fact, separate but equal to white schools.

The second pattern (Proving the desirable or undesirable consequences of a position) also approaches a value question through factual emphasis. In this case, a policy stance is taken; it is then argued that not taking this stance will have undesirable consequences and/or taking this stance will have desirable ones. For example, a segregated society would maintain the cultural integrity of different ethnic groups. This approach can be defended or attacked by verifying whether these assumed relationships do hold up.

Patterns three and four both involve the use of analogies to clarify the depth of commitment to a particular value and the consistency of a position. In pattern three, we try to determine the range of situations over which a position would hold. (If we believe in sexual equality, do we also believe in integrating the sexes in bathrooms and gym classes? Is our position on sex and age discrimination the same as our position on racial discrimination? How far are we willing to go with our value?) In pattern four, analogies are used to justify a claim that one value has priority over another, provided that the second value is not grossly violated. (In the segregation case, some argued that equality was not extremely violated by separate schools, whereas state's rights—local control—would have been extremely violated if the federal government had imposed integration of the schools.)

As a refresher, you may want to reread the discussion of voting rights in the Theory and Overview section in which, you may recall, the teacher used several patterns of argumentation to explore the student's position on the voting rights issue.

One of the tasks in planning for the Jurisprudential Model is to develop situations that are analogous to the issue under consideration. Through such analogies you can test the consistency of the students' positions and the depth of their commitment to a particular value.

EXERCISE 3

In the following exercise, develop each of the four lines of argumentation on the public policy issue: We should have a plan of socialized medicine in order to provide adequate medical care for all people. Take a position *against* the issue. For each pattern of argumentation, write two or three statements reflecting that pattern. Which pattern seems to be the strongest line of reasoning on this particular issue?

1. Establish the point at which the value is violated (factual emphasis). (Hint: What value(s) are at issue here?)
2. Prove desirable or undesirable consequences of a position (factual emphasis).
3. Clarify the values conflict through analogies.
4. Assert priority of one value over another and demonstrate lack of gross violation of the second value.

Implementing the Jurisprudential Strategy

At this point you may be wondering how you actually go about using the Jurisprudential Model with your students. In the remainder of this reading, we hope to show you how these ideas come together in the various phases and activities of the model.

Getting Started

The burden of directing activities in the Jurisprudential Model is borne by you, the teacher. But it is important to know that, if your students understand what steps you plan to lead them through and what the goals of the process are, the whole experience will be smoother and more effective. This is especially true the first few times you try the model with a group of students. We have found it useful to start with a short orientation to the model—a little talk in which you explain the importance of learning how to deal with complicated social and personal issues in a systematic and thoughtful way. For instance, you might note that every citizen makes choices and expresses preferences on controversial issues. The Jurisprudential Model offers a useful method for developing and supporting a strong stance on the kinds of social issues that everyone must eventually confront. You might ask your students to identify current social problems or issues they are facing.

After you have discussed the general purpose and importance of the model, it is useful to define the important concepts that are the building blocks of the model: public policy issue, values, balance of values, and rational consent. These concepts should be defined and illustrated briefly in your own words. The goal here is to give your students a feeling for the kind of tools they will be working with, not to teach formal definitions.

Finally, you might list the phases of the Jurisprudential Model on the chalkboard, again using your own words to briefly describe the steps that you will be taking. If possible, leave the list of phases on the chalkboard and refer to each of them in turn as you move through the model. This will help the students (and you) stay aware of the structure of the model and how each phase leads into the next. Be sure to encourage your students to ask questions for clarification at this time. When you are satisfied that everyone knows generally what to expect, you are ready to introduce the case.

Phase One: Introducing the Case

You should prepare enough copies of the case description so that each student can have one to read. Read the case aloud while the students follow on their own copies. After you have read the case, ask a few questions to insure that the students understand the facts presented. For example, you could ask a student to define a key word or idea mentioned in the case.

When you feel that your students understand the main ideas, ask them to give you the highlights of the case. Write the highlights on the chalkboard as they are given. This will serve as a useful memory aid as you begin to analyze the case together.

Phase Two: Identifying the Legal-Ethical Issue

Now that you and your students have a common understanding of the facts, you are ready to begin analyzing the case. Explain again that the purposes of this phase of the model are to identify the public policy issue(s) inherent in the case and to make explicit which values are in conflict. It might be helpful at this time to review what is meant by public policy issue and values.

In many cases, more than one public policy issue can be identified. Encourage your students to think of different public policy issues, and write them on the chalkboard. Try not to evaluate or criticize any of these contributions as they are made. The goal here is to place many ideas before the group and to encourage analytic thinking about the case.

When you feel that most of the reasonable candidates for public policy issues have been mentioned, you are ready to choose or formulate the one public policy issue that you will explore in the current session. This choice can be made by you or by the whole group. It is important to agree on the wording of the public policy issue that is chosen and to write this wording on the chalkboard. The identification of values and facts and the definition of terms will be based on the statement of the public policy issue.

Now ask the students to think about the issue and to write down, in their own words, the values that seem to be in conflict. Allow a few minutes for them to put their ideas down and then ask students to suggest values. Write the nominations on the chalkboard. Be prepared to make nominations of your own and to help reword student suggestions. The end product should be a pair of values clearly in conflict in the case.

Finally, the group must identify the facts to be established and the definitional questions to be answered in the process of developing a strong stand on the public policy issue. Ask the students to point out which terms are central to the issue and write them on the chalkboard. Do not attempt to define these terms or establish critical facts at this time; simply list them as they are identified.

Phase Three: Taking a Position

At this stage, the students know enough about the case to take a tentative stand on the question. Explain to the group that taking a position means choosing a solution to a controversial situation so that the values in conflict are balanced as evenly as possible. That is, the values should be minimally violated. Remind the students that they should be able to defend their choice of a position by explaining to the group how their position reflects a sensible balance between conflicting values.

Ask the students to write down a position and their reasons for taking it. Allow at least five minutes for this. Then ask two or three volunteers to read their positions and supporting reasons aloud. At this point, it is helpful to emphasize that the purpose of the whole exercise is for the entire group to develop the most defensible position for this case. Each individual should have something to contribute, and no single student should be expected to have all the "right answers."

Often, the process of analyzing the case and determining its underlying policy questions, value conflicts, and actual and definitional questions will take considerable time. The function of this phase is to help students consider these points *before* they take their stance. If these activities are lengthy, perhaps an hour, it might be wise to take two sessions—one for analyzing the case (Phases One, Two, and Three) and one for exploring and revising the stance (Phases Four, Five, and Six).

Phase Four: Exploring the Stance

At this point, you might ask the students to summarize what the group has done so far. This review is especially useful if you have taken a break before beginning this phase. Refer to the list of phases of the Jurisprudential Model that was written on the chalkboard to show where you have been and where you are headed.

Explain to your students that now the purposes of arguing the case are to refine the position on the controversial issue and to develop support and justification for it. The group should develop the strongest position possible on the issue in question. Some students may have changed their position on the issue while others have maintained the same position but revised their basis.

By now, each student has taken a position on the controversial issue. You should now help the group state a single position that reflects the many individual positions. Use the chalkboard and work on the wording of this group position until everyone is satisfied that it is adequate. (It may happen that two diametrically opposed positions emerge from subgroups of your students. In this case, it will be more effective to develop a position with each group of students separately.)

Once the group (or groups) has agreed on the statement of a position, ask for a student volunteer to defend the position. Defending the position takes the form of a Socratic dialogue in which you, as teacher, probe the stand taken by the group. You should use one or more of the patterns of argumentation described above to provide the student volunteer with an opportunity to support and defend the group position. Allow ample opportunity for the student to "think aloud" as he or she formulates responses to your questions and statements. *Be careful not to force your position upon the group, but at the same time provide enough of a challenge to stimulate analytic thinking.* You are a challenger, not an advocate. Have the class spend between ten and fifteen minutes defending the position.

Phase Five: Refining and Qualifying the Position

After exploring the position, provide your students with an opportunity to change or qualify the position taken earlier. Ask the group for suggestions for changing the wording of the position and for a list of conditions or qualifications in which the revised position would (or would not) be appropriate. One technique for doing this is to ask the group which argument they found most convincing. Write the final version of the group's position and the list of qualifications on the chalkboard.

Phase Six: Testing the Position

The final phase of the Jurisprudential Model is a quick check of the assumptions, consequences, and relevance of the final position. Take care not to let this phase become a reiteration of the process of arguing the case. Ask one student to list the assumptions on which the final position is based. Are these reasonable assumptions? Ask another student to predict some immediate and long-range consequences of resolving the controversial issue in the way favored by the group. Are you willing to live with these consequences? Finally, discuss the relevance of this issue to the lives of students, parents, teachers, and citizens generally. This discussion should bring to a close the entire process of analysis and deliberation that is the Jurisprudential Model of teaching.

THEORY CHECKUP FOR THE JURISPRUDENTIAL MODEL

Instructions: Circle the response that best answers the question or completes the statement. Check your answers with the key that follows.

1. Which of the following is *not* characteristic of the Jurisprudential Model?

    a. vigorous debate
    b. logic
    c. values
    d. metaphoric activity

2. If either Oliver or Shaver were president of the United States during the 1960s, would he have looked favorably upon the civil rights movement, and the resistance to the war in Vietnam?

    a. yes
    b. no

3. List the three areas of competence that a skillful analyzer and discusser of public issues must develop.

4. Which of the following terms is not part of the Socratic role?

    a. adversary
    b. dialectical
    c. accepting
    d. challenging

5. List the phases of the Jurisprudential Model.

6. A public issue:

    a. is a disagreement.
    b. is a question that requires a decision.
    c. involves decisions about the aims and goals of our society.
    d. involves decisions about the aims and goals of our society and actions or policies taken by individuals to attain societal goals.

7. Bill Smith, a student in Ms. Jones's class, said that the Vietnam protestors who went to Canada should be punished by having certain rights taken away. Ms. Jones replied, "That's one way of looking at the problem." If she had taken the Socratic role, she would probably have responded with:

    a. a value.
    b. an analogy.
    c. a definition.
    d. a question asking someone else what he thought.

8. Which of the following is *not* a legal-ethical value?
   a. due process
   b. right to own property
   c. monogamy
   d. group life style

9. List the three types of problems that usually arise in public policy issues.
   a.
   b.
   c.

10. Which of the following is a public policy question?
   a. How many people under 21 voted in the last election?
   b. Should I join an exclusive tennis club?
   c. Should the United States join the Common Market?
   d. Should I invest in Arabian companies?

Theory Checkup Key

1. d

2. a

3. values framework based on the American creed
   discussion skills (the process of rational consent)
   knowledge of contemporary public issues

4. c

5. Phase One: Orientation to the Case
   Phase Two: Identifying the Issues
   Phase Three: Taking a Position
   Phase Four: Arguing the Case
   Phase Five: Refining and Qualifying the Position
   Phase Six: Testing the Factual Assumptions

6. d

7. b

8. d

9. factual
   definitional
   value

10. c

Component II

VIEWING
THE MODEL

One of the purposes of Component II is to provide examples of actual sessions in which the Jurisprudential Model is the strategy being used. Reading the demonstration transcript that follows, hearing a tape of a teacher and students, or viewing a videotape of class activity are alternate means of illustrating the "model in action."

As you study any of these alternatives, you will be introduced to the Teaching Analysis Guide for analyzing the model. This same Guide will also be used in Component III to analyze the peer teaching and microteaching lessons. We want you to become familiar with the Guide now, however, as it will sharpen your perception of the demonstration lesson.

The two activities in this component are (1) reading the Teaching Analysis Guide and (2) viewing (reading) the lesson. Before going on to them, you may wish to reread the material in the Introduction to this book that discusses the purposes and philosophy of the Teaching Analysis Guide.

Analyzing Teaching: Activity 1

The Teaching Analysis Guide for the Jurisprudential Model consists of twenty-six questions. Most of the questions refer to a specific activity that takes place in a particular phase. We are concerned with whether the activity occurred

143

and, very roughly, how well it was carried out. Does it need strengthening? The questions in the Teaching Analysis Guide are designed to assess three aspects of the Jurisprudential Model:

1. the basic activities
2. orientation to the model and its concepts
3. the characteristics of Socratic dialogue

Read through the questions in the Guide and identify items that you do not understand. Try to determine which of the three aspects listed above each of these items refers to. Discuss any difficulties you may have with your instructor or with a peer.

TEACHING ANALYSIS GUIDE FOR THE JURISPRUDENTIAL MODEL

This Guide is designed to help you analyze the process of teaching as you practice the Jurisprudential Model. The analysis focuses on aspects of teaching that are important to the syntax of the model, the teacher's role, and specific teaching skills.

The Guide consists of a series of questions and phrases. As you observe a practice session (whether peer teaching or microteaching), analyze the teaching using the rating scale that appears opposite each question and statement. This scale uses the following items:

Thoroughly. This item signifies that the teacher engaged in the behavior to the point where students were responding comfortably and fluently. Appropriateness varies from situation to situation. Students familiar with the Jurisprudential Model may not need a review in the major concepts.

Partially. This item signifies that the teacher engaged in appropriate behavior, but not as thoroughly as possible. There is some doubt about whether the students are responding fully.

Missing. The teacher did not engage in the behavior; there appears to be a loss in student response or probably will be one.

Not Needed. The teacher did not explicitly manifest the behavior, but there is no loss. Either the behavior was included in others or the students began to respond appropriately without being led to.

For each question or statement in the Guide, circle the term that best describes the teacher's behavior.

Phase One: Orientation to the Case

1. Did the teacher orient students to the model—to the idea of issues and of taking a stance on issues, for example?	Thoroughly	Partially	Missing	Not Needed
2. Did the teacher introduce the case?	Thoroughly	Partially	Missing	Not Needed
3. Did the teacher ask for or respond to students' requests for clarification of the case material?	Thoroughly	Partially	Missing	Not Needed
4. Did the teacher ask the students to identify the most important facts of the case?	Thoroughly	Partially	Missing	Not Needed

Phase Two: Identifying the Issues

5. Did the teacher explain the purposes of this phase—to identify policy questions and value, factual, and definitional issues?	Thoroughly	Partially	Missing	Not Needed
6. Did the teacher ask the students to synthesize the facts of the case into public policy questions?	Thoroughly	Partially	Missing	Not Needed
7. Did the teacher explain the idea of a policy question and provide an example of it?	Thoroughly	Partially	Missing	Not Needed
8. Did the teacher have students select one policy question to explore?	Thoroughly	Partially	Missing	Not Needed

145

TEACHING ANALYSIS GUIDE FOR THE JURISPRUDENTIAL MODEL

9. Did the students identify the values and value conflicts at issue in the public policy question?	Thoroughly	Partially	Missing	Not Needed
10. Did the teacher explain the concepts of factual and definitional issues?	Thoroughly	Partially	Missing	Not Needed
11. Did the teacher ask the students to identify factual or definitional questions pertinent to the public policy question?	Thoroughly	Partially	Missing	Not Needed

Phase Three: Taking a Position

12. Did the teacher ask students to take a position on the public policy question and give their reasons for their stance?	Thoroughly	Partially	Missing	Not Needed
13. Did some of the students share their position with the rest of the group?	Thoroughly	Partially	Missing	Not Needed

Phase Four: Exploring the Stances

14. Did the students summarize what they had done so far in the model?	Thoroughly	Partially	Missing	Not Needed
15. Did the teacher explain the purposes and procedures of arguing the case?	Thoroughly	Partially	Missing	Not Needed
16. Did the teacher explore the issue with one or more students (or groups of students)?	Thoroughly	Partially	Missing	Not Needed
17. Did the teacher maintain a Socratic style of dialogue in questioning students' assumptions?	Thoroughly	Partially	Missing	Not Needed
18. Did the teacher avoid advocating a stand and trying to convince the students to adopt an alternative stand?	Thoroughly	Partially	Missing	Not Needed
19. Did the teacher use one or more of the following patterns of argumentation?				
a. factual emphasis: establishing the point at which the value is violated	Thoroughly	Partially	Missing	Not Needed
b. factual emphasis: proving desirable or undesirable consequences of an action	Thoroughly	Partially	Missing	Not Needed
c. clarifying the value conflict	Thoroughly	Partially	Missing	Not Needed
d. asserting the priority of one value over another and the lack of gross violation of the second value	Thoroughly	Partially	Missing	Not Needed
20. While exploring the students' stances, did the teacher probe the students' ideas for:				

TEACHING ANALYSIS GUIDE FOR THE JURISPRUDENTIAL MODEL

a. relevance?	Thoroughly	Partially	Missing	Not Needed
b. consistency?	Thoroughly	Partially	Missing	Not Needed
c. specificity?	Thoroughly	Partially	Missing	Not Needed
d. generality?	Thoroughly	Partially	Missing	Not Needed
e. definitional clarity?	Thoroughly	Partially	Missing	Not Needed
21. While exploring the students' stances, did the teacher enforce and maintain continuity of thought?	Thoroughly	Partially	Missing	Not Needed

Phase Five: Refining and Qualifying the Position

22. Did the students identify the most convincing position(s)?	Thoroughly	Partially	Missing	Not Needed
23. Did the students identify a number of similar situations in order to test the strength of the position(s)?	Thoroughly	Partially	Missing	Not Needed
24. Did the students qualify the position?	Thoroughly	Partially	Missing	Not Needed

Phase Six: Testing Factual Assumptions Behind the Qualified Position

25. Did the students test the position(s) by identifying factual assumptions and determining their relevance?	Thoroughly	Partially	Missing	Not Needed
26. Did the students determine the predicted consequences of the position(s) and whether they are likely to occur?	Thoroughly	Partially	Missing	Not Needed

Viewing the Lesson: Activity 2

We'd like you now to read the demonstration transcript that follows, identifying the phases of the model and commenting on the lesson as an illustration of the model. On your own or with a group of your peers, record the occurrence of the phases and comment on the model as it is presented here.

Phase One: Orientation to the Case	Adequate	Minimal	Not at All
Phase Two: Identifying the Issues	Adequate	Minimal	Not at All

147

Phase Three: Taking a Stand	Adequate	Minimal	Not at All
Phase Four: Exploring the Stances	Adequate	Minimal	Not at All
Phase Five: Refining and Qualifying the Position	Adequate	Minimal	Not at All
Phase Six: Testing the Position	Adequate	Minimal	Not at All

Analyzing the Lesson: Activity 3 (Optional)

View a live, taped, or filmed demonstration and analyze the lesson using the Teaching Analysis Guide. You can do this in two ways: either complete the form as the tape is viewed, or complete it afterward. If you are working in a group, you may want to divide the task of analysis, with one or more of your colleagues taking a particular phase or aspect of analysis.

DEMONSTRATION TRANSCRIPT: JURISPRUDENTIAL MODEL

Michael McKibbin taught this lesson to a high school group that included Spanish-speaking students.

T: ALL RIGHT. WHAT WE ARE GOING TO DO THIS AFTERNOON IS CALLED THE JURISPRUDENTIAL MODEL, WHICH TAKES A CASE, LOOKS AT THE DIFFERENT SIDES AND DIFFERENT ISSUES AND THE KINDS OF VALUES AND THE FACTS AND THAT SORT OF THING THAT ARE IN THE CASE. THE JURISPRUDENTIAL MODEL WAS DEVELOPED AT HARVARD BY TWO MEN NAMED OLIVER AND SHAVER. THEIR IDEA IS THAT THIS IS THE SORT OF THING THAT IS ESSENTIAL FOR CITIZENSHIP. YOU'VE GOT TO BE ABLE TO TAKE STANDS ON VARIOUS ISSUES, AND YOU'VE GOT TO BE ABLE TO DEFEND WHAT YOU BELIEVE. NOT ONLY THAT, BUT YOU MUST BE ABLE TO LISTEN TO WHAT OTHER PEOPLE STAND FOR, AND BELIEVE, AND TALK ABOUT. AND BESIDES, AFTER YOU'VE DONE ALL OF THESE THINGS, THEN YOU WILL BE ABLE TO MODIFY YOUR STANDARDS ACCORDING TO THE NEW FACTS AND NEW VALUES THAT COME UP. AND THAT'S WHAT WE ARE GOING TO DO HERE.	**Phase One: Orientation to the Case** Teacher explains the model in general terms.
TAKE THE CASE THAT YOU HAVE IN FRONT OF YOU. YOU KNOW, THERE ARE TWO SIDES OF THE STORY. AND, YOU KNOW, REGARDLESS OF LAW OR WHATEVER, THERE ARE STILL GOING TO BE TWO SIDES TO THE ISSUE AND THERE WILL ALWAYS BE CONFLICTS. BUT AFTER LOOKING AT THE FACTS, LOOKING AT THE VARIOUS VALUES, AND IN THIS CASE, CONFLICTING VALUES, AND	Teacher introduces the case.

TRYING TO FIGURE OUT WHAT IS WHAT, THEN YOU TAKE A STAND.

THE CASE THAT YOU HAVE NOW IS ACTUALLY A REAL EVENT THAT HAPPENED AND IT HAS BEEN RESOLVED IN VARIOUS WAYS, BUT TO A LOT OF PEOPLE IT HAS NEVER BEEN RESOLVED SATISFACTORILY. THE PERSON'S NAME IS LOUIS DELGADO. PLEASE TAKE YOUR TIME AND READ THE CASE NOW. (Students read the case.)

T: OK, ARE WE ALL FINISHED? WHY DON'T YOU TELL ME WHAT YOU KNOW ABOUT THE CASE? WHY DON'T YOU KIND OF TELL ME THE FACTS OF THE CASE?

S: TERRANCE HAD A HIGHER GRADE POINT AVERAGE THAN LOUIS DID.

T: OK. WHAT ELSE? WHAT ARE THEY BOTH GOING AFTER?

S: THEY'RE GOING TO GO TO BLUE RIDGE SCHOOL.

T: WHAT KIND OF SCHOOL IS IT?

S: MEDICAL.

T: WHAT ELSE DO WE KNOW?

S: TERRANCE'S MCAT SCORE IS HIGHER.

T: THEY'RE SOMEWHAT HIGHER TOO—HIS OTHER SCORES, HIS MEDICAL SCHOOL ADMISSIONS.

S: TEST, IS THAT WHAT THAT IS?

S: YEAH.

T: FINE. WHAT ELSE? WHAT DO THEY DO WITH THE APPLICATIONS? HOW ARE THE APPLICATIONS HANDLED?

S: IF YOU GET A CERTAIN SCORE, YOU'RE PUT INTO IT. IF IT IS LOWER, YOU'RE JUST PUT INTO A POOL.

T: GOOD. HIGH TEST SCORES AUTOMATICALLY GO IN. THEN YOU'VE GOT ANOTHER SET OF TEST SCORES THAT ARE PUT INTO A POOL. WHAT HAPPENS TO THE ONES THAT ARE PUT INTO A POOL?

S: SOMETIMES THEY ARE REJECTED.

T: SOMETIMES REJECTED, OK. WHERE DO TERRANCE AND LOUIS FIT IN THIS WHOLE GROUP OF APPLICATIONS AND THAT SORT OF THING? ARE THEY IN THE TOP GROUP OR ARE THEY IN THE POOL GROUP OR WHAT?

S: THEY'RE IN THE POOL.

T: AND WHAT HAPPENS TO POOL APPLICATIONS? ARE THEY DEALT WITH IN ANY SPECIAL WAYS OR WHAT?

S: MINORITIES GET FIRST CHANCE.

T: FINE. IS THERE GENERAL AGREEMENT THAT THIS IS THE WAY IT IS—ACCORDING TO BLUE RIDGE MEDICAL SCHOOL, MINORITIES GET FIRST CHANCE, RIGHT? ANY OTHER FACTS THAT WE

Phase Two: Reviewing Facts

NEED TO KNOW ABOUT THE CASE? RONNIE? JOHN?

S: IT SAYS THAT BELOW 74.5 ARE REJECTED, AND LOUIS HAD 73.8.

T: SO UNDER MOST CIRCUMSTANCES LOUIS WOULD HAVE BEEN REJECTED, WOULD NOT HAVE GOTTEN INTO MEDICAL SCHOOL. RIGHT?

S: RIGHT.

T: NOW, IF WE ARE PRETTY MUCH AGREED THAT THESE ARE ALL OF THE FACTS OF THE CASE, LET'S BEGIN TO IDENTIFY THE ISSUES IN THIS CASE, WHAT WE CALL A PUBLIC POLICY ISSUE. A PUBLIC POLICY ISSUE IS SOMETHING THAT IS BASED UPON A CHOICE OR SOMETHING THAT WE HAVE TO MAKE A DECISION OR ACTION ON AS A PEOPLE. AN EXAMPLE OF THIS WOULD BE—A BROAD ISSUE—LIKE SHOULD THE UNITED STATES GIVE AID TO ISRAEL IS A PUBLIC POLICY ISSUE. IT IS SOMETHING YOU ACT UPON; THERE IS SOME CHOICE, ONE WAY OR ANOTHER. MOST PUBLIC POLICY QUESTIONS START OUT WITH "SHOULD."

ANOTHER ONE WOULD BE: SHOULD THE FEDERAL GOVERNMENT CONTROL AUTOMOBILE DESIGN, FOR EXAMPLE, PUTTING IN SEAT BELTS AND THAT SORT OF THING? CAN YOU THINK OF A PUBLIC POLICY ISSUE, NOT NECESSARILY RELATED TO THIS CASE, BUT AN EXAMPLE OF, SAY, SOMETHING CONNECTED WITH SCHOOL?

S: SHOULD STUDENTS BE ABLE TO SMOKE ON SCHOOL GROUNDS?

T: GOOD. THAT'S EXACTLY IT. ANYTHING ELSE? CAN YOU THINK OF ANOTHER ONE?

S: SHOULD STUDENTS BE ALLOWED TO LEAVE THE CAMPUS DURING SCHOOL HOURS?

T: OK? DOES IT HAVE A CHOICE? IS THERE SOME CHOICE IN WHAT HE SAYS?

S: YEAH.

T: YOU THINK SO? THERE IS A DECISION TO BE MADE TOO, ISN'T THERE? THAT'S EXACTLY IT, THAT'S EXACTLY THE SORT OF THING WE'RE TALKING ABOUT. NOW LET'S SEE, WHAT ARE THE POLICY ISSUES HERE? I'M GOING TO WRITE THEM ON THE BOARD FOR YOU. AFTER WE HAVE SEVERAL, WE'LL DEAL WITH THE ONE THAT SEEMS TO BE THE MOST POINTED QUESTION,— THE ONE THAT REALLY HITS US BETWEEN THE EYES. OK? ARE YOU READY TO GO ON THAT?

S: SHOULD LOUIS BE GIVEN SPECIAL RIGHTS ON ENTRANCE? CAUSE IT SAYS HERE THAT ANYONE WITH A GRADE POINT, WELL, WITH A PFYA AVERAGE BELOW 74.5 SHOULD BE REJECTED.

T: RIGHT.

S: AND LOUIS HAD LESS THAN THAT, BUT HE WAS PUT INTO A SPECIAL GROUP WITH THE MINOR-

Phase Two: Identifying the Issues

Teacher gives an example.

Public policy issue—Should. . .

ITIES, WHICH GAVE HIM ANOTHER CHANCE TO GO IN. SO...

T: ANY OTHER PUBLIC POLICY ISSUES? CAN YOU THINK OF ANOTHER ONE? IF WE DON'T, WE CAN WORK WITH THAT ONE. HAVE YOU GOT ONE?

S: NO.

T: OKAY. ANYBODY ELSE GOT ONE? NO? WELL, LET'S BEGIN WITH THIS ONE: SHOULD MINORITIES BE GIVEN SPECIAL RIGHTS ON ENTRANCE TO MEDICAL SCHOOLS?

NOW, WHAT I WANT YOU TO DO IS TO IDENTIFY THE VALUES AND VALUE CONFLICTS IN OUR POLICY STATEMENT. FOR EXAMPLE, IF WE WERE MAKING A DECISION ABOUT WHETHER STUDENTS HAD THE RIGHT TO PUBLISH WHATEVER THEY WANTED IN THEIR SCHOOL NEWSPAPER, WHAT VALUES WOULD BE IN CONFLICT THERE? THE SCHOOL ADMINISTRATION SAYS NO, WE HAVE THE RIGHT TO CENSOR, YOU KNOW, WHEN YOU'RE USING SWEAR WORDS AND THAT SORT OF THING IN YOUR NEWSPAPER; AND THE STUDENTS SAY WE CAN PRINT WHATEVER WE WANT IN OUR OWN NEWSPAPER. WHAT KIND OF VALUES ARE IN CONFLICT THERE? GOT IT?

S: THE GRADE SCORES.

T: ALL RIGHT. ONE OF THE THINGS THAT IS AT ISSUE IS IN THE HANDLING OF THE GRADE SCORES. WHAT DO YOU MEAN?

S: WELL, TERRANCE, FOR SURE, SHOULD HAVE GOT POOLED, BUT LOUIS SHOULD HAVE BEEN DROPPED AUTOMATICALLY.

S: IT'S JUST THE GRADE SCORES LIKE THIS WHERE LIKE LOUIS, FOR INSTANCE, HE GOT 73.8 AND THE GRADE SCORE TO BE IN THE POOL IS 74.5— HE SHOULD HAVE BEEN DROPPED AUTOMATICALLY.

S: REJECTED.

T: OK. THE SELECTION BASED ON ACHIEVEMENT, BASED UPON MERIT. THAT IS THE ONE CONFLICT, RIGHT? WHAT IS IN CONFLICT THERE?

S: THE REJECTION?

T: WHAT'S THE OTHER SIDE OF IT? THE IDEA OF THEIR PICKING LOUIS?

S: DISCRIMINATION?

T: WHAT DO YOU MEAN, DISCRIMINATION?

S: LOUIS IS A MINORITY; HE WAS PICKED TO PROVE THAT THEY WEREN'T FAVORABLE TO ANYBODY.

T: IN OTHER WORDS, YOU'RE SAYING THAT IT IS A REVERSE DISCRIMINATION IN THIS SENSE?

S: YEAH.

T: LET'S TALK A LITTLE BIT ABOUT MINORITY DOCTORS. ARE THERE A LOT OF THEM?

Students select policy question to explore.

Students identify the values and value conflicts.

Value conflict.

S: NO.

T: OK, SO WHAT IS THE ISSUE?

S: THAT MINORITIES SHOULD HAVE THE RIGHT TO HAVE JOBS JUST LIKE OTHER DOCTORS WITH A HIGHER GRADE POINT AVERAGE.

T: IN OTHER WORDS, REPRESENTATION? IS THAT KIND OF WHAT YOU'RE GETTING AT?

S: YEAH.

T: IS THIS MINORITY REPRESENTATION?

S: THERE'S BEEN SO MANY WHITES THAT ARE DOCTORS THAT A MINORITY, A MEXICAN OR WHATEVER, SHOULD HAVE A CHANCE.

T: OK. THE OTHER SIDE IS THAT THERE IS SUCH A NEED FOR MINORITY DOCTORS THAT THEY OUGHT TO BE GIVEN A CHANCE. FIRST IS THE VALUE, IS THE NEED FOR MINORITY DOCTORS, IS THAT WHAT YOU ARE SAYING?

S: YES.

T: ARE THERE ANY OTHER CONFLICTS OR VALUES THAT OUGHT TO BE RAISED IN THIS THING?

S: THE IDEA OF LEARNING?

T: LEARNING? WHAT DO YOU MEAN?

S: WELL, LIKE SOMEONE WHO IS REALLY TRYING TO GET INTO THIS COLLEGE AND HE IS TRYING TO LEARN, AND YOU KNOW, HE IS REALLY, REALLY TRYING, AGAINST SOMEONE WHO JUST WANTS TO GET INTO THERE BECAUSE OF HIS MINORITY GROUP OR SOMETHING.

T: THOSE ARE TWO GOOD ONES. THAT'S FINE. NOW, I WANT YOU TO LOOK AT OUR PUBLIC POLICY QUESTION—OUR ISSUE—AND WE HAVE SOME TERMS AND SOME FACTS THAT I WANT TO MAKE SURE YOU UNDERSTAND. WHAT DO YOU MEAN BY MINORITIES? YOU HAVE TO DEFINE THAT FOR ME. DOES THAT MEAN THAT SOMEBODY FIRST GENERATION FROM POLAND IS A MINORITY? OR ARE YOU JUST TALKING ABOUT WHAT WE CALL TODAY THE VISIBLE MINORITIES?

Clarifying terms.

Teacher points out factual and definitional issues.

S: PEOPLE WHO AREN'T GIVEN THE CHANCE TO TRY AND LIVE UP TO WHAT THE BASIC SOCIETY'S MADE UP TO BE.

S: IT ISN'T UP TO WHAT PEOPLE BELIEVE.

T: MOST EVERYBODY COULD GET INTO THAT, COULDN'T THEY? EVERYBODY IS A MINORITY IN THAT DEFINITION, IN ONE WAY OR ANOTHER, AREN'T THEY?

S: NOT REALLY.

T: HOW ARE THEY NOT?

S: THERE ARE SPECIAL GROUPS OF PEOPLE, YOU KNOW, THAT HAVE BEEN DISCRIMINATED AGAINST BECAUSE OF THEIR COLOR OR SEX AND EVERYTHING, AND PEOPLE HAVE LOOKED DOWN

UPON THEM, YOU KNOW, BLAMING THEM FOR MOST OF THE PROBLEMS ARISING IN THE UNITED STATES. SO, THEY JUST STAY DOWN IN PEOPLE'S MINDS. YET THOSE PEOPLE ARE THE PEOPLE WHO HAVE A CHANCE TO DO EVERYTHING ELSE THAT PEOPLE WHO ARE BEING DISCRIMINATED AGAINST CAN'T DO.

T: YOUR DEFINITION IS BASED UPON OPPORTUNITY, RIGHT? ALL RIGHT. WOULD YOU RATHER HAVE THE DEFINITION OF MINORITY BASED UPON OP-PORTUNITY, BASED UPON RACE, COLOR, OR HOW ARE WE GOING TO DEFINE MINORITY? DO YOU HAVE AN IDEA?

S: WELL, MINORITY SHOULD BE BASED UPON RACE.

T: THAT'S VERY OFTEN THE WAY. I WOULD BET THAT'S PROBABLY THE WAY BLUE RIDGE COL-LEGE IS DOING IT. PROBABLY THEY ARE USING THE DEFINITION OF VISIBLE MINORITIES, WHICH MEANS BLACKS, CHICANOS, NATIVE AMERICANS, PEOPLE THAT HAVE COME FROM PUERTO RICO, AND THAT SORT OF THING, RATHER THAN WHAT WE CALL THE WHITE ETHNICS, THE PEOPLE FROM POLAND AND ITALY AND GREECE AND THAT KIND OF THING. AND THEN, OTHER PEOPLE WOULD DEFINE AS A MINORITY, WOMEN, AL-THOUGH WOMEN ARE 52 PERCENT OF THE WHOLE COUNTRY'S POPULATION. BY OPPORTUN-ITY, WOMEN ARE A MINORITY. BY RACE AND COLOR, THEY ARE NOT. WHICH ONE WOULD YOU LIKE TO HAVE AS A DEFINITION?

Teacher asks students to identify factual or definitional question.

S: RACE.

S: COLOR.

T: RACE AND COLOR? OK. VISIBLE MINORITIES IS WHAT WE MEAN. WOMEN WOULD NOT BELONG UNLESS THEY ARE A VISIBLE MINORITY.

S: OK.

T: ANY OTHERS? WHAT DO YOU MEAN BY SPECIAL RIGHTS? SPECIAL RIGHTS HAVE TO DO WITH SCORES AND THAT SORT OF THING?

S: YEAH.

S: SPECIAL OPPORTUNITIES.

T: WOULD YOU RATHER REPLACE THE WORD "RIGHTS" WITH "OPPORTUNITIES"? OR IS RIGHTS ALL RIGHT?

S: RIGHTS IS ALL RIGHT.

T: NOW, WHAT I'D LIKE YOU TO DO IS TO TAKE A POSITION. WHAT THIS MEANS IS TAKING A STAND, STATING WHY YOU WANT TO BE ON ONE SIDE OR ANOTHER. I'D LIKE YOU TO TAKE A POSITION BASED UPON YOUR VALUES AND WHAT YOU THINK THE CONSEQUENCES OF SUCH A POSITION MIGHT BE. WRITE DOWN YOUR POSITION ON THE BLUE RIDGE CASE. (Students write.)

HAVE WE ALL TAKEN OUR STANCES AND GIVEN

Phase Three: Taking a position
Teacher asks students to take a position and give reason for their stance.

OUR REASONS FOR THEM? I WOULD LIKE TO READ YOUR POSITION PAPERS AND THEN, BASED UPON HOW YOU STAND, WE ARE GOING TO DIVIDE YOU INTO GROUPS.

S: MY STANCE IS FOR NOT GIVING MINORITIES THAT SPECIAL RIGHT TO ENTER MEDICAL SCHOOL BECAUSE OF THEIR STATUS. I BELIEVE THAT IF THEY REALLY WANTED TO ENTER THAT COLLEGE, THEY WOULD HAVE STRIVED REALLY HARD AND THEY WOULD HAVE ACHIEVED A HIGHER SCORE ON THE EXAM, WHICH THEY WERE SUPPOSED TO HAVE STUDIED FOR. LOUIS' SCORE WAS KIND OF LOW, YOU KNOW.

S: WELL, I DON'T THINK MINORITIES SHOULD GET SPECIAL RIGHTS, BECAUSE WE WANT PEOPLE WHO KNOW WHAT THEY ARE DOING AS DOCTORS AND NOT TO BE PICKED JUST BECAUSE OF THEIR RACE. FOR EXAMPLE, LOUIS HAD SPECIAL RIGHTS BECAUSE OF HIS RACE, ALTHOUGH TERRANCE HAD A HIGHER SCORE, YET HE WASN'T PICKED.

T: OK. SO YOU THINK THAT YOU'RE IN FAVOR OF THE "MERIT" SIDE?

S: RIGHT.

T: JOHN, HOW DO YOU THINK?

S: I THINK THEY SHOULD BE GIVEN THE RIGHTS—SPECIAL RIGHTS, BECAUSE IT IS HARDER FOR A MINORITY TO GET INTO A SCHOOL WHERE THERE'S ALL THE RACES.

T: OK. THAT'S FINE. VERONICA?

S: MINORITIES SHOULD NOT BE GIVEN SPECIAL RIGHTS, BECAUSE IF THEY DON'T QUALIFY TO BE SENT TO MEDICAL SCHOOL, THEN THEY OUGHT NOT TO BE DOCTORS.

T: TONY?

S: MINORITIES SHOULD NOT BE GIVEN EXTRA OPPORTUNITIES, BECAUSE PEOPLE WITH BEST SCORES SHOULD BE CONSIDERED FIRST. MINORITIES WITHOUT GOOD SCORES SHOULD NOT BE GIVEN THOSE SPECIAL RIGHTS TO MEDICAL SCHOOLS BECAUSE THEY MIGHT KNOW ENOUGH TO BE IN THAT SCHOOL AND YET A WHITE PERSON WHO IS REJECTED MIGHT KNOW MORE THAN THAT MINORITY.

T: OK. FINE.

S: MINORITIES SHOULD HAVE THE RIGHT TO BE ACCEPTED, BECAUSE THEY HAVEN'T HAD THE SAME TRAINING LIKE ANY OTHER AMERICAN FAMILY THAT IS RICH AND SENT THEIR KID TO A FANCY SCHOOL. WELL, THE MINORITIES COULDN'T HAVE HAD TRAINING AS MUCH AS THE OTHER ONES. IF AN AMERICAN DOCTOR HAD A PATIENT THAT WAS PUERTO RICAN OR JAPANESE OR MEXICAN, HOW WOULD HE TALK TO THEM, HOW WOULD HE TREAT THEM? SO WE NEED MINORITIES TO TREAT THEM.

T: SO WE HAVE THE TWO DIFFERENT POSITIONS

Students share their positions.

REPRESENTED. I GUESS WE HAVE FOUR PEOPLE THAT THINK ON THE SIDE OF MERIT, AND WE HAVE TWO PEOPLE THAT ARE ON THE SIDE OF REPRESENTATION. WHAT WE ARE GOING TO DO NOW IS DIVIDE UP INTO A COUPLE OF GROUPS. I'D LIKE THE TWO PEOPLE THAT TAKE THE POSITION IN TERMS OF REPRESENTATION—JOHN, WHY DON'T YOU CHANGE CHAIRS WITH TONY, AND THEN, TONY AND MONICA, WHY DON'T YOU COME MEET DOWN HERE AT THIS CORNER AND KIND OF WORK OUT YOUR POSITION. I WANT YOU TO FIRM UP YOUR STAND NOW, AND WHAT WE'LL DO WHEN WE COME BACK IS ARGUE THE CASE. YOU FOUR WILL BE PRESENTING A KIND OF A UNITED POSITION BASED UPON WHERE YOU STAND, AND THE OTHER TWO WILL GO THE OTHER WAY. I'M GOING TO BE WORKING WITH THESE PEOPLE TO KIND OF HELP THEM WITH THEIR STAND, SINCE THEY AREN'T AS MANY AS YOU ARE. THAT SEEMS ONLY FAIR. (Students prepare their discussions.)

T: ARE YOU GUYS READY? GO ON, MARY.

S: ALL RIGHT. I BELIEVE THAT THE MINORITIES SHOULDN'T HAVE ANY SPECIAL RIGHTS. AS I SAID BEFORE, IF HE DOESN'T QUALIFY IN MEDICAL SCHOOL, THEN HE SHOULDN'T BE GIVEN THE CHANCE JUST BECAUSE HE IS A MINORITY.

T: WHY? WHAT IF HE DOESN'T HAVE THE QUALIFICATIONS?

S: IF HE DOESN'T HAVE THE QUALIFICATIONS AND HE PASSES TO MEDICAL SCHOOL JUST BECAUSE HE IS A MINORITY, THEN WHAT HAPPENS WHEN HE GETS INTO PRACTICE AND HE DESTROYS A PERSON? SOMETHING GOES WRONG. . .

S: WHAT IF HE HAD TRAINING JUST LIKE ANY OTHER DOCTORS AND WAS JUST AS SMART?

S: PERHAPS IF HE WOULD HAVE STUDIED A LITTLE HARDER. . .

S: MAYBE HIS PARENTS DIDN'T HAVE THE MONEY TO SEND HIM TO A COLLEGE THAT WAS RESPECTABLE AND THAT HAD A LITTLE MORE, YOU KNOW, HAD THE MONEY AND THE CLASSES IN CHEMISTRY AND OTHER THINGS.

T: NOW, LET'S HEAR FROM THE OTHER SIDE.

S: I BELIEVE THAT MINORITIES SHOULD HAVE IT, BECAUSE IF THEY HAD THE SAME STUDIES AS ANY OTHER, EVEN IF THE GUY IS NOT WHITE, IF HE HAD THE MONEY, HIS PARENTS WOULD SEND HIM TO A SCHOOL THAT WAS GOOD. HE WOULD HAVE THE SAME RESPECTABLE CLASSES AND BRAIN JUST LIKE ANY OTHER MAN AND HE WOULD GET IN THAT COLLEGE.

T: HOW DO YOU REACT TO THE OTHER SIDE'S STATEMENT THAT IF YOU ADMIT PEOPLE THAT HAD POOR SCORES ON THEIR TESTS, YOU'RE LIABLE TO END UP WITH POOR DOCTORS.

S: IF THAT DOCTOR HAD THE TRAINING, IF HE

Students divide into groups.

Phase Four: Exploring the Stance(s)

Students present their positions.

Teacher explores issues with group.
Teacher moves into Socratic mode.

GOT SENT TO THAT COLLEGE AND HE STARTED TRAINING WITH ANY OTHER DOCTOR, HE'LL HAVE THE SAME STUDIES AND HE'LL KNOW WHAT TO DO; HE'LL BE JUST AS GOOD AS ANY OTHER DOCTOR. BUT JUST BECAUSE HE DOESN'T HAVE THE GRADE POINT AVERAGE, THAT DOESN'T MEAN THAT HE ISN'T A GOOD DOCTOR.

T: YOU'RE SAYING THAT THE PROBLEMS WITH THE TESTS AND THE THING IS THAT IF HE DOES HAVE GOOD TRAINING, HE WILL BECOME A GOOD DOCTOR.

S: YES.

T: (To the other group.) WOULD YOU LIKE TO REACT TO THAT?

S: WHAT HE IS SAYING IS THAT IF HE DIDN'T QUALIFY FOR THIS SCHOOL, HE SHOULD BE GIVEN A CHANCE JUST TO GO TO CLASSES RIGHT AWAY, RIGHT?

T: IS THAT WHAT YOU ARE SAYING?

S: I'M SAYING THAT HE SHOULD BE ACCEPTED SO THAT HE COULD BECOME JUST AS GOOD AS ANY OTHER DOCTOR.

S: AND HE JUST PROVED HIMSELF NOT TO BE BY HIS GRADE POINT AVERAGE.

S: HIS GRADE POINT AVERAGE WASN'T AS GOOD AS OTHERS, BECAUSE HE WASN'T IN A GOOD SCHOOL LIKE THE OTHER PERSON WAS.

S: AND WHAT IF LATER ON THROUGH HIS TRAINING, HE JUST DOESN'T GET THROUGH. THEN THAT IS A LOT OF WASTED MONEY ON HIM.

(The discussion continues back and forth.)

T: LET'S ASSUME THAT THE LOUIS DELGADOS OF THE WORLD ARE NOT ALLOWED INTO MEDICAL SCHOOL AND WE END UP WITH MOSTLY WHITE DOCTORS. RIGHT? WHAT HAPPENS WHEN THE WOMAN THAT SPEAKS ONLY SPANISH COMES TO TERRANCE ROYCE'S PLACE AND HE CANNOT SPEAK SPANISH OR DOESN'T REALLY UNDERSTAND THE MEXICAN AMERICAN CULTURE OR THE MEXICAN CULTURE. WHAT IS GOING TO HAPPEN? WHAT ARE THE CONSEQUENCES OF THAT SIDE OF IT?

S: LET'S SAY YOU HAVE A MEXICAN WHO'S BECOME A DOCTOR, AND PERHAPS HE WOULD BE ABLE TO HELP THAT PATIENT BECAUSE SHE DID SPEAK SPANISH, BUT IS HE GOING TO BE ABLE TO HELP AN ORIENTAL BECAUSE HE IS JAPANESE?

T: PROBABLY NOT.

S: IT IS JUST LIKE THE AMERICAN. THE AMERICAN WOULD JUST HAVE THE SAME PROBLEMS AS THE MEXICAN WILL.

S: ALL HE HAS TO DO IS SEND HER TO ANOTHER DOCTOR, SOMEONE WHO CAN HELP HER.

S: EVERYBODY HAS THE QUALIFICATIONS.

Teacher questions whether other values are violated.

S: OK. YOU SEND AWAY FOR A DOCTOR AND THE DOCTOR'S WHITE AND THE PATIENT IS MEXICAN, AND THE LADY IS IN CONVULSIONS; WHAT IS HE GOING TO DO THEN?

S: WELL, THEN HE TREATS HER FOR CONVULSIONS. WHO NEEDS TO KNOW. . .

S: IF HE KNOWS THE SYMPTOMS. . .

S: BUT IF SHE DIDN'T KNOW IT AT THE TIME AND HE'S JUST SITTING THERE LOOKING AT THE LADY. . .

S: I DON'T THINK HE WOULD DO THAT.

T: IF YOU WENT TO A GRADE SCHOOL THAT HAD BAD TEACHERS, WHAT IS THE POTENTIAL FOR YOU BEING A GOOD HIGH SCHOOL STUDENT? DOES THAT HAVE ANYTHING TO DO WITH YOUR BASIC INTELLIGENCE? DO YOU WANT TO CARRY THAT, TONY? ALL RIGHT, WHAT'S THE RELATIONSHIP BETWEEN THAT AND MEDICAL SCHOOL AND HOW GOOD A DOCTOR YOU'RE GOING TO BE, BASED UPON YOUR EARLIER SCHOOLING? DO ANY OF YOU THINK YOU WERE A BETTER HIGH SCHOOL STUDENT THAN YOU WERE AN ELEMENTARY SCHOOL STUDENT?

S: HM HM.

T: WHY?

S: BECAUSE WE LEARNED MORE.

T: WHY?

S: I THINK IT WAS BECAUSE OF THE TEACHERS.

T: WHAT WAS IT BECAUSE OF?

S: BECAUSE WE WANTED TO LEARN.

S: AND THAT IS THE ONLY REASON WHY WE'RE IN HIGH SCHOOL NOW, BECAUSE WE WANT TO KNOW, WE WANT TO LEARN.

(The students debate early schooling and later achievement. After a time the teacher introduces a new idea.)

T: OKAY. LET'S GO TO ANOTHER POINT. WHICH IS MORE IMPORTANT? IS IT MORE IMPORTANT TO HAVE MERIT OR TO HAVE REPRESENTATION? I THINK THAT'S WHAT IT COMES DOWN TO.

S: I WANT ONE THAT WOULD BE A GOOD DOCTOR.

T: WHAT KIND OF A DOCTOR WOULD YOU LIKE TO GO TO, ONE THAT COMES FROM YOUR OWN ETHNIC GROUP OR ONE THAT MAY HAVE GOT HIGHER ADMISSION SCORES IN THE COLLEGE?

S: WELL, LIKE PRETEND THAT YOU'RE A MEXICAN, AND WOULD YOU GO TO AN AMERICAN DOCTOR THAT WE KNOW? YOU ONLY SPEAK SPANISH. WOULD YOU GO TO A DOCTOR THAT ONLY SPEAKS AMERICAN, OR WOULD YOU GO TO A DOCTOR THAT COULD SPEAK SPANISH TOO?

T: I THINK THAT I WOULD PROBABLY GO TO ONE THAT SPOKE SPANISH BECAUSE I WOULD FEEL MORE COMFORTABLE.

Teacher uses analogy.

Teacher introduces idea of priorities of one value over another.

S: WELL, IT'S HARD. I WOULD GO TO THE ONE THAT KNEW WHAT HE WAS DOING, YOU KNOW, THAT HAD A BETTER EDUCATION, BUT MAYBE I WOULD FEEL COMFORTABLE WITH THE OTHER DOCTOR.

T: YOU'D FEEL MORE COMFORTABLE, HUH, WITH THE SPANISH DOCTOR?

S: YEAH, BUT I'D GO TO THE GOOD ONE.

T: YOU'D STILL GO TO THE ONE THAT DIDN'T SPEAK SPANISH. YOU STILL WOULD?

LET'S KIND OF MOVE ON TO ANOTHER PHASE. I WANT YOU TO TURN YOUR PAPER OVER AND TELL ME WHERE YOU STAND AGAIN. YOU CAN KEEP, MODIFY, OR SWITCH YOUR POSITION. (Students write again.)

Phase Five: Refining and Qualifying the Position

Student has choice of maintaining, modifying, or changing position.

T: I THINK WE'LL START WITH ALICIA THIS TIME AND JUST KIND OF READ AROUND, BECAUSE WE STARTED WITH ROBERT LAST TIME. OK, GO AHEAD.

S: I MODIFIED MY POSITION BECAUSE I THINK RACE SHOULDN'T INTERFERE WITH ANY KIND OF WORK, ESPECIALLY A DOCTOR, BUT I THINK THE MINORITIES SHOULD HAVE A CHANCE BECAUSE, I MEAN, THEY COULD HAVE COME FROM BAD SCHOOLING, BUT YET THEY WANTED TO ACHIEVE A GOAL OF BEING A DOCTOR. THAT'S ALL, BUT THEY DIDN'T HAVE THE RIGHT SCHOOLING FOR THOSE TESTS.

Students present positions again.

T: SO YOU'VE MODIFIED YOUR POSITION TO A CERTAIN POINT?

S: I'VE MAINTAINED THAT THE MINORITIES SHOULD BE GIVEN A CHANCE TO SHOW THEY ARE AS GOOD AS THE OTHERS. THEY HAVE TO GET ADMITTED BEFORE THEY CAN DO THAT. I'VE MAINTAINED THAT MINORITIES SHOW THAT THEY ARE JUST AS GOOD AS ANY DOCTOR THAT HAD A GRADE POINT AVERAGE.

(The students take turns. No one changed positions, but several modified their stance and argument. Now the teacher pushes the group toward policy.)

T: SUPPOSE YOU PEOPLE HERE ARE A POLICY GROUP THAT IS MAKING POLICY FOR THE WHOLE COUNTRY, AND YOU HAD TO MAKE A DECISION ON WHETHER PEOPLE IN A PROFESSION, LIKE THE MEDICAL PROFESSION, SHOULD BE THERE— EQUALLY REPRESENTED OR REASONABLY REPRESENTED OR BASED SOLELY ON MERIT. WHAT KIND OF POLICY WOULD YOU STATE? YOU'RE A POLICY MAKING GROUP. YOU'VE GOT TO MAKE THIS DECISION.

The policy level is introduced.

S: IS THIS FOR THE WHOLE COUNTRY?

T: THE WHOLE COUNTRY. THINK ABOUT IT FOR A MINUTE AND I'LL COME BACK. I'LL GIVE YOU ABOUT FIVE MINUTES.

(The discussion then deals with the policy issue, the facts needed to make policy, and the assumptions behind policies.)

Component III

PLANNING

AND

PEER TEACHING

In this component you will plan a lesson using the Jurisprudential Model, teach this lesson to a small group of your peers, and then analyze the lesson using the Teaching Analysis Guide.

Four steps in planning and organizing Jurisprudential lessons have been identified. Short discussions of the considerations involved in each of these steps are provided to guide you through planning a Jurisprudential lesson. The four planning steps are:

1. developing case materials
2. analyzing issues
3. preparing analogies and patterns of argumentation
4. organizing for Socratic dialogue

The sections on planning should be read in conjunction with your preparation of the peer teaching lesson and completion of the Planning Guide that appears at the end of this component.

Step 1 (developing case materials) discusses the development of case materials and presents examples of several cases. Step 2 discusses four aspects of case analysis—determining the policy issue(s) and identifying the value, definitional, and factual questions underlying the issue. Step 3 comments on the preparation of analogies and patterns of argumentation that might be used during Phase Four (exploring the stance). These analogies and patterns of argumentation will form the basis of the dialogue between students and teacher. Step 4 explains the nature of the Socratic dialogue so that the students will understand the process. In other words, Step 4 explains the model to the students.

DEVELOPING CASE MATERIALS

Many complex problems face our society—racial and economic inequality, the concentration and abuse of power by labor, business, and public officials, and the increase in crime, to name but a few. It is virtually impossible to live through a single day without being exposed to an incident that reflects one of these pressing social concerns. It is therefore surprising that schools have not systematically and directly prepared students to deal with public issues and social problems. Oliver and Shaver take the position that previous curricular and instructional approaches to controversial issues have been inadequate in one way or another in cultivating and combining the interests, skills, and understanding that create a skillful citizen.

Ideally, Oliver and Shaver would like to see a curriculum in which students are systematically exposed to all of the major problems of our times. The objective of such a curriculum would be to have students consider and take a personal stance on the social and political value problems in each problem area. This objective can be achieved by using the Jurisprudential Model of teaching with appropriate controversial case materials.

A controversial case describes a specific situation about which there are conflicting ethical, legal, factual, or definitional interpretations. The case may consist of a classic historical or legal situation, such as *Plessy* v. *Ferguson* in race relations, or the Wagner Act or the Kohler strike in labor relations; or it may be a short story or fictionalized account of a societal controversy, such as Orwell's *Animal Farm*.

If you look through your newspaper you will find each page contains three or four articles that either explicitly or implicitly present an important public policy question. Usually some of the facts of the situation are presented, but the original situation that provoked the controversy is not described in full detail. Newspapers generally summarize the facts and then provide their own commentary, or comments from involved parties. Because newspaper accounts are not true case studies, it is hard to use them to form stances on policy questions with the aid of the tools of legal reasoning. It is possible to develop case materials based on articles or issues in newspapers by reconstructing or making up the facts, as in Example 2 below.

Example 1 is a newspaper story with some factual detail. It concerns two sisters aged 12 and 13 who have lived happily with their foster parents for three years but who are suddenly forced to return to their natural mother because she wants them back with her. Perhaps you or one of your students has been in situations that involved a conflict of basic values and included important public policy implications. It is important to recognize that public policy questions grow out of the plight of individuals as well as the policies of governments, unions, and corporations.

It is relatively easy to develop case materials for the Jurisprudential Model. The distinguishing feature of a case approach is that the cases are accounts of real or hypothetical situations. It is essential that all the pertinent facts of the situation be included in the case material or the case will be vague and frustrating.

Example 1: Foster Home Case

Mineola, N.Y. Two young sisters, who said a court order returning them to their natural mother was "expecting a child to turn off his entire life, like a faucet," tearfully surrendered to authorities yesterday, ending six days as fugitives from the law.

Their faces mirroring their unhappiness, Cheryl Wallace, 13, and her sister Patricia, 12, left a court building yesterday for a temporary foster home.

Three hours earlier, they had turned themselves in to police, ending a search that began last Saturday when they ran away from another foster home to protest a court order returning them to their natural mother, 34-year-old Patricia Wallace of Long Beach, N.Y.

Police said during their six-day disappearance, Cheryl and Patricia had been given shelter by the Organization of Foster Families for Equality and Reform, a private group promoting the rights of foster children.

Before they left the courthouse, Cheryl read a statement indicating she and her sister have all but lost hope of any reunion with the George Lhotans of Hicksville, N.C., the foster parents with whom they lived for more than three years.

Reading in a monotone, Cheryl said, "It was and still is our desire to be reunited with our sisters and our Mom and Dad, George and Dorothy Lhotan, as soon as possible."

In what appeared to be a dig at her natural mother, Cheryl added, "Whether social workers and grownups realize it or not, it's keeping in touch that lets you know what love is. Parents who don't keep in touch lose their children to those who are there.

"It doesn't mean giving presents or special treats . . . It means not expecting a child to turn off his entire life like a faucet if he is called back across the gap of time by the parent who gave birth to him."

The girls waited in a private room in the courthouse as Justice Albert Oppido said that a June, 1975, ruling by Justice Bernard McCaffrey, awarding their mother custody of the two girls, would have to be honored.

The court order requires their return to Wallace no later than October 6.[1]

United Press

Example 2: The Armband Case

You notice the following article in the morning paper on July 24, 2010:

The war in South America has been going on now for nearly eleven years. Our country became involved almost immediately by giving aid to Bolivia, one of the combatants. First, our government sent only financial aid and some

[1] *San Francisco Chronicle*, June 12, 1976. Reprinted by permission of United Press International.

military advisers, but our level of involvement has gradually increased to the point where there are now nearly 500,000 American troops fighting in Bolivia.

Although public opinion originally ran strongly in favor of the government's aid program, support has fallen off sharply in recent years, especially among the young.

Louise Alcott, Benjamin Brith, and Ed Burke are all students at Lee High School in St. Louis. They and their families are among those who have become disenchanted with the war in South America. On a recent evening, they have all gotten together and decided to speak out against the war by wearing black armbands to school as a symbol of mourning for those who have been killed in the war.

Lee has 1,500 students and, like most other schools, its students have divergent views on the question of American involvement in the war in South America.

The principal of Lee, Elmer Grant, learned of the plan to wear armbands and adopted a policy that anyone wearing an armband would be asked to remove it, and if they refused to do so they would be suspended until they were ready to come back to school without the armband.

Yesterday, Louise, Bennie, and Ed were suspended from school for wearing the armbands.

In an interview yesterday afternoon, Mr. Grant explained that he had issued the no-armband policy to avoid disruption of the educational process at Lee. He said, "If we allow students to wear these protest armbands, it will cause heated debate about the war, which will interfere with scheduled classroom activities. I'm also afraid that it might lead to violence among the kids and polarize the student body."[2]

Where do you stand? You are to assume that wearing armbands is a form of speech; that is, by wearing armbands the students were speaking out against the war in South America. Further, school policy in effect until this time was that items such as buttons were permitted unless they were obscene.

Using Case Materials

Case materials are accounts of the essential facts of a conflict situation; they *describe* the conflict. Case materials are not comments about events, nor are they dramatic human-interest stories. In developing case materials, it is important to include the pertinent information about the participants, the events, and the circumstances surrounding the events.

Cases can be chosen because of interest in the particular conflict situation or because of the issues involved in it. Some teachers prefer to begin with the issue and develop a hypothetical or real case; others prefer to introduce a familiar, high-interest conflict situation, regardless of the issue. In either situation, you will probably want to revise the case once you have analyzed it in terms of its value conflicts and definitional and factual problems. Then you will be sure you have incorporated into the case material the information pertaining to these three problem areas. The following pages contain three cases for you to read through; each case is followed by discussion of the ethical or legal issues involved.

[2] The cases in this component were all developed by Ralph Pais of Stanford University Center for Research and Development in Teaching. We are especially grateful for his assistance in developing these materials.

Case 1: The Medical School Admissions Case[3]

Luis Delgado applied for admission to the first-year class at the Blue Ridge Mountain Medical School. Luis is from New Mexico; he was an undergraduate at a state university there. He had an undergraduate cumulative grade-point average (GPA) of 3.4 (on a scale of 4). He took the Medical College Admissions Test (MCAT), on which he achieved a score of 566 (the range is from 200 to 800).

Terrance D. Broyce also applied for admission to Blue Ridge. He was an undergraduate at Green River College (the companion school to Blue Ridge). He had an undergraduate GPA of 3.75 and an MCAT score of 688.

The medical school received 1,800 applications for 160 openings in its entering class. In evaluating applicants the school assigned a "Predicted First-Year Average" (PFYA), based on undergraduate grades and test scores. Applications were evaluated by the Admissions Committee, which consists of seven faculty members and four students. *Generally*, applicants whose PFYA was 77 or above were admitted and those below 74.5 were rejected. Those in between were placed in a separate pool. Also placed in the pool were the applications of all "minority" applicants, regardless of PFYA. Terrance's PFYA was 76.4; Luis's was 73.8. Both applications were placed in the pool. Ultimately, Luis was admitted to the medical school and Terrance was rejected.

Terrance was unhappy about being rejected and consulted his family's lawyer, Jeremiah Smith of Stone, Steel, Hardrock, and Flint. After some consultation, Terrance decided to file suit against the medical school on the grounds that he had been discriminated against because of race. That is, Terrance maintained that he was denied equal protection of the laws because minority applicants less qualified than he, who would have been rejected but for their minority status, were admitted.

Given the above facts, where do you stand?

Discussion

This is a racial discrimination problem. It is somewhat unusual because the person who may have been discriminated against is white rather than a minority-group member. The medical school's action is based on its admissions policy of giving preferential treatment to minority students. The reason for this policy is to help increase the number of practicing doctors who are members of minority groups. The medical school would like to judge all applicants on the same basis, but if it did so, nearly all of its entering class would consist of white students.

Is this sufficient justification for Terrance's rejection? What are the competing interests? Terrance has a personal interest in going to medical school and becoming a doctor. Luis' interest appears to be the same. The medical school has an interest in helping to eliminate the effects of past racial discrimination in the medical profession. Society has an interest in having an integrated medical profession, but it also has an interest in insuring that doctors are adequately qualified. The courts have generally condemned racial discrimination that is designed to stamp those discriminated against as inferior. Is that the purpose of the discrimination involved here? Is it valid for admissions officers to consider an applicant's race, or should they evaluate grades and test scores only? How

[3]The transcript lesson in Component II presents a lively class discussion of this case.

useful are records of past performance in evaluating potential success in a new experience?

(At this time, the United States Supreme Court has not decided the issues raised in this problem. The state court that considered the case ruled that this type of discrimination was permissible because it was designed to eliminate the effects of past racial discrimination. This information should be supplied only upon request, and only at the end of the discussion.)

Case 2: The Search of Student Locker Case

Howard Norman is a junior at Weber High School. Students at Weber are issued lockers at the beginning of each school year for their use during the year. Students do not pay any charge for the use of the lockers. It is made clear to students at the beginning of the year that, although they are given permission to use the lockers for the year, the lockers are owned by the school.

School officials at Weber are concerned about the use of drugs (primarily marijuana) on school grounds, and they have undertaken efforts to locate those students involved in on-campus drug sales and use. The principal and staff would like to eliminate the use of drugs at Weber because they feel that this type of behavior is incompatible with a successful academic program.

Howard is an excellent student and vice president of the student body; he will probably go to college after he graduates from Weber. However, several of his teachers are suspicious that Howard is involved with the drug scene at Weber. They are not sure that he uses or sells drugs, but some of them have observed him in whispered discussions in the halls with other students suspected of using drugs. None of the teachers has ever seen Howard sell drugs, nor have they ever observed him in a condition suggesting he had used drugs.

Nevertheless, on the basis of the teachers' observations, the principal calls Howard to his office. The principal and his assistant question Howard about his involvement with drugs. Howard denies any involvement or knowledge of drug use by others. After about ten minutes of this questioning, Howard is sent back to class.

The principal, not satisfied, decides to look through Howard's locker, to which he obtains access by using the master key. In the bottom of the locker he finds a plastic bag containing a very small amount of what appears to be marijuana. The principal realizes that there would be no sense in involving the police, since the amount of marijuana in the bag is not enough to bring criminal charges. Besides, the principal sees this situation as a matter of school discipline; as such, it should be handled within the school. Further, the principal sees himself as more an agent of the parents than of the state.

The principal has Howard brought to his office and confronts him with the bag. He tells Howard that the school cannot tolerate drug use. Because he wants to punish Howard and because he wants to set a clear example for the rest of the student body by dealing firmly with this student "leader," the principal suspends Howard for three weeks. Howard attempts to present his side of the story, but is not allowed to do so.

(If Howard had been allowed to present his side of the story, he would have pointed out that the substance in the bag was herb tea.)

What are the issues, and where do you stand?

Discussion

There are two broad issues in this problem: the right of the school officials to search Howard's locker, and the suspension of Howard from school without a hearing. The specific issues that could be discussed are set forth below.

What are the competing interests represented by the locker? Does Howard have an ownership interest in his locker? Is the degree of ownership related to how much privacy should be expected in the use of the locker? On the basis of the facts presented, can the search of the locker be justified?

The principal is described as seeing himself as more an agent of the parents than of the state. Where do you stand on this question? At some point, it should be explained that the constitutional protection against unreasonable searches applies only to the conduct of state officials.

Regarding Howard's suspension, should there have been a procedure that would have allowed Howard to present his side of the story? In depriving someone of the right to an education, what sort of procedure should be followed? (The Supreme Court has recently held that students being suspended should at least be notified of the charges for which they are being disciplined and be given an opportunity to refute these charges.) All suspensions are noted on a student's records; how does this affect the need for impartial proceedings?

Partway through the discussion of this case, students could be asked if their positions are affected by the following facts. Three days following Howard's suspension, the principal called him at home and told him to come to school the following day for a hearing on his case. At this hearing, Howard was able to convince the principal that the substance in the bag had, in fact, been tea. The principal told Howard that he could return to school the following day. The fact of his suspension would remain in his records.

Case 3: The Unreasonable Search Case

On the evening of May 29, 1976, Karen Bruce was in the bar at the Litter Inn in San Mateo, California, with five of her friends. The group had gone to the bar to celebrate Karen's twenty-first birthday, which was coming up the following week. The group was sitting quietly at a corner table enjoying drinks; they had been in the bar for about an hour. The bartender did not ask any of the group for proof of age the first time he served them. At about 10:30 P.M. two agents from the Alcoholic Beverage Control Commission (ABC) entered the bar and looked around the premises. (These agents' job is to enforce the laws regarding the sale of alcoholic beverages and insure that persons under the age of twenty-one are not served.)

The agents looked around the bar and observed the groups of people. After a few minutes, the agents approached Karen and her friends and asked them all to produce identification to prove that they were over twenty-one. Everyone produced their driver's license except Karen, who informed the agents that she did not have her license with her. The agents then asked her when she had graduated from high school and she stated 1973. They then asked her how old she was, to which she replied that she was twenty-one. Following this exchange, the agents arrested Karen, saying that she was underage.

After arresting Karen, the agents decided that they would take her to the San Mateo police station in order to run a computer check to verify her age. (A computer check can be used for this purpose because all drivers' licenses are cross-indexed by name and number, making verification of identity a relatively simple task.) After arriving at the police station and entering the pertinent information into the computer, the agents decided that while they were waiting for the computer to process the information, they would examine Karen's purse to see if they could find any proof of her age. They opened her purse and began to look through it. In examining her purse the agents found five packages of cigarettes, which one of the agents found somewhat unusual. Because of this, he removed all five packages from her purse, laid them on the table, and decided to open each one and look through it. The first three packages contained only regular cigarettes. However on opening the fourth package, the agent found what appeared to be marijuana cigarettes. By this time, the computer had returned the requested information. The agents charged Karen with: (1) being in a bar while under the age of twenty-one, (2) consuming alcoholic beverages while being under twenty-one, and (3) possession of marijuana. A short time later, Karen was released and allowed to return home. The following day, she consulted her family's lawyer, who agreed to defend her in the criminal action being brought against her by the district attorney.

(In the discussion of Karen's problem, some of the students might be asked to consider the issues that would be raised by Karen's attorney, and others might be asked to take the position of the prosecutor.)

Discussion

The discussion of this problem should not be allowed to focus on whether or not the ABC agents had the authority to undertake the actions they did. If this question is raised, it should be disposed of simply by stating that the ABC agents, as agents of the state, are granted the authority by law to do the things they did. If the discussion wanders off on this question, the group will get absolutely nowhere with the problem.

The primary issues raised by this problem concern the Fourth Amendment to the U.S. Constitution and its prohibition against unreasonable searches and seizures. The discussion of this problem should focus on what searches and what seizures took place, and whether or not they were reasonable. For any search or seizure to be reasonable, there should be enough evidence to create probable cause. Therefore, the discussion should first attempt to define which acts of the agents constitute searches or seizures. Then, it should be determined whether there was probable cause to conduct the searches or seizures; if there was, they will have been reasonable.

It is very difficult to precisely define probable cause; courts deal with it on a case-by-case basis, evaluating the facts present in a particular case. The discussion of probable cause in the present situation should focus on which facts could have given rise to a reason to believe that a crime was being committed by Karen. There is no predetermined way in which to argue the facts; students should be encouraged to carefully weigh each fact and not just make broad conclusionary statements.

Chronologically, the first issue that arises from the facts in this situation is whether the ABC agents had probable cause to arrest Karen for being underage. The agents approached the group, perhaps assuming that they looked somewhat young, and asked all of them to produce identification. All but Karen were able to comply. She told the agents that she did not have her driver's license with her at the time. When they asked her when she graduated from high school, she replied 1973; the agents had calculated that since most people are seventeen when they graduate from high school, Karen must now be twenty and therefore underage. Are the combined absence of a driver's license and the statement regarding high school graduation sufficient to constitute probable cause to arrest Karen for underage drinking? Obviously, there could be any number of legitimate reasons why Karen might in fact have forgotten her driver's license, and the year of graduation from high school may have little bearing on how old one actually is. These issues should be developed to some extent. It should also not be forgotten that the arrest of Karen is a seizure of the person. If it is determined that the agents have probable cause to believe Karen was under twenty-one and that therefore a crime was being committed, then it was reasonable for them to arrest her. If the opposite was true, then perhaps the arrest was unreasonable.

There are a number of issues raised by the agent's conduct at the police station. Not much time should be spent on whether it was appropriate for the agents to conduct a computer check, since this is really not relevant to the focus of discussion—the searches and seizures that took place in this case. Attention should be focused at this point on the search of Karen's purse. Hopefully, the students will realize that more than one search was conducted. The agents not only searched the purse, they also searched the cigarette packages. It should be pointed out in the discussion that these are two separate searches and must be considered separately. The same standards that were used in evaluating the arrest should be used in evaluating the agents' conduct with regard to these searches. That is, did the agent have probable cause to examine the contents of Karen's purse? It can easily be argued that since the agents were attempting to locate proof of Karen's age, it was appropriate for them to examine her purse for a driver's license. On the other hand, since the agents were already using the computer to check Karen's age, this alternate approach to determining her age might not have been necessary, and may therefore have been unreasonable. It would probably not have been unreasonable for the agents to assume that most women carry their driver's license in their purse. However, the agents had no reason to suspect that Karen had any contraband in her purse. There was no indication that she had been using drugs, nor had the agents arrested her on that basis. The only reason for looking in Karen's purse was to attempt to locate proof of age. What proof of age could be found inside a cigarette package? It would be realistic for the discussion regarding the search of these packages to conclude with the finding that those searches were unreasonable under the circumstances.

It might be useful at the end of the discussion to point out that although this case has revealed some of the general principles of law involved in the concept of search, it does not offer a definitive statement of an individual's Fourth-Amendment rights under all circumstances. It has been used simply as a problem for discussion and as a demonstration of the Jurisprudential Model.

This problem is based on an actual case. In real life, the woman's lawyer made a motion to the court that the marijuana evidence not be admitted because it had been obtained as the result of an illegal search; that motion was granted by the court. Following this, the woman pleaded guilty to the charge of drinking while under the age of twenty-one. The district attorney decided to drop the other charge—being in a bar while underage. This last fact might open up an entirely new discussion—on plea bargaining—but it should probably not be included in this problem.

EXERCISE 1

We would like you to develop your own case materials for use in peer teaching. At this point, however, some of you may prefer to use the case materials above rather than developing your own. If you choose to develop our materials, complete Exercise 1. If you are developing your own case materials, complete Exercise 2. If there are more than four persons in your peer teaching group, some will have to develop their own materials. We hope that several in each group will do this.

Take one of the three cases presented above, and in two or three sentences describe the case and develop a list of the pertinent facts in the case. Do this by completing Part I of the Planning Guide.

EXERCISE 2

Select a situation (or a value conflict) and develop case materials that you can use with your peers. Then complete Part I of the Planning Guide.

ANALYZING THE ISSUES

Analyzing issues involves four steps:

1. identifying the public policy question(s) in the case
2. determining the values and value conflicts in the case
3. determining the important factual questions in the conflict
4. determining the definitional problems in the conflict

Most conflicts contain several public policy issues, each of which can be formulated at a different level of generality (or specificity) and complexity. The first step in analyzing the issue is to identify beforehand the one issue that will be explored. Then you will be able to analyze the value, definitional, and factual problems in the issue and prepare analogies. As you (and your students) gain experience with the Jurisprudential Model and with legal-ethical concepts, you can leave the choice of issues up to the students. In beginning Jurisprudential sessions, it is best to prepare for only *one* issue.

Students discover quickly that how the policy issue is formulated has important implications for the stances that they are likely to take on it. It should not surprise you to find them struggling with the wording, making suggestions to one another, and revising the level of abstractness at which the issue is expressed.

Once you have selected the one issue that students will take a stance on, you can begin to analyze that issue. First, you will want to determine the values at stake in this issue and the value conflicts. Once again, any case can usually be argued from several points of view, or value stances. For example, in the armband case (pertaining to the students' right to protest the war in South America), the values of equal protection under the law (students' right to freedom of speech) and due process (students' right to a hearing or a notice of impending action) were in conflict with the values of preservation of peace and order and promotion of the general welfare (the school is viewed as a community). Some participants saw the issue in terms of one group of students (the protesters) versus the majority. These people saw the value conflict as one of personal liberty versus equal protection (the majority of students' right to an uninterrupted education).

Once the value issues and their context in the specific case are determined, you can then reflect upon factual and definitional problems. If the armband case is analyzed in terms of personal liberty versus equal protection, one definitional question centers on what is educational. Some people, especially social-studies teachers, could argue that participating in social action is educational; to have the whole school truly involved in a social issue might be an ideal educational experience. A factual question might be: Would the wearing of armbands actually disrupt the school?

EXERCISE 3

Figure 1 is a sample of the planning you will do in Part II of the Planning Guide. It presents some of the public policy questions and value, factual, and definitional problems involved in school integration cases. After you read the sample answers, complete Part II of the Planning Guide for the case you have decided to peer teach.

II. Analyzing the Issues
   A. What are the basic public policy questions?
      A. Should a whole section of the country be forced to go through a period of increased tension, violence, and civil strife in order to give Negroes equal educational rights?
      B. Should the people of the South be allowed to work out the problem themselves, perhaps very gradually, so that there will be less threat of violence and less disruption of the normal activities of the community?
   B. Select one issue you want to focus on. What are the value (or legal) conflicts in the issue?
      A. Peace and order versus equal educational opportunity.
   C. What are some important factual questions in the conflict?
      A. Will there actually be violence and civil strife if we try to desegregate the schools?
      B. Is the violence caused by desegregation itself, or by radical and unstable people within the community who simply use desegregation as an opportunity to vent their pent-up hostilities?
      C. Can the more subtle forms of violence (economic reprisal, intimidation by anonymous phone calls, etc.) be controlled by law-enforcement agencies?
      D. Will both Negro and white suffer more through attempts at desegregation than if everyone accepted separate-but-equal as a principle?
   D. What are the definitional problems in this conflict?
      A. What do we really mean by violence?
      B. Are tensions and threats violence?
      C. Are boycotts, economic sanctions, or threats of being fired violence?
      D. Is mass picketing and jeering violence?

Figure 1. *Sample Answers to Part II of the Planning Guide.*

PREPARING ANALOGIES
AND DEVELOPING PATTERNS OF ARGUMENTATION

One of the most difficult aspects of this model is probing the students' positions, because it is hard to predict exactly what stances the students will take and what the bases for their positions will be. Two ways to help prepare for the Socratic dialogue are (1) developing analogies and (2) formulating questions or statements that reflect the different patterns of argumentation. Analogies test the consistency of a student's position across more general and/or more specific situations and also clarify the circumstances and limits under which the value applies. The patterns of argumentation provide alternative lines of reasoning that the student must account for. Not all of these patterns or analogies will be used in the exploration of student positions, but they will encourage you to reason your way through the argumentation and be well acquainted with the issues and problems in the case.

Sample answers to Parts III and IV of the Planning Guide appear in Figure 2. These answers pertain to a school integration case. After you have read these sample answers, complete Parts III and IV of the Planning Guide for the case you are planning to peer teach.

ORGANIZING FOR SOCRATIC DIALOGUE

The organization of instruction for the Jurisprudential Model does not present too many unusual problems except during Phase Four and perhaps Phase Five. Naturally, it is easier to maintain the involvement of a smaller group of students, say ten or twelve, than a class of twenty-five. Remember, the essence of the Socratic style of dialogue is to probe one line of thinking to its logical conclusion, continually questioning assumptions and testing consistency. With as many stances as students, this can be difficult. If you jump around from student to student, you will have difficulty enforcing one line of thinking. If the students debate one another, the discussion becomes just that—a debate instead of a dialogue—one stand versus another instead of a questioning of reasoning. There are subtle differences among the various types of discussion, and it is not absolutely necessary to use a Socratic approach. We prefer the Socratic style because, done well, it works the policy stance thoroughly and leads to a strengthening of it or a changing of it to a more rationally defensible stance.

We have found it helpful to have all the students record their policy stance on cards or paper. Then, prior to the exploration of the stances (Phase Four) small groups of four or five students can be formed on the basis of similarity of stances. Each group can pool ideas and develop the strongest possible position. One person can volunteer to explore this position, first with the teacher and perhaps later with students in other groups. At times, other members of the original group may take over the position of spokesman. It seems to us that this is one way of organizing instruction that permits continuity of thought and at the same time maintains the involvement of all the students.

We have also found it useful in Phase Five, after all students have heard the exploration of the stances, for them to reach a consensus on one or two positions they felt were the strongest, and to clearly state these positions.

III. Preparing Analogies

Describe at least two analogies for each side of the value conflict.

A. Analogies emphasizing the importance of basic rights and justifying violence:
   1. The American Revolution
   2. World War II
   3. A man is giving a lecture. Several people start shouting him down and heckling him. Do the police have the right to forcibly remove the hecklers from the hall?
   4. You and your friends enter a public playground. Several boys threaten to prevent you from using the baseball field. Should you go ahead and use the field, even though there may be a fight?

B. Analogies emphasizing peace and order:
   1. The Hungarian Revolution of 1956: should we have risked atomic war to free the Hungarian people?
   2. The seizure of Tibet by Communist China
   3. A store manager is enraged at a clerk for knocking over a box of cans. You know the clerk did not do it. Should you get into the argument, even though you know that the manager is likely to become very angry with you?

IV. Patterns of Argumentation

Which of the following patterns of argumentation do you anticipate will be most appropriate in this case? (Check one or more, as appropriate.)

A. Factual emphasis: establishing the point at which a value is violated. Example: Are separate black schools and white schools really equal?

B. Factual emphasis: proving the desirable or undesirable consequences of a position. Example: Segregation promotes cultural unity and integrity. Integration leads to mutual respect.

C. Clarifying the value conflict with analogies. Example: When does liberty become anarchy and irresponsibility?

D. Setting value priorities: asserting the priority of one value over another and demonstrating the lack of gross violation of the second value. Example: Separate-but-equal maintains states' rights and local control but does not violate the value of equality to an excessive degree.

Figure 2. *Sample Answers to Parts III and IV of the Planning Guide.*

Completing the Planning Guide

We have developed a Planning Guide in order to help you organize the Jurisprudential lesson you are about to peer teach. This Guide is especially useful the first few times you use the model. After that, such extensive planning is probably not necessary.

By now, you should have completed Parts I-V of the Guide. The remaining part asks you to develop initiating moves for each of the phases of the model. Complete Part VI of the Planning Guide now, and then move on to your peer teaching and microteaching.

PLANNING GUIDE FOR THE JURISPRUDENTIAL MODEL

I. Briefly describe the case, and outline its major facts.

II. Analyzing the Issues

   A. What is the basic public policy question(s)?

   B. Select one issue you want to focus on. What are the value (or legal) conflicts in the issue?

   C. What are some important factual questions in the conflict?

   D. What are the definitional problems in this conflict?

172

III. Preparing Analogies

Describe at least two analogies for each side of the value conflict.

IV. Patterns of Argumentation

Which of the following patterns of argumentation do you anticipate will be the most appropriate in this case? (Check one or more, as appropriate.)

A. Factual emphasis: establishing the point at which a value is violated. Example:

B. Factual emphasis: proving the desirable and undesirable consequences of a position. Example:

C. Clarifying the value conflict with analogies. Example:

D. Setting value priorities: asserting the priority of one value over another and demonstrating the lack of gross violation of the second value. Example:

V. Educational Objectives

List at least two behavioral objectives that you will teach for in this lesson.

VI. Phases of the Model

List your initiating moves for each phase of the model.

Phase One

Phase Two

Phase Three

Phase Four

Phase Five

Phase Six

Analyzing the Peer Teaching Lesson

The questions in the Teaching Analysis Guide ask you to check that important features of the model are taken into account in the peer teaching. Feel free to comment on other aspects of your lesson, and the lessons of your colleagues, and help your colleagues reflect on the aspects of a Jurisprudential lesson that are pointed out in the Teaching Analysis Guide. Duplicate as many copies of the Guide as are necessary to analyze the peer teaching and micro-teaching of all members of the group.

TEACHING ANALYSIS GUIDE FOR THE JURISPRUDENTIAL MODEL

This Guide is designed to help you analyze the process of teaching as you practice the Jurisprudential Model. The analysis focuses on aspects of teaching that are important to the syntax of the model, the teacher's role, and specific teaching skills.

The Guide consists of a series of questions and phrases. As you observe a practice session (whether peer teaching or microteaching), analyze the teaching using the rating scale that appears opposite each question and statement. This scale uses the following items:

Thoroughly. This item signifies that the teacher engaged in the behavior to the point where students were responding comfortably and fluently. Appropriateness varies from situation to situation.

Partially. This item signifies that the teacher engaged in appropriate behavior, but not as thoroughly as possible. There is some doubt about whether the students are responding fully.

Missing. The teacher did not engage in the behavior; there appears to be a loss in student response or probably will be one.

Not Needed. The teacher did not explicitly manifest the behavior, but there is no loss. Either the behavior was included in others or the students began to respond appropriately without being led to.

For each question or statement in the Guide, circle the term that best describes the teacher's behavior.

Phase One: Orientation to the Case

1. Did the teacher orient students to the model—to the idea of issues and of taking a stance on issues, for example?	Thoroughly	Partially	Missing	Not Needed
2. Did the teacher introduce the case?	Thoroughly	Partially	Missing	Not Needed
3. Did the teacher ask for or respond to students' requests for clarification of the case material?	Thoroughly	Partially	Missing	Not Needed
4. Did the teacher ask the students to identify the most important facts of the case?	Thoroughly	Partially	Missing	Not Needed

Phase Two: Identifying the Issues

5. Did the teacher explain the purposes of this phase—to identify policy questions and value, factual, and definitional issues?	Thoroughly	Partially	Missing	Not Needed
6. Did the teacher ask the students to synthesize the facts of the case into public policy questions?	Thoroughly	Partially	Missing	Not Needed
7. Did the teacher explain the idea of a policy question and provide an example of it?	Thoroughly	Partially	Missing	Not Needed
8. Did the teacher have students select one policy question to explore?	Thoroughly	Partially	Missing	Not Needed

175

TEACHING ANALYSIS GUIDE FOR THE JURISPRUDENTIAL MODEL

9. Did the students identify the values and value conflicts at issue in the public policy question?	Thoroughly	Partially	Missing	Not Needed
10. Did the teacher explain the concepts of factual and definitional issues?	Thoroughly	Partially	Missing	Not Needed
11. Did the teacher ask the students to identify factual or definitional questions pertinent to the public policy question?	Thoroughly	Partially	Missing	Not Needed

Phase Three: Taking a Position

12. Did the teacher ask students to take a position on the public policy question and give their reasons for their stance?	Thoroughly	Partially	Missing	Not Needed
13. Did some of the students share their position with the rest of the group?	Thoroughly	Partially	Missing	Not Needed

Phase Four: Exploring the Stances

14. Did the students summarize what they had done so far in the model?	Thoroughly	Partially	Missing	Not Needed
15. Did the teacher explain the purposes and procedures of arguing the case?	Thoroughly	Partially	Missing	Not Needed
16. Did the teacher explore the issue with one or more students (or groups of students)?	Thoroughly	Partially	Missing	Not Needed
17. Did the teacher maintain a Socratic style of dialogue in questioning students' assumptions?	Thoroughly	Partially	Missing	Not Needed
18. Did the teacher avoid advocating a stand and trying to convince the students to adopt an alternative stand?	Thoroughly	Partially	Missing	Not Needed
19. Did the teacher use one or more of the following patterns of argumentation?				
a. factual emphasis: establishing the point at which the value is violated	Thoroughly	Partially	Missing	Not Needed
b. factual emphasis: proving desirable or undesirable consequences of an action	Thoroughly	Partially	Missing	Not Needed
c. clarifying the value conflict	Thoroughly	Partially	Missing	Not Needed
d. asserting the priority of one value over another and the lack of gross violation of the second value	Thoroughly	Partially	Missing	Not Needed
20. While exploring the students' stances, did the teacher probe the students' ideas for:				

TEACHING ANALYSIS GUIDE FOR THE JURISPRUDENTIAL MODEL

a. relevance?	Thoroughly	Partially	Missing	Not Needed
b. consistency?	Thoroughly	Partially	Missing	Not Needed
c. specificity?	Thoroughly	Partially	Missing	Not Needed
d. generality?	Thoroughly	Partially	Missing	Not Needed
e. definitional clarity?	Thoroughly	Partially	Missing	Not Needed
21. While exploring the students' stances, did the teacher enforce and maintain continuity of thought?	Thoroughly	Partially	Missing	Not Needed

Phase Five: Refining and Qualifying the Position

22. Did the students identify the most convincing position(s)?	Thoroughly	Partially	Missing	Not Needed
23. Did the students identify a number of similar situations in order to test the strength of the position(s)?	Thoroughly	Partially	Missing	Not Needed
24. Did the students qualify the position?	Thoroughly	Partially	Missing	Not Needed

Phase Six: Testing Factual Assumptions Behind the Qualified Position

25. Did the students test the position(s) by identifying factual assumptions and determining their relevance?	Thoroughly	Partially	Missing	Not Needed
26. Did the students determine the predicted consequences of the position(s) and whether they are likely to occur?	Thoroughly	Partially	Missing	Not Needed

AFTER PEER TEACHING: MICROTEACHING

Peer teaching was an opportunity to "walk through" the pattern of activities of the model you are using. It should have helped you identify areas of understanding or performance that were amiss for you!

Aside from the specifics of the Teaching Analysis Guide, we would like you to reflect intuitively on your peer teaching experience. Did you feel that the essence of the Jurisprudential Model was incorporated into the learning activity? Were you able to maintain the teacher's role as you had anticipated?

As you prepare your first Jurisprudential lesson for a small group of students, identify aspects of the Jurisprudential Model that you want to improve upon or include. We suggest walking yourself mentally through the microteaching before actually engaging in it.

It is natural in microteaching to wonder, "Am I doing this right?" Except for any glaring omissions or commissions that may have emerged in your peer teaching, the pursuit of excellence in a model is more a matter of refinement, style, and personal goals for the teaching situation. If you have been operating in the "Did I get this right?" frame of mind, now is the time to change to "What do *I* want to get across or elicit in this first teaching situation? How will I go about doing that?" If you have internalized the *basic* goals, principles, and procedures of the model, now is the time to shift from an external way of thinking to an internal one. Build the variations that seem appropriate to you.

We suggest audio-taping your first microteaching session so that you can reflect on the lesson afterwards. Students will respond differently from your peers. It is a good idea to use the Teaching Analysis Guide with your microteaching lesson. You may also want to share the experience with your colleagues and receive their comments and suggestions.

The fourth and last component of the Jurisprudential Model suggests ways to use the model over a long-term curricular sequence and ways to adapt curricular materials to it. The emphasis of your training in this model will gradually shift now from mastering the basic elements of teaching to curriculum design and application.

Component IV

ADAPTING
THE MODEL

Oliver and Shaver wrote *Teaching Public Issues in the High School* and developed curriculum materials to support it with the purpose of providing an alternative framework for teaching social studies courses in high schools. They were concerned with substance as well as process. That is, they were concerned both with what would be taught and how it would be taught.[1] Consequently, the model provides a framework for developing contemporary course content in public affairs and for developing a process for dealing with conflict in the public domain, leading students to an examination of values.

Essentially, the direct application of this model is in the construction of courses or units of courses in secondary school settings. As such it can be sufficient on its own. It is limited to older students and must be modified considerably for use at the junior high school and middle school levels with any but the most able students. We have successfully carried out the model with extremely able seventh and eighth grade students but have had little success with younger children.

[1] Donald Oliver and James P. Shaver, *Teaching Public Issues in the High School* (Boston: Houghton Mifflin, 1966).

COMBINING THE JURISPRUDENTIAL MODEL WITH OTHER MODELS OF TEACHING

At this point, we believe that it is possible to build curriculums that intersperse the Jurisprudential Model framework with that of a variety of other models. A course in political science, for example, could open with a unit about the legal structure of the United States government that is built around either an inductive model of teaching or structured with advance organizers. This could be followed by a unit built around the Jurisprudential Model, utilizing cases involving governmental processes. In the first unit, the students would develop information and concepts about governmental process; in the second they would begin to explore the value conflicts and issues involved in the dynamics of governance. This unit would also train students in the jurisprudential methodology. Subsequent units of the course could move into specific areas such as environmental protection, transportation, medical care, and housing with units that help the students gain information and develop concepts. These could be interspersed with further explorations from the jurisprudential view.

Similarly, an instructor who wishes to build the year's work around group investigation (with students helping to determine course content and identifying issues to be studied) could introduce the Jurisprudential Model in order to provide the students with tools of inquiry into public issues and values.

For many years instructors have organized social studies courses around cases; the Jurisprudential Model provides a way to heighten the vigor and intensity with which such cases are studied. Of course, cases that do not have public issues or value conflicts embedded in them would not lend themselves readily to the jurisprudential approach. But it is worthwhile to speculate that, unless social studies courses do deal with values, both personal and public, then they will have missed the vital mainstream of social concern. Thus, this model provides a criterion for the selection of cases for social studies courses.

As was the case with the Role Playing Model, once students become fluent in the use of the Jurisprudential Model, it can be applied to conflicts that occur in and around their own lives. The scenario at the beginning of this model provided an example of students' application of the Jurisprudential Model to an issue that touched their own lives.

Without such application, we speculate that the study of public issues, even vigorously pursued, can seem abstract and irrelevant to the lives of school children. Public issues are endemic in public life. Children live in communities where issues abound. Their study of values should not be confined to cases far removed from them, but should be applied to the dynamics of their own lives and the community around them.

SIMULATION

MODEL

SCENARIO FOR THE SIMULATION MODEL

Students in a driver education course in a secondary school in Chicago, Illinois, are taking turns driving a simulated car on a simulated street. A motion-picture camera projects an image of the roadway ahead. Obstacles appear. A child steps out from behind two parked cars; the "driver" turns the wheel and misses the child. A stop sign appears suddenly beyond a parked truck; the driver slams on the brakes. The driver makes a turn and a roadway narrows suddenly; again the driver brakes. One by one the students experience driving under simulated conditions. As students complete the "course," the instructor and the other students debrief them, questioning their reactions and various ways of driving defensively.

In another classroom, this time in the suburbs of Boston, Massachusetts, a class is watching a television show. The actors are portraying the members of the United States Cabinet facing a crisis. After discussing the crisis, the class examines the issues under consideration. They reach a conclusion. One of the students reaches for the telephone in the classroom, dials a number, and speaks to the actors in the studio, suggesting how they might play their roles differently in order to

181

resolve the crisis. Twenty-five other classrooms are simultaneously debating the issues seen on television and communicating their views to the actors in the studio. The next day the show resumes. In various ways, the actors play out the suggestions made by the classes. The other members of the Cabinet react. The students in the twenty-five classrooms not only see their ideas brought to life on the television screen, but they also see the consequences of their recommendations.

In an inner city school in Toronto, Canada, another class—this time an elementary school class—is watching a television screen. On the screen, an announcer portrays a countdown as a rocket attempts to break free from the gravity of the moon but fails to do so. Class members then take the role of members of the crew of the spaceship. Instructions from the Royal Canadian Space Administration divide them into teams and they prepare to work together to conserve their life-support systems and to manage their relationships in the rocketship until repairs can be made.

In San Antonio, Texas, two groups of children enter a room. One group represents the Alpha culture, the other the Beta culture. Their task is to learn how to communicate with others who have learned rules and patterns of behavior from a different society. Gradually, they learn to master communication patterns. Simultaneously, they become aware that, as members of a culture, they have inherited powerful patterns that strongly influence their personality and their ways of communicating with other people.

In Philadelphia, Pennsylvania, a class is engaged in a caribou hunt. As they progress through the hunt, which the Netsilik Eskimos operate, they learn behavior patterns of the Netsilik and begin to compare and contrast those patterns with the ones they carry on in their everyday lives.

In a suburb of San Francisco, California, a group of students tries to face a problem posed by the Secretary of State of the United States. Agronomists have developed a nutrient that, when added to the food of beef cattle, increases their weight tremendously. Only a limited amount of this nutrient is available, and the students must determine how the nutrient will be divided among the needy nations of the world. Congress has imposed the following restraints: the recipient nations must have a reasonable supply of beef cattle, must not be aligned with the "hard-core" communist bloc of nations, must not be vegetarians, and must have a population that exceeds a certain size. The students debate the alternatives. Some countries are ruled out immediately. Of the remaining countries, some seem attractive at first, yet less attractive later. The students grapple with the problems of humanity and ideology and with practical situations. In simulation they face the problems of the committees of scientists who continuallly advise the United States government on various courses of action.

These students are all involved in simulations. They are playing the roles of persons engaged in real-life pursuits. Simulation allows the students to face realistic conditions and develop realistic solutions to them. Simulation brings into the classroom elements of the real world. These elements are simplified and presented in a form that can be contained inside the classroom rather than outside in the hurly-burly of the active daily life of adults.

In order to progress through the tasks of the simulation, students have to develop concepts and skills necessary for performance in the area to which the simulation pertains. The young drivers have to develop concepts and skills for driving effectively. The young caribou hunters have to learn concepts about culture. The young members of the Cabinet need to learn about international relations and the problems of conducting a major state.

In simulation, students learn from the consequences of their actions. The driver who does not turn rapidly enough "hits" the child she is trying to avoid; she must learn to turn more quickly. Yet if she turns too quickly, the car goes out of control and veers to the other side of the street. She has to learn to correct her initial move while keeping her eyes on the road and looking for yet other obstacles. The students who do poorly in the caribou hunt learn what happens if the culture does not function efficiently, or if its members shrink from carrying out its mandates.

In this component, we shall explore simulations of various kinds. Some of these simulations are presented in a game format. Some of them are games with a goal. The familiar parlor game *Monopoly* is such a game. It simulates the activity of real-estate speculators and incorporates many of the elements of real-life speculation. The players play to win in this type of game simulation.

Other simulations are simply activities in which the players attempt to reach a goal in a noncompetitive way. No score is kept, but interactions are recorded and analyzed later. An example is the *Life Career* game, in which the students play out the life cycle of a human being: they select mates, choose careers, decide whether to obtain various amounts of education, and learn through the consequences of their decisions how these decisions can affect their real life.

Unlike many other models of teaching, game-type simulations depend on *software*; that is, the game has paraphernalia of various kinds. The game of *Monopoly* has a game board, pieces that represent the players, houses, hotels, cards that insert chance events into the situation, and paper money. Without these, the game of *Monopoly* cannot be played. Similarly, driver simulators, games involving "Cabinets" in crises, human relations games such as *Star Power*, and many other simulations all require pieces of material that are used to represent the real world to the students in a simulated form. Much of the model of teaching that we call Simulation involves learning to use this software effectively. Whereas other models of teaching depend on the interpersonal skill of the teacher (understanding of concepts, skillful moves that help the students explore important ideas), in the Simulation Model the teacher blends the already prepared game or other simulation into the curriculum and learns to use what developers have created.

OUTLINE OF ACTIVITIES FOR THE SIMULATION MODEL

Objectives	Materials	Activity
COMPONENT I: DESCRIBING AND UNDERSTANDING THE MODEL		
1. To recognize the goals, assumptions, and procedures of the Simulation Model and to understand the nature of simulation.	Theory and Overview	Reading
2. To gain a sense of the model in action.	Theory in Practice	Reading
3. To become familiar with the fundamentals of the Simulation Model and the roles of the teacher in simulation.	Theory and Overview	Reading
4. To recognize the learning principles operating for students during simulation.	Taking Theory Into Action	Reading
5. To evaluate your understanding of the Simulation Model.	Theory Checkup	Writing
COMPONENT II: VIEWING THE MODEL		
1. To become familiar with the Teaching Analysis Guide, and identify items you do not understand.	Teaching Analysis Guide	Reading
2. To identify phases of the model and comment on the lesson.	Demonstration Transcript	Reading/Writing/Discussion
3. **Option:** To apply the Teaching Analysis Guide to other demonstration lessons.	Live demonstration or videotape/Teaching Analysis Guide	Viewing/Group or Individual Analysis
COMPONENT III: PLANNING AND PEER TEACHING		
1. To become familiar with the various types of simulations.	Games and Simulations: Overviews	Reading
2. To provide a sample Planning Guide of a simulation game to which you may compare your own planning.	Sample Planning Guide	Reading
3. To complete the Planning Guide for the Simulation Model.	Planning Guide	Reading/Writing
4. To peer teach the Simulation Model.	3 or 4 peers; simulation game	Teaching
5. To analyze the simulation lesson using the Teaching Analysis Guide.	Teaching Analysis Guide	Writing/Group Discussion or Individual Analysis

184

OUTLINE OF ACTIVITIES FOR THE SIMULATION MODEL

COMPONENT IV: ADAPTING THE MODEL

1. To apply Simulation to curriculum areas.	Curriculum Applications	Reading
2. To combine Simulation with other models.	Combining Simulation with Other Models of Teaching	Reading

Component I

DESCRIBING
AND UNDERSTANDING
THE MODEL

THEORY AND OVERVIEW

Game-type simulations and simulations that do not involve games have been used increasingly in education over the last thirty years. The Simulation Model did not, however, originate within the field of education. Rather, it is an application of the principles of a branch of psychology called *cybernetics*.

Cybernetic Principles

From one perspective, cybernetic psychology represents the machine's contribution to the humanization of man. The cybernetic psychologist conceptualizes the learner as a self-regulating feedback system, making an analogy between humans and machines.

Cybernetics as a discipline "has been described as the comparative study of the human (or biological) control mechanism, and electromechanical systems such as computers."[1] The central focus is the apparent similarity between

[1] Karl U. Smith and Margaret Foltz Smith, *Cybernetic Principles of Learning and Educational Design* (New York: Holt, Rinehart and Winston, 1966), p. 202.

186

the feedback-control mechanisms of electromechanical systems and human systems. "A feedback control system incorporates three primary functions: it generates movement of the system toward a target or defined path; it compares the effects of this action with the true path and detects error; and it utilizes this error signal to redirect the system."[2] For example, the automatic pilot of a boat continually corrects the helm of the ship, depending on the readings of the compass. When the ship begins to swing in a certain direction and the compass moves off the desired heading more than a certain amount, a motor is switched on and the helm is moved over. When the ship returns to course, the helm is straightened out again and the ship continues on its way. The automatic pilot operates in essentially the same way as does a human pilot. Both watch the compass, and both move the wheel to the left or right, depending on what is going on. Both initiate action in terms of a specified goal ("Let's go north") and, depending on the feedback or error signal, both redirect the initial action. Very complex self-regulating mechanical systems have been developed to control devices such as guided missiles, ocean liners, and satellites.

The cybernetic psychologist interprets the human being as a control system that generates a course of action and then redirects or corrects the action by means of feedback. This can be a very complicated process—as when the Secretary of State reevaluates foreign policy—or a very simple one—as when we notice that our sailboat is heading into the wind too much and we ease off on our course just a little. In using the analogy of mechanical systems as a frame of reference for analyzing human beings, psychologists came up with the central idea "that performance and learning must be analyzed in terms of the control relationships between a human operator and an instrumental situation. That is, learning was understood to be determined by the nature of the individual, as well as by the design of the learning situation."[3]

Cybernetics in a Learning Environment

In any learning situation we must be able to identify and characterize the pertinent human capabilities and the components of the learning environment. More important, we have to specify the relationships between the capacities of the learner and the instrumentalities of the learning situation. The basis for this analysis is the sensorimotor capabilities of the learner. Based on these capacities and instrumentalities, the learning situation can be designed to match the feedback capabilities of the learner. Since the learner can apprehend the consequences of his or her actions (get feedback from them), the system can be designed to maximize such feedback. Individuals use feedback as a means of controlling their behavior, hopefully to reach their goals and potentials.

All human behavior, according to cybernetic psychology, involves a perceptible pattern of motion. This includes both covert behavior, such as thinking and symbolic behavior, and overt behavior. In any given situation, individuals modify their behavior according to the feedback they receive from the environment. They organize their movements and their response patterns in relation to this feedback. Thus, their own sensorimotor capabilities form the basis of their feedback system.

[2] *Ibid.*, p. 203.
[3] *Ibid.*, p. vii.

This ability to receive feedback constitutes the human system's mechanism for receiving and sending information. As human beings develop greater linguistic capability, they are able to utilize indirect as well as direct feedback, thereby expanding their control over the physical and social environment. That is, they are less dependent on the concrete realities of the environment because they can utilize its symbolic representations. The essence, then, of cybernetic psychology is the principle of sense-oriented feedback that is intrinsic to the individual (he "feels" the effects of his decisions) and is the basis for self-corrective choices. Individuals can "feel" the effects of their decisions because the environment responds *in full*, rather than simply "You're right" or "Wrong! Try again." That is, the environmental consequences of their choices are played back to them. Learning in cybernetic terms is sensorially experiencing the environmental consequences of one's behavior and engaging in self-corrective behavior. Instruction in cybernetic terms is designed to create an environment for the learner in which this full feedback takes place.

Simulators and Simulation Games

The application of cybernetic principles to educational procedures is seen perhaps most dramatically and clearly in the development of *simulators*. A simulator is a training device that represents reality very closely, but in which the complexity of events can be controlled. For example, a simulated automobile has been constructed in which the driver sees a road (by means of a motion picture), has a wheel to turn, a clutch and a brake to operate, a gearshift, a turn signal, and all the other devices of a contemporary automobile. She can start this simulated automobile, and when she turns the key she hears the noise of a motor running. When she presses the accelerator the noise increases in volume, so she has the sensation of having actually increased the flow of gas to a real engine. As she drives, the film shows her curves in the road and, as she turns the wheel, she may experience the illusion that her automobile is turning. The operation of the automobile on the road has been reproduced in a simulation. The simulator can present the student with learning tasks to which she can respond, but her responses do not have the same consequences that they would have in a real-life situation: her simulated automobile does not crash into anything, although it may look like it is crashing from her point of view. And in the manner of training psychology, the tasks presented can be made less complex than those she would have to execute in the real world; this way, it is easier for her to acquire the skills she will need later for actual driving. For example, in a driving simulator the student can simply practice shifting from one gear to another until she has it down pat. She can also practice applying the brakes and turning the wheel until she has a feel for how the automobile responds when she does those things.

The advantages of a simulator are several. As we noted above, the learning tasks can be made much less complex than they are in the real world, so that the students may have the opportunity to master tasks that would be extremely difficult when all the factors of real-world operations impinge upon them. A very good example of this is the flying of an airplane. Learning how to fly a complex airplane without the aid of a simulator leaves very little room for error: the student pilot has to do everything adequately the first time, or the plane is in difficulty. With the use of a simulator the training can be staged. The trainee can be introduced to simple tasks, and then more complex ones, until he builds a repertoire of skills adequate for piloting the plane. Also, difficulties of various kinds can be simulated, such as storms and mechanical problems, and the student can learn how to cope with them. Thus, by the time the student actually begins flying, he has built the repertoire of skills necessary to do so.

A second advantage of simulators is that they permit the students to learn from self-generated feedback that they experience themselves. As the student pilot turns the wheel of the great plane to the right, for example, he can feel the plane bank, he can feel the loss of speed in some respects, and he can learn how to trim the craft during the turn. In other words, he can learn through his own senses, rather than simply through verbal descriptions, the corrective behaviors that are necessary. In the driving simulation, if the driver heads into curves too rapidly and then has to jerk the wheel in order to avoid going off the road, this feedback permits her to adjust her behavior so that when she is on a real road she will turn more gingerly as she approaches sharp curves. The cybernetic psychologist designs simulators so that the feedback about the consequences of behavior enables the learners to modify their responses and develop a repertoire of appropriate behaviors.

Some very elaborate applications of cybernetic psychology have been made in military training. For example, there is a submarine simulator in which several members of the crew can communicate with one another by radio and other devices. They are able to take their "submarine" under water, maneuver it against enemy ships, raise their periscope, sight ships through it, and fire torpedoes. The simulator is constructed so it can be attacked by enemy destroyers and can emerge and engage in evasive action, the crew hearing the enemy only over sonar and other undersea listening devices.

Thus far, the applications of cybernetics within normal elementary and secondary education are somewhat less spectacular. Exceptions are an urban simulator, which is being used experimentally with children from the upper elementary grades,[4] and Omar Khayyam Moore's famous talking typewriter, which simulates a human being who talks back to the student as he presses typewriter keys representing particular words or letters. Most other applications of cybernetics to education up to this point are fairly simple. We shall describe some of them here and the cybernetic principles will be made more explicit.

The Life Career Game

This game was developed to assist guidance counselors and students in their mutual task of planning for the future, a task that requires the student to take into account many factors, such as job opportunities, labor-market demands, social trends, and educational requirements.[5] Vocational and educational guidance personnel seek to help students become aware of these multiple factors, evaluate their significance, and generate alternative decisions. In the *Life Career Game* students are able to interact with these various components of the environment. They make decisions about jobs, further education or training, family life, and the

[4] Developed by the Washington Center for Metropolitan Studies, 1717 Massachusetts Ave., Washington, D.C.
[5] See: Barbara B. Varenhorst, "The Life Career Game: Practice in Decision-Making," in *Simulating Games in Learning*, ed. Sarane Boocock and E. O. Schild (Beverly Hills, Calif.: Sage Publications, 1968).

use of leisure time, and receive feedback on the probable consequences of these decisions. The environment in this case is represented by other persons or organizations. That is, the probable consequences of the student's decisions are represented by responses from persons playing the roles of teachers, college-admissions officers, employers, and marriage partners. As the players move through the different environments of school, work, family, and leisure, they are able to see the interrelationships among their decisions and among the components of their lives. The game is played as follows:

> The Life Career Game can be played by any number of teams, each consisting of two to four players. Each team works with a profile or case history of a fictitious person (a student about the age of the players).
>
> The game is organized into rounds or decision periods, each of which represents one year in the life of this person. During each decision period, players plan their person's schedule of activities for a typical week, allocating his time among school, studying, job, family responsibilities, and leisure time activities. Most activities require certain investments of time, training, money and so on (for example a full-time job takes a certain amount of time and often has some educational or experience prerequisites as well; similarly having a child requires considerable expenditure of time, in addition to financial expenses), and a person clearly cannot engage in all the available activities. Thus, the players' problem is to choose the combination of activities which they think will maximize their person's present satisfaction and his chances for a good life in the future. . . .
>
> When players have made their decisions for a given year, scores are computed in four areas—education, occupation, family life, and leisure. Calculations use a set of tables and spinners—based upon U.S. Census and other national survey data which indicate the probability of certain things happening in a person's life, given his personal characteristics, past experiences, and present efforts. A chance or luck factor is built into the game by the use of spinners and dice.
>
> A game usually runs for a designated number of rounds (usually ten to twelve) and the team with the highest total score at the end is the winner.[6]

The variations of the *Life Career Game* illustrate the educational features of a simulation game as well as the enormous potential of simulation for incorporating several educational objectives into the basic simulation-game design. For instance, every simulation implies a theory about behavior in the area of life being simulated. This theory is implicit in the goal-achievement rules (the objectives of the game) and the rules governing the environmental-responses.

One version of the *Life Career Game* assumes that each person attaches a different amount of importance to the various areas of life. Following this assumption, players determine their own goals by weighing the various areas in terms of their importance to them. At the end of the game, the objective achievements in those areas are converted to subjective satisfaction by means of weighted conversion ratios selected by the player. Alternately, if one of the processes being simulated is the selection and modification of goals contingent

---

[6] This excerpt from "An Experimental Study of the Learning Effects of Two Games with Simulated Environments," by Sarene S. Boocock is reprinted from *Simulation Games in Learning,* Sarene S. Boocock and E. O. Schild, eds., © 1968, p. 108; by permission of the publisher, Sage Publications, Inc.

upon the consequences of one's actions, the player may be asked to weigh the different areas of life at various times during the course of play. In both cases, the student is "playing against" the environment according to a personal criterion rather than an externally determined goal (such as gaining more points in the game than someone else).

The game may also include certain requisite skills, such as actually making formal applications for job and interviews, selecting courses, setting up interviews, or selecting courses from the college catalog. It can also be conducted to allow group discussion at the end of rounds, analyzing and challenging each other's decisions and identifying the values underlying them.

Computer-Based Economics Games

Two computer-based economics games for sixth graders have recently been developed by the Center for Educational Services and Research of the Board of Cooperative Educational Services (BOCES) in Northern Westchester County, New York.[7] The use of the computer makes it possible to individualize the simulation in terms of learning pace, scope, sequence, and difficulty of material. Aside from this feature, the properties of the simulation remain the same as in non-computer-based simulation games.

The Sumerian Game instructs the student in the basic principles of economics as applied to three stages of a primitive economy—an agricultural period, the development of crafts, and the introduction of trade and other changes. The game is set during the time of the Neolithic revolution in Mesopotamia, about 3500 B.C. The student is asked to take the role of the ruler of the city-state of Lagash. The ruler must make certain agricultural decisions for his kingdom at each six-month harvest. For example, he is presented with the following problematic situation: "We have harvested 5,000 bushels of grain to take care of 500 people. How much of this grain will be set aside for next season's planting and how much will be stored in the warehouse?"[8] The student is asked to decide how much grain to allocate for consumption, for production, and for storage.

These situations become more complex as the game continues, for the student must take into account such circumstances as changes in population, the acquisition of new land, and irrigation. Periodically, technological innovations and disasters alter the outcome of his decisions. The effect of each decision upon the economic condition of the kingdom is shown in an immediate progress report. Students are apprised of certain quantitative changes—for example, in population, in the amount of harvested grain, and in the amount of stored grain—and are furnished with some substantive analyses of their decisions—for instance, "The quantity of food the people received last season was far too little."[9] In Phase Two of the *Sumerian Game*, the student can apply his surplus grain to the development of crafts.

Inter-Nation Simulation. Harold Guetzkow and his associates have developed

---

[7] Center for Educational Services and Research, Board of Cooperative Educational Services, 42 Triangle Center, Yorktown Heights, N.Y., 10598.
[8] This excerpt from "Two Computer-Based Economic Games for Sixth Graders," is reprinted from *Simulation Games in Learning*, ed. Boocock and Schild, p. 156; by permission of the publisher, Sage Publications, Inc.
[9] *Ibid.*, p. 164.

a very complex and interesting simulation for teaching students at the high school and upper elementary levels the principles of international relations.[10] This *Inter-Nation Simulation* consists of five "nation" units; in each of these nations, a group of participants act as decision makers and "aspiring decision makers." The simulated relations among the nations are derived from the characteristics of nations and from principles that have been observed to operate among nations in the past. Each of the decision-making teams has available to it information about the country it represents. This information concerns the national economic systems' basic capability, the consumer capability, force capability (the ability of the nation to develop military goods and services), and trade and aid information. Together, the nations play an international-relations game that involves trading and the development of agreements of various kinds. International organizations can be established, for example, or mutual-aid agreements, or trade agreements. The nations can even make war on one another, the outcome being determined by the force capability of one group of allies relative to that of another group.

This simulation enables students to play the roles of decision makers in nations. It requires them to make realistic negotiations of the kinds diplomats and other representatives of nations have to make as nations interact with one another, and it requires them to refer to the economic conditions in their country and the other countries as they do so. In the course of this game-type simulation, the students learn ways in which economic restraints operate on a country. For example, if they are members of the decision-making team of a small country and try to engage in a trade agreement, they find that they have to give something in order to get something. If their country has a largely agricultural economy and they are dealing with an industrialized nation, they find that their country is in a disadvantageous position unless the other nation badly needs the product they have to sell. By receiving feedback about the consequences of their decisions, the students come to an understanding of the kinds of principles that operate in international relations.

Simulation as a Model of Teaching

Syntax of the Model

Simulation has four phases. Phase One—orientation—presents the broad topic of simulation and the introduction of concepts that will be incorporated in the action simulation. Phase Two—training of the participants—involves setting up the scenario (rules, roles, procedures, scoring, types of decisions to be made, and goals), role assignments, and an abbreviated practice session. Phase Three—the actual simulation—includes feedback on the evaluation of environmental stimuli and behavior adaptations that are necessary in reaching the goals. Phase Four is the participant debriefing: guided by the teacher, the students summarize the events of the simulation and their perceptions, difficulties, and insights. They are asked to compare the simulation to the course content and/or the real world. Finally, they are provided the opportunity to appraise and redesign the simulation.

[10] Harold Guetzkow et al., *Simulation in International Relations* (Englewood Cliffs, N.J.: Prentice-Hall, 1963).

Principles of Reaction

The reactions of the teacher are primarily those of a facilitator. Throughout the simulation he or she must maintain a nonevaluative but supportive attitude. It is the teacher's task to first present and then facilitate understanding and interpretation of the rules of the simulation activity. In addition, should interest in the activity begin to dissipate or attention begin to focus on irrelevant issues, he must direct the group to "get on with the game."

Social System

Because the teacher selects the simulation activity and directs the students through carefully delineated activities, the social system of simulation is rigorous. Within this structured system, however, a cooperative, interactive environment can and ideally should flourish. The ultimate success of the simulation, in fact, depends partly on the cooperation and willing participation of the students. Working together, the students share ideas, which are subject to peer evaluation but not teacher evaluation. The peer social system, then, should be nonthreatening and marked by cooperation.

Teacher's Role

Educational simulations enable students to learn from the simulated experiences built into the games, rather than from the teacher's explanations or lectures. The teacher's role in using an educational simulation is one of *explaining, refereeing,* and *coaching.*.

Of course, in using the Simulation Model the teacher still has the responsibility of instructing students in subject matter, as she does in other aspects of the course. However, when the students are engaged directly in the simulation activity, the teacher should suspend her more traditional role. When the students are discussing the game and its outcomes, the teacher plays the important role of assuring that they reflect on the game experience and consider the relationship between the game and the course content to which it is related.

Explaining the Game. To learn from a simulation, the players need to understand the rules sufficiently to carry out most of the activities in the game and to understand the implications of each move they might make. However, it is *not* essential that the students have a complete understanding of the game at the start. As in real life, many of the rules become relevant only as the game is played. The player need only know enough of the mechanics to start playing the game. Thus, repeating the rules of the game and drilling the students is unnecessary; instead, the explanation of the game should be kept to a minimum. Implications of various game moves are much clearer to students *after* they have played, and are best discussed then.

Refereeing (Controlling) the Game. Simulations used in the classroom are designed to provide educational benefits. The teacher should control student participation in the game to assure that these benefits are realized. This means that before the game is played, the teacher must assign students to teams (if the game involves teamwork) so as to best match individual capabilities with the roles in the game and to assure active participation by all students. For example, shy and assertive students should be mixed on teams. One pitfall the teacher should avoid is assigning the apparently more "difficult" roles to brighter students and the more passive roles to less academically talented students. Many simulations call upon a broader range of personal competencies than do typical classroom tasks. Besides, the more academically proficient students have already had experience in leadership roles. Simulations offer an opportunity to distribute such experiences more widely.

The teacher should recognize in advance that simulations are *active* learning situations and thus call for more freedom of movement and more talk among students than other classroom activities. The teacher's control should be like that of a referee who enforces game rules but does his best not to interfere in the game activities.

Coaching the Game. The teacher should assume the role of coach when students need coaching. This means giving players advice that enables them to play better—that is, to exploit the game's possibilities more fully. As a coach, the teacher should be a supportive advisor, *not* a preacher or a disciplinarian. In a game, players have the opportunity to make mistakes and take consequences—and learn. Furthermore, a coach does *not* play. The coaching role of the teacher should consist of offering (but not insisting on) advice only when it is solicited by players, and perhaps making some unsolicited suggestions to players who seem shy.

Discussing the Game. During the game the teacher should explain, referee, and coach. After the game the teacher should be certain to lead the class in discussing how closely the game simulates the real world, what difficulties and insights the students had in playing the game, and what relationships can be discovered between the simulation and the subject matter that the game was meant to supplement. The class might also suggest ways to improve the game!

Support System

Simulation requires support materials ranging from simple teacher-made games, to marketed games (which sell for under ten dollars to more than two hundred dollars), to specially designed simulators such as car-driving or airplane-navigating simulators (whose costs can ascend into the thousands of dollars). Simulations are gaining in popularity, and the number of published materials increases every year. The 1973 *Social Science Education Consortium Data Book* lists more than fifty simulations available for use in social studies instruction alone. (See the SSEC Data Book overviews of published simulations in Component III.) The teacher who is interested in utilizing simulations is directed to publishers' catalogues; the aforementioned *Data Book;* Ronald Klietsch, *Directory of Educational Simulations, Learning Games, and Didactic Units;* David Zuckerman and Robert Horn, *Guide to Simulation Games for Education and Training;* and Ron Stadsklev, *Handbook of Simulation Gaming in Social Education.*[11]

---

[11] *Data Handbook* (Boulder, Colo.: Social Science Education Consortium, 1971, 1972, 1973); Ronald G. Kleitsch, *Directory of Educational Simulations, Learning Games and Didactic Units* (St. Paul, Min.: Instructional Simulations, 1969); David W. Zuckerman and Robert E. Horn, *The Guide to Simulation Games for Education and Training* (Cambridge, Mass.: Information Resources, Inc., 1970); and Ron Stadsklev, *Handbook of Simulation Gaming in Social Education,* I (Textbook) and II (Directory) (Institute of Higher Education Research and Services, University of Alabama, n.d.).

The Value of Simulation Games[12]

How can students best learn from a simulation game? Although this is likely to vary from simulation to simulation and perhaps from teacher to teacher, we can distinguish two main sources of student learning. First, students may learn directly as a result of their experience in the simulation. For example, students playing the roles of decision makers in a relatively powerless nation in an international simulation may, as a direct result, learn to feel a new and heightened sense of empathy or understanding for the problems and limitations of a country like India. Here the game functions, in a sense, as a teacher.

Students may also learn as a result of activities that follow a game and that are used to exploit their experience in the game. Those who have experimented with simulations in the classroom suggest that follow-up discussions are very important if the simulations are to realize their full teaching potential. There may not be a universal way to structure these "post-mortems" on what happened in the game, but there is one strategy that has often proved successful. This is to use the students' experiences in the game as a take-off point for a discussion of their beliefs about the reality that has been simulated. The simulation, in effect, generates a universe of experience that can be compared with the "real world"; more accurately, the students can compare their experiences in the game with what they believe to be true about the real world. . . .

. . .The important thing in teaching with simulations is for the teacher to get the students to be explicit about their experience with and in the game and, from there, to examine their views of the real world or referent situation. The leading question always is, "How do you think the game (or some selected part of it) compares with the real world?" If the students claim the real world is different, then the next logical question is, "How do you think reality is different?" Next, "Why is reality different?" etc. A well-conducted simulation game will stimulate many avenues of thought that can be followed up by further study.

Learning About Competition

For the participants in games, competition and tension produced by striving against obstacles for some objective make the experience an exciting one. The competition may be against the forces of nature, as in the hunting games developed by the Education Development Center (formerly Educational Services, Inc.). . . .

Learning Cooperation

No educational game, however, is designed to teach ruthless competition, and most demonstrate the advantages of cooperative effort. Fifth graders playing "Seal Hunting" soon learn that the alternative to sharing is starvation. . . .

Learning Empathy

The degree to which games successfully foster cooperative or nonaggressive attitudes seems to depend, at least in part, on the extent to which students

[12] William A. Nesbitt, *Simulation Games for the Social Studies Classroom* (New York: Foreign Policy Association, 1971), excerpts from pp. 38-53.

become involved in their roles. The more strongly the player identifies with his role, the more likely he is to develop sensitivity to and understanding of the individual whose role he has assumed. . . .

Learning About the Social System

Moreover, students are not only acting out another person's role and hopefully gaining insights thereby, but are also learning about the social system or process being modeled. Players of "Napoli" learn something about the legislative process, including the desirability of bargaining, the importance of pleasing enough of their constituents to be reelected, and the place and importance of political parties. . . .

Learning Concepts

The importance of teaching concepts—an idea that underlies both the "new math" and the "new social studies"—has generally been enthusiastically endorsed by proponents of games. In their view, in fact, games are uniquely fitted to convey conceptual knowledge. . . .

Developing Efficacy

Teaching a youngster that his behavior can have some effect upon his environment—even the global one—may be fundamental to meaningful learning. James S. Coleman, well known both for his studies of adolescents and for his work with games, wrote, in "Equality of Opportunity," a report for the Department of Health, Education, and Welfare: "If a child feels that his environment is capricious, or random, or beyond his ability to alter, then he may conclude that attempts to affect it are not worthwhile, and stop trying." In the simulated environment of a game, students learn that there is a causal relationship between their behavior and the outcome of events. The Johns Hopkins' "Life Career Game" seems to have been particularly successful in teaching students that what they do now will affect their future. As one participant put it, "The game was delightful and interesting and offered an extremely new way to plan for the future." In short, students who actually see the results of game behavior acquire a greater feeling of efficacy. In the words of Dr. Boocock, they gain "confidence to act upon what is learned." . . .

Learning Skills

While the student is learning through play that his environment is at least somewhat responsive to his own actions, he is also learning some of the necessary skills for attaining his objectives. In the "Life Career Game," for example, the student learns the skill of applying to college as he plans the life of a fictitious person. . . .

Learning to Pay the Penalty

Whether from lack of skill or poor judgment, students are bound to make mistakes in games; indeed, learning by failing may be one of the principal values of classroom simulation. As one game designer put it, "They cannot learn that they have made mistakes unless they can make mistakes—and making a mistake in history means making a wrong decision, not failing to remember a date." And it is important that these mistakes are penalized in games in a manner less damaging than in real life situations. . . .

Dr. Coleman has pointed out the learning advantages that result when penalties are imposed by rules of the game or peers instead of by authority figures. Too often rebellion or hostility toward adult, "square" society interferes with learning valuable behavior, especially during adolescence. In the simulation environment the teacher is without authority, often a mere bystander; so whatever lessons students learn come from the game itself. Sometimes peers do the punishing. Fifth graders who refuse to share seals with their fellow Eskimos in "Seal Hunting" must bear the brunt of bitter resentment from other members of the game community, who are facing starvation. Similarly in "Community Disaster," students who try to put their own selfish interests before the interest of the community as a whole will have to face the disapproval of peers who suffer accordingly. Sometimes the "punishing" is more impersonal, as happens in computer-based games. In the "Sumerian Game" the computer admonishes or congratulates the player by typing such responses to his decisions as, "You have done well, Bobby," or "Your people are starving. What will you do?"

Learning the Role of Chance

Most games introduce some element of chance in order to replicate the real world and teach the student that it is not completely amenable to his manipulation. News releases report false information. Ships are beset by storms and sink in "The Game of Empire," and grain is destroyed by rats in "The Sumerian Game."

. . .The introduction of chance happenings can give students a more realistic sense that while they cannot avoid bad luck they at least can reduce its impact by good planning. For example, in the Johns Hopkins' "Consumer Game" a student who draws a chance card saying that he has had an accident and must pay $100 in doctor's bills learns, hopefully, that if he has some money set aside for emergencies he is not faced with a catastrophe. Or, in the "Life Career Game" a chance card saying that he is faced with a divorce if he and his wife have not graduated from high school is not considered to be a problem if the couple have finished their secondary education before getting married. . . .

Learning to Think Critically

A final value claimed for games is their ability to teach critical thinking to the players: examining alternative strategies, anticipating those of others and analyzing the validity of the simulation. Often students must see through ruses, be prepared for military feints or recognize specious arguments of a legislator pressing for the passage of a bill. In a word, games expose students to the adult requirements of analysis and judgment involved in decision making.

There is general agreement that the most vital part of the learning process in games is the de-briefing or post-mortem period, when the teacher encourages the players to criticize the game on its own terms: whether its rules, playability, and outcomes were satisfactory—indeed, whether the simulation was even worth their time. Students are also asked to consider whether the game really mirrored some reality. Most important of all, they are asked to analyze the defects or shortcomings in the social process or system that was simulated. Through a simulation of the international system, for example, students may discover that peaceful solutions to conflicts are difficult to achieve and may be induced to seek better machinery for the purpose. They may come to understand the cost of armaments in terms of human needs or consumer satisfactions and realize the desirability of arms limitation. Similarly, playing a game simulating the legislative process may lead students to consider the means that could enable legislators to follow their consciences rather than the election returns.

Cybernetic Psychology and the Classroom Teacher

The cybernetic psychologist attempts to study human beings by making analogies between human information processing systems and electronic feedback systems, and attempts to apply those analogies to the development of training devices. Simulators are only one variety of the training devices that have resulted from this application of cybernetic principles, but they are an interesting variety and they show the possibilities in the area. Teachers can use cybernetic principles in two ways. First, of course, they can use game-type simulations, or other simulations, in their own teaching. Social studies teachers can use games prepared by the High School Geography Project,[13] the urban simulator developed by the Urban Studies Council of Washington, D.C., or the *Inter-National Simulation* or any of a wide variety of other games that have been prepared in that area. In driver training and other areas, simulation is frequently used not merely as an aid to instruction but as a primary vehicle for instruction. In fact, the principle of simulation—that is, that people learn from the dynamic consequences of their own action—can be employed by any teacher who will help students to engage in realistic activity, to apprehend the results of their behavior, and to learn to modify their behavior by understanding what they are doing. For example, teacher-trainers now frequently use television tape as an aid: Young teachers are taped as they teach and afterward the tape is played back to them. As they analyze the tape they begin to see more clearly the consequences of their behavior and can attempt to modify it. Some young teachers discover that the type and amount of questions they ask affect the responses of their students. If they ask questions requiring their students to think, the students are more likely to respond with thinking than if they ask questions that permit the students simply to recall information or follow directions. Learning this about students' behavior, the teachers can begin to modify their own behavior—by asking questions that will pull more thinking from the students and challenge them more completely.

Summary

In this section we have introduced the fundamentals of the Simulation Model. We have presented the four phases through which simulation activities progress, and have delineated the teacher's role and principles of reaction. Likewise, we have

[13] Social Science Education Consortium, *High School Geography Project* (New York: Macmillan, 1970).

outlined the environmental social and support systems. The skills to be developed and the knowledge obtained by the students through simulation will be illustrated in the transcript lessons in Components I and II. Further discussion and training in simulation is presented in the Component III of this model.

SUMMARY CHART: THE SIMULATION MODEL

Syntax

Phase One: Orientation
   A. presentation of the broad topic of simulation and the concepts to be incorporated into the simulation activity at hand
   B. explanation of simulation and gaming

Phase Two: Participant Training
   A. setting up the scenario (rules, roles, procedures, scoring, types of decisions to be made, goals)
   B. role assignments
   C. abbreviated practice session

Phase Three: Simulation Operations
   A. game activity and game administration
   B. feedback and evaluation (of performance and effects of decisions)
   C. clarification of misconceptions
   D. continuation of simulation

Phase Four: Participant Debriefing (any or all of the following activities)
   A. summary of events and perceptions
   B. summary of difficulties and insights
   C. analysis of process
   D. Comparison of simulation activity to the real world
   E. relation of simulation activity to course content
   F. appraising and redesigning the simulation

Principles of Reaction
   1. Do not evaluate players' decisions and moves.
   2. Facilitate students' understanding and interpretation of rules.
   3. Encourage participation and help the students cope with uncertainty.
   4. Tell the students to "get on with the game" when necessary.

Social System

The social system is structured by the teacher through selecting materials and directing the simulation. The interactive environment of the class, however, should be non-threatening and marked by cooperation.

The Teacher's Role
   1. manages simulation (takes care of organization and logistics)
   2. explains game
   3. referees game (maintains rules)
   4. coaches (offers advice, prompts)
   5. debriefs (conducts interview or discussion on simulation experience)

Support System

Simulation requires a carefully structured base of resource materials.

Students Skills and Knowledge That Are Developed
1. learning about competition
2. learning cooperation
3. learning empathy
4. learning about the social system
5. learning concepts
6. developing efficacy in simulation activities
7. learning simulation skills
8. learning to pay the penalty
9. learning the role of chance
10. learning to think critically

THEORY IN PRACTICE

No amount of description can convey a sense of a model of teaching as well as an example of the model in practice. In fact, reading too much theory before gaining a rough "image" of the practice can be confusing and, for some people, frustrating and discouraging. So we encourage you, at this point of your study of the Simulation Model, to read the following abbreviated transcript of an actual classroom session. We suggest that you first read only the teacher-student dialogue and then go back to note the annotations. Remember, the goal at this point in your training is to gain a sense of the model—its flow and feeling—not to master the techniques of implementation.

T: THIS GAME IS CALLED HANG UP. WHAT THE GAME IS DESIGNED TO DO IS HELP US WORK ON OUR HANG-UPS. LIKE A PILOT LEARNING TO FLY IN THE SIMULATOR GETS OVER SOME OF HIS PROBLEMS, THIS IS DESIGNED TO HELP US GET OVER SOME OF THE PROBLEMS WE HAVE WITH OUR FEELINGS. BUT WE DO IT RIGHT HERE. FOR EXAMPLE, SOME OF THE THINGS YOU'LL BE ASKED TO DO ARE TO BE VERY ANGRY. NOW WE CAN ACT THAT OUT HERE, YOU KNOW, WITHOUT HURTING ANYBODY AND LEARN HOW TO CONTROL OUR ANGER; WHEREAS OTHERWISE WE GO OUT AND GET ANGRY, YOU KNOW, AND WE HAVE TROUBLE WITH REAL PEOPLE IN REAL SITUATIONS. SO IT IS DESIGNED TO HELP CONTROL OUR FEELINGS. AND YOU'RE GOING TO PLAY IT AND I'M JUST GOING TO KIND OF BE THE MASTER OF CEREMONIES FOR A WHILE. YOU KNOW WHAT I MEAN? AND THEN GRADUALLY I'LL TURN THE GAME OVER TO YOU UNTIL YOU'RE PLAYING THE GAME BY YOURSELVES, BUT JUST TO SAVE TIME, WE'LL JUST JUMP RIGHT IN. SO HOW ABOUT EACH PERSON PICKING ONE OF THESE PIECES. THESE ARE THE PIECES YOU MOVE AROUND THE BOARD. SOMEBODY GETS THE PENNY. PUT THEM OVER THERE NEXT TO "START," AND REMEMBER YOUR COLOR.

Phase One: Orientation
Teacher explains the purpose of the game.

S: MINE'S EASY.

T: OKAY. NOW I'M GOING TO DEAL SOME CARDS TO YOU AND I WANT YOU TO LOOK AT THE CARDS BUT DON'T READ THEM ALOUD. THAT'S IMPORTANT. OK. WE'RE IN BUSINESS. NOW, LET'S HAVE SOMEBODY START.

S: I'LL START.

T: GOOD! OKAY, GIVE US A ROLL OF THE DICE. MOVE YOUR PIECE UP AND I'LL TELL YOU WHAT TO DO NEXT.

S: OH, DOUBLES. WHAT DO I DO—JUST GO?

T: YES, GO ON UP TO SIX, OKAY, NOW SEE THESE? (points to second set of cards) THESE CARDS TELL YOU ABOUT A STRESS SITUATION YOU ARE IN. YOUR SITUATION IS THAT YOU HAVE BEEN IN AN AC-CIDENT AND YOU WAKE UP IN A HOSPITAL. IT'S A HOSPITAL IN WHICH THERE ARE ONLY WHITE PEOPLE. OK? NOW SEE IF YOU HAVE A NUMBER SIX AT THE BOTTOM OF ANY OF YOUR SEVEN CARDS. WHEN YOU COME TO A CARD THAT HAS A SIX ON IT, PULL IT OUT AND READ IT.

T: YOU'RE GOING TO USE THE HANG-UP THAT GOES WITH ALL OF THEM, ALL RIGHT? READ YOUR CARDS. OKAY, WATCH THIS NEXT STEP. READ YOUR CARD—DON'T PEEK, IT'S NOT FAIR. EACH ONE OF YOU READ YOUR CARD JUST FOR A SECOND.

S: THE ONE WITH SIX ON IT?

T: YEAH, THE ONE WITH SIX IF YOU HAVE ONE. BUT IT DOESN'T MATTER. JUST READ ONE CARD TO YOURSELF. NOW, HER CARD IS LIKE YOURS—IT HAS A HANG-UP ON IT. IT'S GOT A PROBLEM AND SHE IS GOING TO PANTOMIME—SHE IS GOING TO ACT OUT THIS HANG-UP, AND WE'RE GOING TO TRY AND GUESS WHAT THE HANG-UP IS. NOW WE'RE GOING TO GIVE ABOUT TWO MINUTES TO THAT, AND IF WE GET IT—YOU KNOW, IF SOME-BODY GETS IT BEFORE THE TWO MINUTES ARE UP—SHE GETS TO DISCARD ONE OF THESE CARDS. SHE GETS TO GET RID OF HER HANG-UP IF SHE WAS ABLE TO TELL US IN PANTOMIME WHAT IT WAS. THE PERSON WHO GUESSES IT, OR IF IT IS A TIE—TWO PEOPLE—ALSO GETS TO GET RID OF A CARD.

S: IT IS KIND OF LIKE A HARD WORD—IT IS HARD TO UNDERSTAND IT TO DO IT.

T: IT'S A TOUGHY. THIS IS A TOUGH GAME.

S: OH BOY.

T: NOW IF ANYBODY NEEDS HELP, WE'LL SNEAK OFF FOR A SECOND AND I'LL EXPLAIN. BUT THAT IS WHAT WE DO, AND THE OBJECT IS TO GET RID OF YOUR HANG-UPS. DO YOU KNOW WHAT I MEAN?

S: YEAH.

T: EVERYBODY HAS BEEN DEALT SEVEN HANG-UPS AND THE FIRST PERSON TO GET RID OF ALL HIS

Phase Two: Participant Training
Teacher leads the participants through the rules and procedures.
Phase Three: Simulation Operations
The first run-through is mainly for practice.

Teacher reads first problem for the participants to act out.

Teacher continues to explain the procedures.

HANG-UPS WINS. ALMA, JUST STAND RIGHT BACK THERE. LET'S ALL TURN AROUND JUST A LITTLE BIT SO WE CAN ALL SEE HER. AND JUST CALL OUT WHEN YOU THINK YOU KNOW WHAT HER HANG-UP IS. HER HANG-UP IS A PROBLEM, SOMETHING LIKE A PROBLEM ON YOUR CARD. PROBABLY NOT THE SAME ONE. OKAY, WE'RE IN YOUR HANDS. REMEMBER THE SITUATION SHE IS IN. SHE HAS BEEN IN AN ACCIDENT, AND SHE FINDS OUT SHE IS IN AN ALL-WHITE HOSPITAL. NOBODY ELSE.

S: SHE'S PREJUDICED.

T: SHE'S PREJUDICED. TALK TO HER. SHE'LL TELL YOU WHEN YOU GET IT.

S: ARE YOU PREJUDICED?

S: NO.

T: KEEP GOING. COME ON. GIVE US THE BUSINESS.

S: WEARY.

S: ARE YOU TRYING TO GET SOMEONE TO HELP YOU?

S: YES, A LITTLE LIKE THAT, YEAH.

T: KEEP GOING, KEEP GOING.

S: GET IN A FIGHT?

S: TEMPERAMENTAL?

S: NO.

S: DESTRUCTIVE?

S: YES, A LITTLE.

T: ALL OF THESE THINGS ARE TEMPERAMENTAL IN A SENSE. YOU ARE IN THE RIGHT PLACE. COME ON, SEE IF YOU CAN GET IT. YOU'VE GOT SOMETHING GOING BACK HERE.

S: NOW THE WHITE PEOPLE IN THE HOSPITAL ARE LOOKING.

S: YEAH.

T: WHAT IS SHE TRYING TO DO?

S: SHE SAYS NOBODY WILL HELP HER, SO SHE'S TRYING TO GET SOME HELP.

S: SHE'S TRYING TO GET SOME HELP FROM THE NURSES.

T: WHAT DOES SHE WANT THE HELP FOR?

S: BECAUSE SHE DOESN'T KNOW WHERE SHE IS AND SHE IS TRYING TO FIND OUT WHERE SHE IS.

S: SHE'S WORRYING.

T: NOT QUITE. UH-UH. SOMETHING ELSE. WHY WOULD SHE GET—SHE'S MAD—TRYING TO GET PEOPLE TO HELP HER. WHAT IS SHE MAD ABOUT?

S: SHE'S IN A WEIRD PLACE. SHE DOESN'T KNOW—

T: RIGHT. WHAT'S WEIRD ABOUT IT? BECAUSE SHE'S STUNNED, DO YOU MEAN FROM THE ACCIDENT?

The student pantomimes the hang-up she has on her card and the others try to figure out what she is acting out.

S: RIGHT.

T: NO. THAT'S NOT QUITE IT. YOU KNOW, SHE DOES LOOK A LITTLE THAT WAY. GIVE US A LITTLE BIT MORE.

S: THIS WAY? OH.

T: YOU EXAGGERATE A STRESS—INTO A CRUSADE AT TIMES. DO YOU KNOW WHAT A CRUSADE IS?

S: YES.

T: AND YOU WANT TO GET PEOPLE GOING. AND WITH YOU AS THE HERO. SO WHAT IS SHE TRYING TO DO?

S: TRYING TO GET PEOPLE NOT TO BE PREJUDICED.

T: RIGHT. SHE'S TRYING TO GET THE HOSPITAL INTEGRATED. SEE, YOU WERE ON THE RIGHT TRACK FROM THE BEGINNING. JUST THE OTHER WAY AROUND. SHE WAS TRYING TO INTEGRATE THE HOSPITAL. SHE GOT MAD, SHE WAS GOING TO BE A HERO, AND SO FORTH. THAT WAS WHAT SHE WAS TRYING TO TELL US.

YOU'RE ON PAUL. ROLL THE DICE. YOU'RE ON NEXT. LET'S SEE WHAT YOU CAN DO WITH THE HANG-UP.

S: FOUR.

T: OK. HERE'S THE HANG-UP. HERE'S THE STRESS SITUATION. YOU HAVE A FACE-TO-FACE ENCOUNTER WITH A SEPARATIST BLACK MILITANT. DO YOU KNOW WHAT THAT MEANS?

S: A PERSON—

T: WHO IS VERY BITTER ABOUT WHITE PEOPLE. DO YOU GET THE IDEA?

S: YEP.

T: IT IS PREJUDICE OF BLACKS TOWARD WHITES.

S: YEAH. RIGHT.

T: IT IS SOMEBODY WHO WANTS TO LIVE SEPARATELY—CREATE A SEPARATE BLACK COMMUNITY. ALL RIGHT.

S: AND GET THE BLACKS AWAY FROM THE WHITES.

T: RIGHT. AND THIS PERSON IS VERY BITTER ABOUT THIS. ALL RIGHT, YOU HAVE YOUR HANG-UP THERE. CAN YOU ACT IT OUT?

S: I DON'T KNOW.

T: DO YOU NEED ANY HELP FROM ME?

S: NO.

T: OK. SORRY.

S: THAT'S A HARD ONE.

T: IT IS.

S: WHEN I GET UP THERE YOU GUYS BETTER GUESS.

T: YOU'LL LIKE THIS ONE.

S: ANGRY.

Teacher helps students figure out the feelings that are being acted out.

Operations continue as another student tries to act out a stressful situation.

T: ANGRY?

S: AT SOMEBODY.

S: HE WANTS TO FIGHT.

T: YEAH. WHY DOES HE WANT TO FIGHT?

S: BECAUSE HE IS PREJUDICED.

S: HE WANTS TO FIGHT BECAUSE HE BELIEVES IN JUST WHITES.

S: DOING THEIR OWN THING.

T: COULD BE.

S: EVERYBODY IS NOT DOING THINGS HIS WAY—HE WANTS IT HIS WAY.

T: VERY NICE. VERY NICE. RIGHT ALONG THE LINE. YOU GET TO DISCARD ONE AND YOU GET TO DIS-CARD YOURS. NOW YOURS WAS ALMOST RIGHT, LANCE, EXCEPT ON THE WHOLE THESE THINGS HAVE TO DO WITH THE WAY YOU FEEL INSIDE. AND YOU KNOW, SOMETHING LIKE PREJUDICE IS KIND OF THE WAY YOU HANDLE IT. YOU CAN EITHER BE PREJUDICED OR NOT BE THE KIND OF PERSON YOU WERE RAISED AS. THAT COULD WORK EITHER WAY. SO THAT IS THE KIND OF THING YOU TRY TO ACT OUT. BUT THAT WAS VERY GOOD. REALLY NICE.

    Teacher evaluates and summarizes the action.

S: ROLL THE DICE.

S: FIVE.

T: OKAY, HERE'S A FIVE. DO YOU HAVE A CARD WITH A FIVE IN IT?

S: YEAH.

T: OKAY. LET ME READ YOU THE STRESS SITUA-TION, OK? WHEN YOU TAKE A LOOK AT YOUR OWN CARD YOU CAN GET SOME IDEA HOW YOU WOULD ACT OUT YOUR HANG-UP. JUST TAKE A LOOK FOR A MINUTE. ALL RIGHT, HERE IS THE PROBLEM. YOU ARE A NEW TEACHER.

S: ALL RIGHT.

T: YOU ARE SURPRISED TO FIND YOURSELF AS-SIGNED TO A POORLY BEHAVED, ALL-BLACK CLASS.

S: OKAY.

T: GOT IT? POORLY BEHAVED. WHY DON'T YOU SEE WHAT YOU CAN DO. WHY DON'T WE GIVE YOU A SHOT, AND THEN IF YOU GET HUNG-UP JUST YELL FOR HELP—WE'LL STAND OUTSIDE FOR A COUPLE OF MINUTES. REMEMBER, WE ARE TRY-ING TO FIGURE OUT HOW HE COPES WITH THIS. OKAY.

S: HE'S KIND OF MAD.

S: HE'S SELF-CONSCIOUS?

S: NO.

S: HE'S TRYING TO MAKE THEM HAPPY?

S: HE'S TRYING TO GO THE OTHER WAY?

S: HE HAS A LOW OPINION OF HIMSELF.

S: HE'S TELLING THEM NOT TO ACT SO SMART.

T: THINK OF HIM. THINK OF HOW HE IS COPING. IT IS HOW HE HANDLES A CRISIS.

S: HE CAN'T HANDLE IT THE SAME WAY THEY ARE.

S: HE HAS TROUBLES WITH THE KIDS THAT HE CAN'T—

S: HE'S TRYING TO HELP—

T: HOW IS HE TRYING TO COPE? HE IS UNDER STRESS—IT ISN'T WORKING.

S: HE'S TRYING TO IGNORE.

T: HE'S TRYING TO IGNORE THEM?

S: YEAH.

S: HE'S TRYING TO HELP THEM.

S: HE'S REALLY MAD BECAUSE THEY ARE NOT LISTENING.

T: IS HE MAD!

S: HE'S KIND OF DEPRESSED.

S: THEY SHOULD KNOW THE ANSWER.

T: WHAT DO YOU WANT ME TO DO?

S: HE CAN'T HELP THE KIDS BECAUSE THEY ARE NOT LISTENING—THEY AREN'T AGREEING WITH HIM.

T: HOW DOES HE FEEL TOWARDS THEM?

S: HE COULDN'T CARE LESS, IN A WAY.

T: WHAT'S HE TRYING TO PRETEND?

S: HE IS TRYING TO GET THE KIDS' ATTENTION.

S: YEAH.

T: THAT'S PRETTY NEAT. LET'S SEE WHICH ONE THAT WAS.

S: (reads hang-up card) I WAS CONTROLLING THE SIT-UATION BY PRETENDING A WARMTH THAT I DIDN'T FEEL.

T: HE WAS TRYING TO MAKE FRIENDS IN A KIND OF WAY, BUT HALF-HEARTEDLY.

S: YEAH.

T: NICE JOB, REALLY, WASN'T THAT A TOUGH ONE?

S: YEAH.

S: DID ANYBODY GET IT?

T: NONE OF US GOT IT. BUT THE ACTING OUT WAS REALLY GREAT.

S: REALLY.

T: UNFORTUNATELY, IT REQUIRES OUR COOPERA-TION.

S: YEAH. (laughs)

(Game continues as students act out various stressful situa-tions.)

T: I WANT TO TALK FOR JUST A MINUTE. WHAT DO YOU THINK YOU LEARNED FROM THIS KIND OF GAME?

S: DIFFERENT HANG-UPS OF DIFFERENT PEOPLE, ESPECIALLY THEIR TYPES OF PERSONALITY COMPARED TO DIFFERENT SITUATIONS.

S: EVERYBODY ACTS IN THE SAME WAY.

T: HOW ABOUT YOURSELVES? DID YOU FIND YOURSELF BEING AFFECTED AS WE WENT ALONG?

S: YES.

T: WHAT HAPPENED TO YOU?

S: I THOUGHT ABOUT HOW OTHER PEOPLE MIGHT ACT IN THE SAME SITUATION.

S: HOW THEY CAN ACT AGAIN AND HOW THEY ARE GOING TO DO IT AND STUFF.

S: IT MADE ME THINK BACK ON PAST EXPERIENCES AND THE WAY I LOOK AT THESE THINGS.

T: YOU BEGIN TO REIN IN YOUR FEELINGS. HOW DID YOU FEEL THIS AFTERNOON WHEN YOU WATCHED FACES, PEOPLE WALKING AROUND, AND ALL THAT?

S: ANGRY.

T: SUPPOSE YOU GOT ANGRY RIGHT NOW. WHAT WOULD YOU DO?

S: TRY NOT TO SHOW YOUR ANGER.

S: CONTROL.

T: DO YOU THINK IT HAS THAT KIND OF EFFECT? THAT'S VERY NICE. THAT'S WHAT IT IS DESIGNED TO DO, TEACH US HOW WE AND OTHERS REACT— HOW MUCH WE HAVE IN COMMON—AND TEACH US TO DO AND LEARN ABOUT STRESS SITUATIONS. WE CAN GET OURSELVES IN TUNE WITH DIFFERENT THINGS. OKAY, IF ANYBODY WANTS TO PLAY FOR A LITTLE WHILE, I'LL BE GLAD TO HAVE YOU DO IT.

Phase Four: Debriefing

Students summarize what they have learned.

Teacher encourages students to examine the insights they have gained through simulation.

Teacher asks students to reflect upon their actions in the "real world."

Teacher summarizes the purpose of this simulation.

TAKING THEORY INTO ACTION

The Phases of Simulation

Simulation games begin with the orientation of the students to the game. The rules are explained and the materials are presented to the students. A second phase of any simulation is the training of the participants to carry out their roles. For example, in some simulations there are leaders who have to organize groups, and these leaders have to be trained. In the case of a driver simulation, the student needs to be introduced to the setting and taught how to carry out the required operations with the simulated devices that are available. Phase Three consists of the simulation operations themselves. The students participate in the game or simulation, carrying out the operations that are presented to them. Phase Four is the debriefing. Here, the experience of the game is analyzed. Debriefing is especially important because the students may not have been aware of what they were learning. Children playing *Monopoly*, for example, may not have any idea about either the "real" property-trading practices they are engaged in or those that are not real. They may have learned principles for being successful in the game, but they may not be able to articulate these yet. Thus, we debrief students in order to help them raise their level of consciousness about the concepts, principles, and skills they have been learning, and to help them become aware of those that they have not learned effectively. Thus, orientation, participant training, simulation operations, and debriefing are carried out in the course of a simulation.

The Simulation Model is somewhat different from many other models of teaching in that it depends on the prior development of a simulation, either by research and development specialists, a commercial company, or a teacher or group of teachers. The simulation itself presents problems to the learners, and the learners deal with those problems as they carry out the simulation operations. The teacher's role in the first phase is to orient, explain, and organize. In the second phase he trains the participants, a task for which he may rely heavily on materials that have already been prepared. In the third phase he supervises the game, sometimes acting as a referee or a coach, and in the fourth phase he acts as a discussion leader, helping the students identify the concepts, principles, and skills that they have acquired in the course of the simulation.

THEORY CHECKUP FOR THE SIMULATION MODEL

Instructions: Circle the response that best answers the question or completes the statement. Check your answers with the key that follows:

1. Simulation Models illustrate the concept of feedback control because:
   a. there is a manager of the simulation.
   b. you can see the effect of your behavior on other persons as they respond to you.
   c. you win or lose at the end.
   d. you have control over your own behavior.

2. The theoretical basis for simulation games is derived from:
   a. reinforcement theory.
   b. role theory.
   c. cybernetic psychology.
   d. principles of learning.

3. The game of *Monopoly* lacks which of the components of simulation?
   a. chance
   b. role playing
   c. model of the system or process
   d. score card

4. List the phases of simulation.

5. A workbook in which students practice multiplying two-digit numbers lacks:
   a. positive reinforcement.
   b. directions to the learner.
   c. feedback control.
   d. careful sequencing.

6. The game of chess is or is not a simulation game?
   a. is
   b. is not

7. Which of the following is not an essential component of simulation?
   a. role playing
   b. resources
   c. goals or objectives
   d. players

8. You walk into a sixth-grade classroom and find three students trying to decide when to distribute the food rations for Day 4. Which phase of activity are they involved in?
   a. Phase Two
   b. Phase Three
   c. Lunch
   d. Phase Four

9. During a simulation game Lisa realized that bookkeeping was "not for her." This illustrates which of the following purposes of simulation?
   a. the concept of power
   b. empathy
   c. knowledge of the economic system
   d. personal growth

10. For which of the following educational activities would you *not* use the Simulation Model?
    a. teaching students to read
    b. teaching the concept of leadership styles
    c. teaching an awareness of social issues
    d. teaching the concept of culture

11. During a simulation game, Ms. Lewis whispered to one of the participants, "See what happens if you withhold the rewards." She was functioning in the capacity of:
    a. discussion leader
    b. referee
    c. coach
    d. disciplinarian

12. At the end of the *Internation Simulation* game, Ms. Lewis asks the students to take out a piece of paper so that she can test them on their knowledge of the different countries involved in the simulation. Instead of doing this, she should have:
    a. explained the rules of the game.
    b. conducted an open-ended debriefing interview.
    c. asked them if they enjoyed the game.
    d. asked them to choose new teams.

13. Programmed-instruction math materials tell students whether their answer is correct or incorrect. Does this exemplify the concept of feedback as cybernetic psychologists discuss it?

    a. yes

    b. no

Key to Theory Checkup

1. b

2. c

3. c

4. Phase One: Orientation
Phase Two: Participant Training
Phase Three: Simulation Operations
Phase Four: Participant Debriefing

5. c

6. a

7. a

8. b

9. d

10. a

11. c

12. b

13. no

Component II

VIEWING
THE MODEL

One of the purposes of Component II is to provide examples of actual sessions in which the Simulation Model is the strategy being used. Reading the demonstration transcript that follows, hearing a tape of a teacher and students, or viewing a videotape of class activity are alternate means of illustrating the "model in action."

As you study any of these alternatives, you will be introduced to the Teaching Analysis Guide for analyzing the model. This same Guide will also be used in Component III to analyze the peer teaching and microteaching lessons. We want you to become familiar with the Guide now, however, as it will sharpen your perception of the demonstration lesson.

The two activities in this component are (1) reading the Teaching Analysis Guide and (2) viewing (reading) the lesson. Before going on to them, you may wish to reread the material in the Introduction to this book that discusses the purposes and philosophy of the Teaching Analysis Guide.

Analyzing the Teaching: Activity 1

The Teaching Analysis Guide for the Simulation Model consists of sixteen questions designed to assess the occurrence of each of the phases and the implementation of the principles of reaction. In addition to the simulation itself, the phases include planning and organizational features, orientation, and participant training. Planning features may not be observable, but planning effectiveness can be inferred.

The Guide can assist you as you read the demonstration transcripts, but at this point you do not need to learn to apply it precisely. Read through the questions in the Guide that follows and identify items that you do not understand. Discuss any difficulties you may have with your instructor or your colleagues.

TEACHING ANALYSIS GUIDE FOR THE SIMULATION MODEL

This Guide is designed to help you analyze the process of teaching as you practice the Simulation Model. The analysis focuses on aspects of teaching that are important to the syntax of the model, the teacher's role, and specific teaching skills.

The Guide consists of a series of questions and phrases. As you observe a practice session (whether peer teaching or microteaching), analyze the teaching using the rating scale that appears opposite each question and statement. This scale uses the following items:

Thoroughly. This item signifies that the teacher engaged in the behavior to the point where students were responding comfortably and fluently. Appropriateness varies from situation to situation. For example, students may have had extensive experience with simulations and the teacher's explanations may be appropriately brief.

Partially. This item signifies that the teacher engaged in appropriate behavior, but not as thoroughly as possible. There is some doubt about whether the students are responding fully.

Missing. The teacher did not engage in the behavior; there appears to be a loss in student response or probably will be one.

Not Needed. The teacher did not explicitly manifest the behavior, but there is no loss. Either the behavior was included in others or the students began to respond appropriately without being led to.

For each question or statement in the Guide, circle the term that best describes the teacher's behavior.

Pre-Run Operations

1. Were all necessary decisions made and planned for?

A. number of participants	Thoroughly	Partially	Missing	Not Needed
B. physical logistics	Thoroughly	Partially	Missing	Not Needed
C. timing and sequence of events	Thoroughly	Partially	Missing	Not Needed

2. Were all support materials developed/available?

A. players' support materials	Thoroughly	Partially	Missing	Not Needed
B. supplementary instructional materials	Thoroughly	Partially	Missing	Not Needed
C. scenario presentation	Thoroughly	Partially	Missing	Not Needed

Phase One: Orientation

3. Was orientation provided:

212

TEACHING ANALYSIS GUIDE FOR THE SIMULATION MODEL

A. for the broad topic of simulation?	Thoroughly	Partially	Missing	Not Needed
B. for concepts?	Thoroughly	Partially	Missing	Not Needed
C. for simulation gaming?	Thoroughly	Partially	Missing	Not Needed

Phase Two: Participant Training

4. Did the simulation manager set up the scenario (explain the game—the rules, roles, procedures, scoring, goals, and types of decisions to be made)?	Thoroughly	Partially	Missing	Not Needed
5. Were role assignments made?	Thoroughly	Partially	Missing	Not Needed
6. Was there an abbreviated practice session?	Thoroughly	Partially	Missing	Not Needed

Phase Three: Simulation Operations

7. Did the gaming activity occur?	Thoroughly	Partially	Missing	Not Needed
8. Were the players provided with feedback and evaluation of their performance and the effect of their decisions?	Thoroughly	Partially	Missing	Not Needed
9. Did the simulation manager clarify misconceptions when necessary?	Thoroughly	Partially	Missing	Not Needed

Phase Four: Participant Debriefing

10. Which of the following focuses were introduced in the debriefing?				
A. summary of events and participants	Thoroughly	Partially	Missing	Not Needed
B. difficulties and insights	Thoroughly	Partially	Missing	Not Needed
C. projection of future events	Thoroughly	Partially	Missing	Not Needed
D. comparison of simulation to the real world	Thoroughly	Partially	Missing	Not Needed
E. relationship of simulation to course content	Thoroughly	Partially	Missing	Not Needed

213

TEACHING ANALYSIS GUIDE FOR THE SIMULATION MODEL

F. appraising and redesigning the simulation	Thoroughly	Partially	Missing	Not Needed
11. Was the teacher's role in the debriefing one of an interviewer?	Thoroughly	Partially	Missing	Not Needed

Principles of Reaction

12. Was the simulation manager non-evaluative of players' decisions and moves?	Thoroughly	Partially	Missing	Not Needed
13. Did the simulation manager facilitate the players' understanding and interpretation of the rules?	Thoroughly	Partially	Missing	Not Needed
14. Did the simulation manager encourage participation and help players cope with uncertainty, where necessary?	Thoroughly	Partially	Missing	Not Needed
15. Did the simulation manager keep the game going ("get on with the game") when players digressed or became bogged down?	Thoroughly	Partially	Missing	Not Needed
16. Did the simulation manager maintain the rules (referee the game) when necessary?	Thoroughly	Partially	Missing	Not Needed

Viewing the Lesson: Activity 2

We would like you now to read the demonstration transcript that follows, identifying the phases of the model and commenting on the lesson as an illustration of the model. On your own or with a group of your peers, record the occurrence of the phases and comment on the simulation as it is presented here.

Phase One _____	Adequate	Minimal	Not at All
Phase Two _____	Adequate	Minimal	Not at All
Phase Three _____	Adequate	Minimal	Not at All
Phase Four _____	Adequate	Minimal	Not at All

Analyzing the Lesson: Activity 3 (Optional)

View a live, filmed, or taped demonstration and analyze the lesson using the Teaching Analysis Guide. This can be done in two ways: either complete the Guide as you view the tape, or complete it afterward.

If you are viewing the lesson in a group, you may want to divide the task of analysis, with one or more of your colleagues taking a particular phase or aspect of analysis. Duplicate as many copies of the Guide as are needed.

DEMONSTRATION TRANSCRIPT

The following transcript introduces you to a group of students who are engaged in a simulation—the game of *Bafa*. *Bafa* organizes students into two groups, and each group learns the characteristics of a simulated culture. The students' task is to learn the traditions and communication devices used by the other group by trying to communicate with one another. The participants are given a brief orientation in which the purposes of the game are explained. They are then divided into two groups, or "cultures." The members of each group are given a set of rules to govern their behavior as members of the new culture.

The Alpha culture is a relaxed culture that values personal contact and intimacy within a sexist and patriarchal structure. The Beta culture, on the other hand, is an aggressive, money-oriented culture in which a person's value is measured by how well he performs in the marketplace.

Each group spends time learning the rules of their new society. Once all of the members understand and feel comfortable with the new way of behaving, observers are exchanged. The observers attempt to learn as much as possible about the values, norms, customs, and reward system of the other culture without directly asking about them. After a fixed time, the observers return to their own group and report on what they saw. Based on the information provided by the observers, each group tries to develop hypotheses about the most effective way to interact with the other culture. After the hypothesis-generating discussion, the cultures proceed as before, except that each person takes a turn trying to interact with the other culture. Once everyone has had a chance to "live off the economy of the other culture," the game is ended and a debriefing is held.

This lesson was taught by Joel Morine and Katie Barreras, who were working with junior and senior high school students from the Alum Rock and Mount Pleasant School Districts in East San Jose, California.

T: SIMULATIONS ARE OPERATING MODELS OF PHYSICAL AND SOCIAL SITUATIONS. AN EXAMPLE OF SIMULATION WOULD BE MATERIALS AND ACTIVITIES THE SPACE PROGRAM USES TO GIVE ASTRONAUTS EXPERIENCES SIMILAR TO THE EXPERIENCES THEY HAVE IN SPACE, BEFORE THEY SEND THEM UP IN SPACE. ANOTHER EXAMPLE OF A SIMULATION WOULD BE A WIND TUNNEL IN WHICH AIRPLANE PARTS ARE TESTED ON THE GROUND. THE PARTS ARE PUT IN A WIND TUNNEL TO SEE HOW THEY WILL ACT WHEN THEY ARE IN HIGH-SPEED WINDS IN THE SKY. THE WORD SIMULATION CAN ALSO REFER TO THE USE OF SYMBOLIC MODELS OF SOCIAL SITUATIONS. HIGH SCHOOL GOVERNMENT CLASSES SOMETIMES HOLD SIMULATIONS OF PRESIDENTIAL ELECTIONS.

THERE ARE TWO THINGS THAT MAKE A SIMULATION QUALITATIVELY DIFFERENT FROM THE REALITY THAT IT REPRESENTS. ONE IS THAT IT'S

Phase One: Orientation
The teacher begins with a brief description of simulation.

REDUCED IN SIZE TO MAKE IT MORE MANAGE-
ABLE. THE SECOND THING IS THAT IT'S SIMPLI-
FIED. IF YOU TAKE THE EXAMPLE OF A HIGH
SCHOOL CLASS DOING A SIMULATION OF A PRESI-
DENTIAL ELECTION, YOU'D USE FEWER VOTERS
AND YOU'D USE LESS TIME FOR THE CAMPAIGN
THAN YOU WOULD IN A REAL ELECTION, SO
THAT IT IS SIMPLER TO DEAL WITH. SOME OF
THE THINGS THAT A REAL PRESIDENTIAL CANDI-
DATE WOULD HAVE TO DO, YOU WOULDN'T DO IN
A CLASS THAT WAS DOING A SIMULATION OF AN
ELECTION. FOR INSTANCE, YOU WOULDN'T HAVE
TO STUFF ENVELOPES WITH LETTERS ASKING
PEOPLE FOR CONTRIBUTIONS.

THIS IS GOING TO BE A SIMULATION OF WHAT IT
IS TO VISIT A DIFFERENT CULTURE FROM YOUR
OWN, A CULTURE THAT BEHAVES WITH DIFFER-
ENT RULES AND EXPECTATIONS THAN YOUR
OWN CULTURE. CULTURE IS LEARNED BEHAVIOR.
IT'S NOT BIOLOGICALLY INHERITED. THE CUL-
TURE OF A TRIBE OR A NATION INCLUDES THE
LIST OF THINGS I'VE GIVEN YOU, AND SOME
OTHER THINGS. YOU MIGHT WANT TO LOOK AT
THE LIST WHILE I'M TALKING ABOUT IT.

THE CULTURE OF A TRIBE OR NATION INCLUDES
THAT SOCIETY'S RELIGION, ART, POLITICS,
TECHNOLOGY, MUSIC, ECONOMY, JOKES, CUS-
TOMS, FOOD, HOLIDAYS, CONDITIONS, VALUES,
CLOTHING, ANY OTHER MATERIAL POSSESSIONS,
STYLE OF COMMUNICATION, TRANSPORTATION.
ALL THOSE THINGS ARE PART OF YOUR CUL-
TURE, AND SOME OF THOSE THINGS CHANGE
FROM ONE CULTURE TO ANOTHER. WITHIN A
CULTURE, WHEN ANY ONE OF THESE THINGS
CHANGES DRASTICALLY, IT CAN CAUSE ANY OF
THE OTHERS TO CHANGE. RECENT CHANGES IN
TECHNOLOGY IN OUR COUNTRY, SUCH AS MOOG
SYNTHESIZERS, HAVE MADE POSSIBLE NEW
KINDS OF AMERICAN MUSIC. INCREASING RE-
SPECT FOR THE OPINIONS AND TALENTS OF WO-
MEN HAS CREATED CHANGES IN OUR ECONOMY,
OUR POLITICS, AND SOME OF OUR CUSTOMS,
SUCH AS DATING AND MARRIAGE. IT HAS
CREATED A WHOLE NEW SET OF JOKES ABOUT
WOMEN'S LIBBERS AND CHAUVINIST PIGS AND
SUCH. SO THAT'S ANOTHER EXAMPLE OF HOW
CHANGES IN ONE PART OF A CULTURE CAN
CHANGE OTHER ASPECTS. SO, VALUES, AN IN-
STITUTION'S BEHAVIOR, AND TECHNOLOGY IN
CULTURE INFLUENCE ONE ANOTHER.

WITHIN ONE NATION OR TRIBE, ALL OF THESE
ASPECTS OF CULTURE MAY CHANGE WITH THE
PASSING OF TIME. THEY CHANGE FROM ONE
CULTURE TO ANOTHER, AND FROM ONE PLACE
TO ANOTHER WITHIN THE SAME NATION OR
TRIBE.

The teacher briefly describes the concept of
culture, which is central to this simulation
game.

NOW I'LL GIVE YOU AN IDEA OF WHAT WE'RE GOING TO DO TODAY. THE OUTLINE ON THE BLACKBOARD IS THE ACTUAL SEQUENCE OF THE GAME ITSELF. WE'LL BE FOLLOWING IT THROUGH, AND YOU'LL GET A DEEPER EXPLANATION OF IT WHEN YOU'VE DIVIDED INTO GROUPS. YOU'LL BE DIVIDED INTO TWO GROUPS, AND JOEL AND I WILL BE TEACHING TWO SEPARATE CULTURES. EACH OF US WILL GIVE YOU THE RULES OF YOUR CULTURE, AND WE WILL TRY TO GIVE YOU THE REASONS FOR LEARNING THEM. AFTER WE FEEL THAT YOU'RE COMFORTABLE WITH THE RULES OF YOUR CULTURE, WE'LL EXCHANGE OBSERVERS; JOEL WILL SEND FOUR TO MY GROUP, AND I WILL SEND FOUR TO HIS GROUP. AFTERWARDS, THE OBSERVERS WILL COME BACK AND WE WILL DISCUSS WHAT THEY HAVE OBSERVED. THEN THERE WILL BE SEVERAL OTHER VISITS BETWEEN THE CULTURES.

WE HAVE THREE GOALS IN MIND THAT WE WANT TO ACCOMPLISH THROUGH THIS GAME. ONE IS TO BE ABLE TO UNDERSTAND WHAT A CULTURE IS. TWO IS TO BE ABLE TO BECOME AWARE OF YOUR OWN FEELINGS ABOUT YOUR ATTEMPTS TO INTERACT WITH ANOTHER CULTURE AND YOUR INTERPRETATIONS OF HOW YOU ARE ABLE TO SENSE WHAT THE OTHER CULTURE IS LIKE. THREE IS TO SEE HOW QUICKLY YOU ARE ABLE TO ADAPT TO A NEW CULTURE. SO, THESE THREE IDEAS OR GOALS WILL BE WHAT WE'LL BE THINKING OF DOING IN A LITTLE WHILE.

(The teacher now addresses only half of the class. The other half is receiving instructions on the second culture—Beta—from the second teacher.)

T: OUR CULTURE IS GOING TO BE ALPHA. WE'RE ALL FROM ALPHA AS SOON AS YOU'VE GOTTEN TIME TO READ THROUGH THE SOCIAL RULES OF ALPHA. ALSO READ THE OTHER SIDE.

AS YOU NOTICE, ALPHA IS SUPPOSED TO BE A VERY WARM CULTURE, FROM WHAT IT SAYS HERE. YOU LOVE TO ENJOY AND DEVELOP FRIENDSHIPS. IT IS UNDERSTOOD THAT EACH OF THE FRIENDSHIPS ARE TO BE TAKEN WITHIN A VERY STRICT SET OF RULES, AND WE WILL GO INTO THESE FURTHER. ALSO, WE ALPHAS HONOR SICK, OLDER PEOPLE. IN THIS CULTURE THE OLDEST MENTOR LEADS THE GROUP. ALSO, FEMALES ARE CONSIDERED TO BE OWNED BY THE MALES OF THE CULTURE, AND STRANGERS DO NOT APPROACH FEMALES WITHOUT APPROVAL OF MALES. NOW, WHEN WE'RE INTERACTING, THIS IS GOING TO BE VERY IMPORTANT BECAUSE IF, BY ANY CHANCE, ANY OF YOU MALES SEE ANY PERSON FROM THE OTHER CULTURE COMING TO APPROACH A FEMALE, YOU MIGHT EITHER TELL THEM TO LEAVE THEM ALONE OR

Phase Two: Paticipant Training

The teacher outlines the purpose and rules of the simulation activity.

The teacher clarifies the goals of the game.

The teacher directs the students to read the rules of the Alpha culture by themselves.

The teacher reviews the rules of the Alpha culture with the class.

KICK THEM OUT. WE MUST HAVE SOME ACTION, BUT VIOLENCE IS NOT PERMISSIBLE IN YOUR CULTURE.

(The teacher demonstrates the activity in an abbreviated practice session.)

(Phase III begins with each culture sending four observers to the other culture. During the observation, each culture behaves according to its norms, simulating the Alpha and Beta cultures. The visitors, returning to their own cultures, tell the members of their culture what they have observed in the other culture. Next, each culture sends four visitors who will attempt to interact with the alien culture. The students visit one another's "cultures," observing the behavior of the newly-formed little society. The teacher is talking with the Alpha culture after the second visitation.)

Phase Three: Simulation Operations

T: LET'S GET A REPORT FROM THE VISITORS TO THE OTHER CULTURE. WHAT WE'RE GOING TO HAVE TO DO NOW IS—FROM OUR INFORMATION THAT WE'VE GATHERED FROM OUR OBSERVERS, FROM THE FIRST VISIT AND THE SECOND VISIT— WE HAVE TO FIGURE OUT WHAT THAT OTHER CULTURE IS LIKE. WHAT ARE ITS VALUES? WHAT RULES DO THEY FOLLOW, AND ARE THERE ANY MORALS—AS, FOR EXAMPLE, OUR NORM THAT NO MALE CAN APPROACH A FEMALE WITHOUT APPROVAL OF MALES? LET'S SEE WHAT THE VISITORS HAVE TO SAY, AND EVERYONE ELSE CAN ASK QUESTIONS. OKAY, WHO WERE THE VISITORS? WHY DON'T EACH OF YOU TAKE A TURN?

The teacher directs the class to give feedback on and evaluations of environmental stimuli they have encountered in their contact with the Beta culture.

S: I THINK WHEN THEY BLINK THEIR EYES THEY WANT TO TRADE WITH YOU. I'M NOT SURE, BUT—

S: OR TO TELL YOU TO GO FIRST.

S: AND WHEN YOU SPOKE ENGLISH TO THEM THEY'D COVER UP THEIR EARS AS IF THEY DIDN'T UNDERSTAND IT OR WOULDN'T SPEAK IT.

S: THEY DIDN'T TALK, AND WHEN YOU TALKED TO THEM THEY'D COVER UP THEIR EARS.

S: CPCT WAS SOME KIND OF NUMBER.

S: I GUESS THEY SAID THAT AS MANY TIMES AS THEY WANTED THE CARD TO BE.

S: I SAID IT THREE TIMES—CPCTCP—AND SHE WENT LIKE THIS (body movements), AND I SAID IT TWICE AND SHE GAVE ME CARDS.

T: WHAT WAS MEANT BY "NO"?

S: LIKE THIS (body movements) OR THIS (body movements), AND THEN I SAID IT TWICE AND SHE GAVE ME A CARD.

T: WHAT WAS THE CARD?

S: THIS ONE.

T: WERE YOU ABLE TO COMMUNICATE WITH THEM? WERE YOU ABLE TO GO THROUGH A WHOLE GAME WITH THEM?

S: I DID, AND THAT'S HOW I FIGURED OUT THE

Note the interaction among the students.

COLORS BY JUST—WHEN I'D PICK UP A CARD, SHE WOULD SAY IT.

T: ANY QUESTIONS?

S: WHEN YOU SAID FOUR—YOU WANT FOUR GREEN CARDS—YOU WENT LIKE THAT (body movement).

S: ON THE CARDS THAT THEY WANT, THEY HAVE THE NUMBERS ON IT.

S: YEAH, BUT I DON'T KNOW IF THAT'S THE WAY, BECAUSE I DID THAT ONE TIME AND I ASKED FOR A GREEN CARD—AND I DID FOUR TIMES—AND I SAW IT IN HER HAND, BUT SHE DIDN'T GIVE IT TO ME. SHE JUST SHRUGGED HER SHOULDERS AND LAUGHED.

S: I ALWAYS PICKED UP THE CARDS—TO SEE IF SHE WOULD GIVE IT TO ME. THE GIRL I ASSOCIATED WITH, SHE DID IT.

T: SO WHAT ARE WE LOOKING FOR IN THEIR CULTURE?

S: THEY DON'T SPEAK ENGLISH.

T: WHAT ELSE?

S: THEY'RE COLOR-ORIENTED.

S: FIRST THEY SAID THE COLOR—RIGHT? THEN THEY'D SAY SOMETHING ELSE. WHAT DOES IT MEAN AFTER THE COLOR—

S: THEY SAID, "CHOO."

T: WHAT DID THAT MEAN?

S: THEY WERE KEEPING SCORE ON THE BOARD, TOO. WE HAD A DIFFERENT SCORE. YOU'D HAND IN THE CARDS AND GET SO MANY POINTS FOR THEM.

S: ONE OF THEM DID TALK ENGLISH. BUT I'D ASK HIM, "HOW COME YOU WANT ALL THE GREENS?" AND HE GOES TO GET A CERTAIN NUMBER, AND THAT'S WHEN I LOOKED ON THE BOARD, 'CAUSE HE'D GO HAND IN ALL HIS GREEN CARDS, AND THEN HE'D CHANGE THE SCORE.

T: OK, WE'VE TALKED ABOUT LANGUAGE. WHAT ABOUT VALUES? DO THEY HAVE ANY VALUES OR ANY RULES YOU MUST FOLLOW AS TO BEHAVING? COMPARED TO WHAT WE'RE LIKE, WHAT DO YOU THINK THEY'RE LIKE?

S: (laughs) THEY DON'T CARE—THAT'S WHAT IT SEEMED LIKE.

S: SHOCKINGLY ENOUGH, WHEN I WAS THERE I SAW A GUY ACTUALLY GO UP TO A GIRL, AND HE DIDN'T EVEN GET PERMISSION FROM ANYBODY.

S: I DON'T THINK THEY HAVE TO, 'CAUSE ALL THE GUYS JUST WALKED UP TO MEET ME, AND ALL THE GIRLS WALKED UP TO WHOEVER THEY WANTED TO.

T: WAS THERE A SHOW OF EMOTION?

S: YEAH, ONE TIME THE TEACHER CAME UP TO ME

The teacher directs the students to make hypotheses about the Beta culture.

Again the teacher directs the students to make hypotheses about the Beta culture.

AND STARTED BLINKING HIS EYES, AND I GO, "CAN YOU SEE?" AND HE COVERED HIS EARS, AND I GO, "CAN YOU HEAR?" AND I'D GO THINGS LIKE THAT, AND THEN WHEN I SPOKE ENGLISH TO HIM HE COVERED HIS EARS AND THEN HE WALKED AWAY, AND THEN HE KEPT COMING BACK TO ME.

T: DO THEY TURN AROUND OR SOMETHING LIKE THAT?

S: YES. AND THEN THEY'D TURN AWAY FROM ME.

T: COMPARING THEM TO OUR CULTURE—AND WE ALL KNOW OUR CULTURE IS WHAT?

S: WE'RE SUPPOSED TO BE VERY FRIENDLY.

T: OKAY, ARE THEY THAT WAY?

S: NO, THEY DIDN'T TALK TO US. THEY'D JUST WALK AWAY.

S: AFTER THEY GOT WHAT THEY WANTED—THEIR CARD THAT THEY WANTED—THEY JUST LEFT RIGHT AWAY. NO SMALL TALK OR FRIENDLINESS, KIND OF RUDE.

S: LIKE THE TEACHER WHO ASSOCIATED WITH ME, HE GOT MAD. HE LOOKED LIKE HE GOT UPSET WHEN I WASN'T SPEAKING HIS LANGUAGE, AND HE TURNED AWAY.

(The second teacher is talking with the Beta culture. This is taking place at the same time as the preceding Alpha-culture discussion.)

T: SINCE A FEMALE CANNOT APPROACH A MALE, THE MALE MUST COME TO THE FEMALE, BUT THEY MUST HAVE THE SIGNATURE OF THE ELDER. AND HE DID NOT GET THE SIGNATURE FROM THE ELDER AND WAS EXPELLED FROM THE CULTURE. ANY OTHER IMPRESSIONS ON HOW YOU FELT THIS GAME SIMULATION AFFECTED YOU? IS IT ABLE TO MAKE YOU UNDERSTAND WHAT THE CONCEPT OF CULTURE IS? IN WHAT WAY, LAURIE?

S: IT'S JUST LIKE LEARNING TO TALK THIS WAY.

T: HOW MANY DIFFERENT THINGS WERE THERE THAT WE GOT CROSSED UP ON GOING FROM ONE CULTURE TO ANOTHER? HOW MANY DIFFERENT, INCOMPREHENSIBLE THINGS?

The teacher prompts the class to bring out different aspects of the other culture.

S: LANGUAGE.

T: ANYTHING ELSE?

S: THE WAY THAT WE USED OUR HANDS AND OUR HEAD.

S: HOW WE WERE SAYING IT.

T: OK, ANYTHING ELSE THAT DIDN'T MAKE SENSE WHEN YOU WERE OVER THERE?

S: THE TYPE OF GAME.

T: WHAT ABOUT THE TYPE OF GAME?

S: OURS WAS FOR POINTS AND THEIRS WASN'T.

T: SO WE WERE TRYING TO GET POINTS AND THEY WEREN'T—WHICH IS WHAT? GOALS, CALL IT GOALS—VALUES—THE RULES. THAT'S FOUR THINGS—LANGUAGE, GESTURES, GOALS, RULES. ARE THERE ANY OTHERS?

S: YOUR FEELINGS TOWARD THE OTHER PERSON.

T: HOW DO YOU MEAN?

S: WELL, WHEN THE PEOPLE THAT CAME OVER HERE WERE TRYING TO BE NICE TO US. WE JUST, LIKE, WANTED TO GET WHAT WE WANTED AND THAT WAS IT.

T: HOW DID YOU FEEL WHILE YOU WERE TRYING TO LEARN THE RULES OF THE MAKE-BELIEVE CULTURE?

S: WEIRD.

T: WHAT WAS YOUR—HOW DID YOU FEEL BEING PUT IN A SITUATION AND TOLD WHAT TO DO AND HOW TO BEHAVE?

S: IT WAS HARD, BECAUSE I'D TRY TO FIGURE OUT ONE THING AND I'D THINK THAT I HAD ONE THING FIGURED OUT—THE WAY IT WAS—AND THEN YOU'D GO TALK TO SOMEBODY ELSE AND THEY'D CHANGE IT ALL AROUND, AND IT WAS REAL HARD TRYING TO PUT IT ALL TOGETHER— SO YOU CAN FIND OUT WHAT THEIR CULTURE IS.

T: WAS IT EASIER FOR YOU TO ADAPT TO THE CUL- TURE YOU WERE LEARNING IN COMPARISON TO THE CULTURE THAT YOU WERE ACTUALLY IN- TERACTING WITH?

S: YEAH, IT WAS A LOT EASIER LEARNING THIS ONE. YOU KNEW HOW EVERYTHING WAS SET UP— HOW EVERYTHING WAS SUPPOSED TO GO—BUT THE OTHER ONE—YOU'RE JUST THROWN IN THERE—HAD TO GO BY WHATEVER YOUR REAC- TIONS WERE.

T: WHICH WAS MORE INTERESTING—MAYBE A SHOW OF HANDS—WHO FOUND IT MORE INTERESTING LEARNING THEIR OWN CULTURE THAN BEING A VISITOR TO THE OTHER CULTURE?

S: I LIKED VISITING THEM, 'CAUSE IT'S MORE OF A CHALLENGE. IT WAS SOMETHING—WE ALREADY KNOW OUR CULTURE AND WE WANTED TO KNOW OTHER PEOPLE'S CULTURE, HOW THEY LIVED, WHAT THEY DID. WE ARE MORE OR LESS LEARN- ING MORE FROM THEIR—WE WERE JUST LEARN- ING MORE OVERALL. IT WAS THE CHALLENGE OF TRYING TO FIGURE OUT HOW THEY LIVED— WHAT THEY DO.

T: ANYONE ELSE WANT TO ADD TO WHAT SHE SAID?

S: YES, SOMETHING THAT COMES TO EVERYBODY IS BEING CURIOUS. SO YOU KNOW YOU'RE REALLY INTERESTED IN FINDING OUT WHAT EVERYBODY ELSE IS DOING. INSTEAD OF THEM COMING OVER HERE AND YOU LEARN YOUR OWN THING, YOU

The teacher here condenses and labels all points made thus far.

Note that the teacher does not evaluate the stu- dent's response; she simply accepts it.

GO OVER TO ANOTHER CULTURE AND YOU TRY AND FIGURE IT OUT—TRY AND UNDERSTAND IT BETTER, INSTEAD OF HAVING IT EXPLAINED TO YOU. YOU'LL PROBABLY LEARN IT BETTER BY JUST GOING OVER AND TRYING TO FIGURE IT OUT BY YOURSELF.

T: WHICH OF THE FEELINGS THAT YOU HAD VISITING THE OTHER CULTURE—I'VE HEARD CURIOSITY MENTIONED, AND I'VE HEARD THE FEELING THAT YOU'RE STUPID, AN OUT-OF-PLACE FEELING, OR THAT YOU'RE KIND OF INSULTING, AND ALSO THE FEELING THAT YOU'VE BEEN INSULTED. WHICH OF THOSE FEELINGS DO YOU THINK YOU WOULD ALSO EXPERIENCE IF YOU WERE TO GO TO SOME FOREIGN COUNTRY WHERE THEY SPOKE ANOTHER LANGUAGE—SAY GERMANY OR RUSSIA OR CHINA OR VIETNAM—ANY OF THOSE COUNTRIES?

The teacher now directs the class to compare their simulation experience to the real world.

S: YOU'D BE KIND OF SCARED AND OUT OF PLACE AND NOT KNOWING WHAT TO SAY AND BE AFRAID YOU MIGHT SAY THE WRONG THING AND OFFEND SOMEONE OR DO SOMETHING WRONG THAT OFFENDS ANOTHER PERSON. YOU JUST FEEL SO MUCH AFRAID TO DO THINGS YOU NORMALLY WOULD DO. IN OTHER WORDS, YOU'D KIND OF, IN YOUR OWN WAY, YOU'D BE CHANGING BECAUSE YOU'D TRY TO ADAPT TO THEIR—YOU'D BE SO AFRAID TO DO THE WRONG THING THAT YOU'D BE FORCED TO DO WHAT THEY DID.

T: HAS ANYBODY HERE EVER DONE THAT? GONE TO A TOTALLY FOREIGN PLACE WHERE YOU DIDN'T KNOW THE LANGUAGE? (pause) GUESS NOT.

S: (general applause)

(At this point the Alphas and Betas prepare for a meeting at which each group gives its impressions of the other culture. Then they discuss problems of relating to other societies, learning other cultures, and dealing with feelings as well as content.)

Component III

PLANNING
AND
PEER TEACHING

The planning of a simulation activity begins with an identification of the student skills to be developed or knowledge to be increased through simulation (for instance, developing the skills of driving a car, or increasing knowledge on the operations of the United States Senate). These having been identified, the next step is to locate or develop the materials necessary for the simulation. Possible sources of simulation games are the Social Science Education Consortium's *Data Handbook*, Ronald Klietsch's *Directory of Educational Simulations, Learning Games, and Didactic Units*, David Zuckerman and Robert Horn's *The Guide to Simulation Games for Education and Training*, and Ron Stadsklev's *Handbook of Simulation Gaming in Education.*[1]

The selection of the simulation activity should be done carefully; a poorly selected activity can be a total classroom failure, even when taught by the best teacher. In addition to identifying an activity that you will use in teaching specific

[1] *Data Handbook* (Boulder, Colorado: Social Science Education Consortium, 1971, 1972, 1973); Ronald G. Klietsch, *Directory of Educational Simulations, Learning Games and Didactic Units* (St. Paul, Minn.: Instructional Simulations, 1969); David W. Zuckerman and Robert E. Horn, *The Guide to Simulation Games for Education and Training* (Cambridge, Mass.: Information Resources, Inc., 1970); and Ron Stadsklev, *Handbook of Simulation Gaming in Social Education, I (Textbook) and II (Directory)* (Institute of Higher Education Research and Services, University of Alabama, n.d.).

skills or increasing specific knowledge, you must be sure the activity you select is appropriate for the group with which it is to be used. The questions to be considered in selecting a simulation activity include:

1. Does everyone in the class have the skills to understand and perform the activity?
2. Will the activity be acceptable to the school and classroom culture?
3. Do you have the skills and knowledge to direct the activity?
4. Do you have the time and all the support materials necessary to successfully complete the activity?

When you have selected, collected, and organized the appropriate support materials, you are ready to begin instruction. Remember that your role (already partially filled by your structuring of the activity) is one of explaining, refereeing, coaching, and debriefing. Your mode of reaction must always be a nonevaluative, supportive one.

OVERVIEWS OF GAMES AND SIMULATIONS

The following games and simulations, taken from the Social Science Education Consortium's 1973 *Data Book* cover a wide range of topics—consumer education, political decision-making, city planning, economics, ecology, family management and budgeting, and career planning.[2] These are just a few of the seventy games described in the SSEC *Data Book*, but are enough to provide a sense of the possibilities. Major sources of simulation games listed in the *Data Book* include:

ABT Associates, Inc.
55 Wheeler Street
Cambridge, Massachusetts 02139

Academic Games Associates, Inc.
430 East 33 Street
Baltimore, Maryland 21218

Interact
Box 262
Lakeside, California 92040

Instructional Simulations Inc.
2147 University Avenue
St. Paul, Minnesota 55114

Western Behavioral Sciences Institute
1150 Silverado
La Jolla, California 92037

[2] Games descriptions abstracted from data sheets published by the Social Science Education Consortium, Inc.

BaFa BaFa

BaFa BaFa was developed for the Personnel Research and Development Center, U. S. Navy, to help prepare Navy personnel for living in another culture. Participants are divided into two groups, the friendly and relaxed Alpha culture and the hardworking and materialistic Beta culture. A series of transactions and social activities, regulated by cultural rules and behaviors unknown to the other group, are undertaken. Visitors are exchanged between cultures in an effort to understand one another. After a fixed period of time they return to their own group to report their findings. Each group then attempts to develop hypotheses regarding the most effective way to interact with the other culture. After all participants have visited the other culture, a debriefing is conducted in which members of one culture attempt to explain the norms and values of the other culture. The goal of the simulation is to foster an understanding of the concept of culture, create feelings similar to those encountered when in another culture, and provide experience in observing and interacting with a different way of life.

Campaign

Campaign is a sophisticated and highly realistic simulation game that deals with the American political campaign system. This game is designed to allow senior high school students and adults to participate in decision making involving the tacts and strategies necessary to produce a winning political campaign. Precinct workers, pressure groups, nominating conventions, political platforms, speech making, vote switching, and news coverage are among the elements of the political process that are simulated. The game is complex and challenging but can be an exciting and effective instructional device.

Consumer

Consumer is designed to involve students in the day to day decision-making problems which face American adults in the marketplace. The participants have to decide whether to use income or credit for their purchases. They learn that borrowing from loan agencies or buying on credit is more costly then deferring purchases until they can pay cash. The game can be adapted to groups of varying abilities and backgrounds. The number of players who participate and the number of rounds which are played is also flexible.

Czar Power

Czar Power simulates the political forces at work during the reign of Czar Alexander II of Russia in the mid-19th century. Individual roles with appropriate biographical information are assigned to each participant. Five social classes are represented including nobility, clergy, civil service and military, merchants and craftsmen, and serfs and peasants. In a series of timed problem-solving sessions the participants play out their roles as both individuals and groups in efforts to influence the Czar, who finally decides what course of action to take on each problem. Participants compute their gains or losses based on their own choice from among the allowed alternative actions.

Democracy

Democracy is a set of eight games which develop from simple to complex; the set represents various stages of decision making in the democratic process. Participants play the roles of legislators in Game 1 and citizens in Game 2. Game 3 links the roles of legislators and citizens and shows the relationship between these roles in a representative democracy. The advanced games are variations of Game 1 and teach more complex principles of political decision making.

Dangerous Parallel

Originally conceived by Roger Mastrude of the Foreign Policy Association and designed by ABT Associates, *Dangerous Parallel* introduces students to "a realistic laboratory experience of international decision making and its consequences." Six imaginary nations must resolve a conflict between two bordering small nations or face world war. Working within the profiles of their nations, participants assume the roles of top cabinet leaders who must allocate their resources to achieve national goals in international conflict while at the same time trying to avoid war. Participants will not only gain insight into the nature of high governmental leadership positions but will also have an opportunity to practice analysis of goals and develop communication skills.

Dig

Dig was developed by Jerry Lipetzky, a high school teacher with David Yount and Paul Dekock of the Interact Company, at El Capitan High School in Lakeside, California. *Dig* has been designed to be the basis of a four-week instructional activity incorporating gaming and simulation components with study of anthropological concepts and archeological field experience. Although designed for use with high school students, the game can be used with a wide range of student age groups. Teachers need no background in anthropology; however, some background, specifically archeology, would be helpful.

Ecology

This is an instructional board game that illustrates the relationships between man's activities and his natural environment. Players compete for land area space in a world in which population density continually increases. The incidence of war is inevitable in the course of the game. The winner of the game is the first player with the required balance of people, money, inventions, and ecology points who passes the Ecology Test in any of the four ages of development—Hunting, Agricultural, Industrial, and Environmental. The game relies largely on chance and can be used more effectively with upper elementary and junior high school age students than with older students. It is one of the few ecology games available for elementary students.

Economic System

Economic System is a complex simulation game for junior high, high school, and adult students built upon the discipline of economics. Starting with a simple model (Level I), the game moves to more sophisticated levels of economic activity (Levels II-IV). To successfully play this simulation game, the teacher must do careful planning and become thoroughly familiar with game procedures.

Explorers I

Explorers I is a simulation game designed to provide students in upper elementary grades with the opportunity to "experience the thrills and disappointments of the early explorers of North America." Students are formed into teams of explorers who travel across the ocean; and, when they discover land, make decisions whether to continue exploring or to settle. Because the game lends itself to a variety of adaptations, it can be played a number of times by the same students.

Family Life Income Patterns

Instructional Simulations, Inc. (ISI) believes that student behavior is changed through "doing." They have used an approach to learning which involves specific learning tasks and performance goals. *Family Life Income Patterns* (*FLIP*) is centered around the task of budgeting for a family. Students encounter the problems of credit management, investment, and interest, in terms of family goals.

Generation Gap

Generation Gap is a simulation game which was designed by Erling O. Schild and Sarane S. Boocock of Academic Games Associates, Inc. at Johns Hopkins University. The game is intended for use primarily by upper-elementary grade students. Cognitive emphasis is minimal and only elementary reading and mathematics skills are required. It is intended that, through discussion techniques, students will acquire greater insight into problem-solving between parents and teenagers and will be able to more effectively solve problems in all of their interpersonal relationships.

Life Career

Life Career was designed to familiarize students with the decision-making problems which are a part of adulthood. Game participants work with a profile of a fictitious person who must allot his time and activities with respect to further education, job training, family life, work, and leisure time. At various intervals in the game, players experience the consequences of their decisions in the form of satisfaction points which reflect how successful they are in achieving the objectives they have planned. *Life Career* encourages students to appreciate the responsibilities and pressures of adulthood and to make rational plans for their lives after leaving school.

Powderhorn

Powderhorn is the elementary school version of *Starpower*. Students assume the roles of frontiersmen and establish a three-tiered society through the process of trading items common to the frontier such as rifles, traps, and pelts. The game is structured so that a few participants receive more valued things than other participants. Thus, the simulation usually ends in a revolt. The content focus of *Powderhorn* encourages students to explore the dimensions and uses of power. Procedures for conducting the simulation are carefully spelled out and should be followed precisely. Debriefing is critical to establishing useful learning from participation in the simulation.

Starpower

Recently developed by R. Garry Shirts for Western Behavioral Sciences Institute, *Starpower* explores the personal accumulation, use, and abuse of power. The game is structured so that a few participants receive a greater amount of high-value wealth chips than the other participants; these same few participants are also provided the opportunity to change the rules of the game to protect their consolidation of power. The purpose of the game is to have the rules break down, as the disenfranchised powerless participants realize that they cannot win within the structure of the rules and they react against their competitors who have abused the power which they had been given by the unequal distribution of wealth chips and privileges. *Starpower* encourages the students to explore the dimensions of power and competitive society.

Tracts

TRACTS is a strongly realistic simulation which illustrates the problems of land use in the city. It is designed to allow students to participate in a decision-making process in order to understand the operations of various interest groups which are involved in city planning. In addition to communication skills, students will learn the importance of negotiation and compromise in making decisions. Although *TRACTS* was designed for use in the high school classroom, it can be used as a training or orientation exercise for city planners and service groups interested in city planning.

A SAMPLE SIMULATION GAME

The following description of the simulation game *Hang Up* was taken from the Social Science Education Consortium's 1973 *Data Book* and is reproduced here in order to provide you with a sample of a professional evaluation of the activity, to which you may compare your own evaluation.[3]

Hang Up

Developer:	Synectics Education Systems and the Unitarian Universalist Association
Publisher:	The Unitarian Universalist Association 25 Beacon Street Boston, Massachusetts 02108
Publication Date:	1969
Availability:	From publisher
Grade Level:	6-12 (Adults)
Subject Area:	Human Relations, Psychology, and Sociology
Number of Players:	6 (2—As many as desired)

[3] Analysis of "Hang Up" reprinted in its entirety with the permission of Social Science Education Consortium, Inc., Boulder, Colorado, 80302.

Overview

This game has been designed to focus attention on racial "hang ups." In playing the game, each participant is given a number of hang ups which he must then try to rid himself of during the game. As he moves around the game board and encounters various stress situations, he tries to pantomime his hang ups successfully. The other participants try to identify correctly each hang up being demonstrated. Both the student whose hang up is guessed and the student who correctly identifies the hang up may discard a hang up card. The winner is the first player to pass the finish line without any hang ups. The game has been used successfully with 6th grade students through adults. It requires little teacher preparation but considerable tact and sensitivity throughout the game play and in the debriefing.

Materials and Cost

Materials Package: Cardboard cylinder, $14'' \times 4''$, contains the following:

Coordinator's Manual: 9 pp., $6\frac{1}{4}'' \times 8''$, stapled paper cover; includes introduction, procedures, suggestions for modification, and rationale

Additional Materials: 57 blue Hang Up Cards; 37 tan Stress Situation Cards on a ring; 23 red Wild Cards; 23 yellow Wild Cards; Tiles, one of each of the following colors: yellow, blue, maroon, turquoise, violet, green; plastic playing board; 6 Clue Lists; 2 dice; 12 blank yellow Wild Cards; 11 blank red Wild Cards; 17 blank blue Hang Up Cards; 18 blank tan Stress Situation Cards

Total Package: $8.00

Required or Suggested Time

A minimum of two hours is necessary to play this game, including briefing and debriefing activities.

Intended User Characteristics

Participants need only elementary arithmetic and reading skills to play this game. The teacher does not have to spend much time in preparing to play the game; however, success in debriefing depends upon the teacher's ability to assist students in gaining real insight into their own game behavior.

Rationale and General Objectives

The purpose of this game is to focus attention on racial attitudes and stereotypic thinking. The developers' rationale in designing this game is based on Gordon Allport's studies in his book, *The Nature of Prejudice*. Allport's findings indicate that people who have a highly developed empathy for other human beings tend to be more tolerant, to be less prejudiced, and to have greater self-insight. Therefore, Hang Up has been designed to stimulate empathetic awareness in students through a process of charading stressful and comical situations based on race relations. The developers believe that through a process of charade and analysis, participants' sensitivity to their own and to others' racial attitudes and prejudices will be heightened. It is intended that each actor will generate, within himself and the other participants, a feeling for and understanding of the situation he is portraying. When each participant tries to pantomime a hang up in a stress situation, he frequently and unconsciously reveals latent racist strains which can then be analyzed in the debriefing process.

Content

In the process of this game, students are involved in trying to identify themselves with situations that they may never have experienced in real life. They are required to analyze how certain types of people might feel and react in specific circumstances. Most of these situations involve hypothetical interaction between people of different racial derivations. As the student tries to role play various stressful situations, he invariably projects some of his own attitudes and feelings. A participant can be given a hang up card that says, "You are the type of person who tries to hide your low opinion of yourself by using a false front of superiority," while at the same time, "Your black friend is beginning to prefer being with other blacks." He has already rolled the dice to discover that he himself is white. Students reveal their own attitudes and feelings not only in the role play but also by the hang up cards they choose to discard when they have the opportunity to discard those of their choice.

The value of the game for students' cognitive and affective growth lies in its potential for analysis of both implicit and explicit prejudices in ways that maximize students' emotional and instructional involvement in the analysis. Skills in self-expression, verbal, and non-verbal communication can also be heightened in game play. Hang Up is also designed so that students can provide their own input by creating their own role-play situations.

Procedures

Each player is dealt seven hang up cards. As he moves around the game board, he lands on different numbered squares, each number representing a specific stress situation. If any of the hang up cards in his hand fit the stress situation on which he lands, he checks the dice to see if he is a black man or a white man (even number black; odd number white). If the player's race eliminates the stress aspect of the situation, he then picks two wild cards and acts them out. One card is an adjective; the other is a noun (e.g., rich, clown). If his acting out of the wild cards is correctly identified, he can discard one hang up card of his choice; if it is not identified, he must draw another hang up card. If the player's race does not eliminate the stress situation, he goes ahead without selecting wild cards and acts out his hang up, taking into consideration the participant's race and his situation. All participants have a printed sheet that lists all possible hang ups. The other players then try to identify which hang up the student is acting out. Each player, however, has only one guess. If another player correctly identifies his hang up, the student has a chance to discard that hang up card and the person who identified it may discard any hang up card in his hand. If the hang up is not identified, the participant who played the role must discard that particular hang up and draw two new ones. The player may, if he wishes, pass up his opportunity to act out a hang up card and wait instead for his next turn. The first player to pass the finish line on the game board without any of his hang ups is the winner.

Evaluative Comments and Suggestions

The developers state in the Coordinator's Manual that "this game has been tested with blacks and whites and adults and young people. It has proved successful both in terms of fun and of learning. . . .The game is designed for players to substitute their own relevant concerns for the ones proposed by the game." This can be an exciting and effective game. Some of the pantomime, however, is difficult; for example, it is not always easy to act out a concept like "self-contained aggression." As a result, it is helpful if the game coordinator immediately makes the rule that words cannot be spelled out by letters in the air. It is also helpful to have the participants keep their hang up cards hidden from sight; sometimes players guess a person's hang up incorrectly on purpose, just so the game doesn't end. The game is effective and adaptable for use at a wide range of age and maturity levels. One conspicuous weakness is the fact that the Manual does not provide any assistance or suggestions for debriefing. The developers do, however, furnish a phone number in the Coordinator's Manual and tell anyone who has questions about the game to call them collect!

Completing the Planning Guide

We have developed the following Planning Guide in order to help you organize your Simulation lesson. The guide is especially useful the first few occasions you use the Simulation Model. After that you will probably not find it necessary to write such extensive plans, although you may still want to informally consider each of the steps in the Guide. A completed Planning Guide has been provided as a model. The lesson described utilizes the simulation game Bafa, which was illustrated in the transcript in Component II. Read through the sample Guide that follows and then complete the Planning Guide that follows it for your peer teaching lesson.

SAMPLE PLANNING GUIDE FOR THE SIMULATION MODEL

1. Identify the goals of this simulation.

   a. *To understand and experience the concept of culture.*

   b. *To become aware of our own attitudes, feelings, and responses when we are in a foreign culture.*

   c. *To acquire concepts for analyzing particular cultures.*

   d. *To experience two different types of cultures and share insights and feelings about the cultures.*

2. Identify and describe the simulation.

   a. Name *Bafa*

   b. Publisher or developer *R. Gary Shirts of Simile II*
      1150 Silverado
      La Jolla, California 92037

   c. Materials provided: *Alpha cards*
      Beta cards
      Buttons

   d. Is the simulation of a model of

      ✓ 1. a social process(es)

      ✓ 2. a social system(s)

      ___ 3. the interrelationship among social systems and social processes

      ___ 4. a historical event

   e. How do the rules and limits of the model reflect the realities of the system or process?

      Second language
      Sanctions for violating the norms of the culture.
      Norms and values of the culture.

3. What student skills are required to understand and perform the activity?

    a. Observation skills with respect to social interaction.

    b. Self-awareness, especially of one's own feelings.

4. Describe relevant aspects of the school or class culture that might enhance or interfere with this activity.

    a. Students are used to teacher-directed, formal instruction and traditional subject-matter content. They are unaccustomed to experience-based learning and gaming activities. Consequently, some students initially may not see this as a learning experience

    b. The class meets for 45-minute periods each day. Bafa will have to be organized around this time constraint.

5. What skills does the teacher need to direct this activity?

    a. Organizing the procedures and logistics.

    b. Moderating during debriefing.

    c. Managerial skills.

6. How much time will be required for the activity?   2 - 2½ hours

7. What support materials, besides those provided in the game, will you need?

    a. Extra chips.

    b. Extra cards for cultures.

    c. Blackboard for Beta culture.

    d. Separate classroom close by.

    e. One student or teacher aide to assist in management of the game.

    f. Tagboard listing activities of the simulation.

8. Identify and describe the roles or role groups.

    a. Director and assistant director: conduct orientation; manage simulation, especially time, pace of activities; responsible for instructional materials, and for conducting debriefing, and instructing in the rules of the culture.

    b. Alpha Culture: set of observers and visitors to Beta culture

    c. Beta Culture: set of observers and visitors to Alpha culture

9. Identify the learning objectives in this simulation and then describe the specific skill, concept, etc.

   ✓   1. Skills *Observation Skills*

   ✓   2. Concepts *Culture, norms, sanctions, role, values, customs*

        3. Social Process

        4. Social Systems

   ✓   5. Attitude Development *Attitude towards "differentness"*

   ✓   6. Personal Growth

> *Awareness of feelings in a strange new environment; in a relaxed culture with a "sexist, patriarchal structure" and in an "aggressive, money-oriented" culture.*

10. Outline the stages of the simulation operations (Phase Three) and your role as coordinator during that period. Specifically what must you do?

> *a. Divide into cultures and learn the new culture (30 minutes).*
> *b. Select and instruct observers. Exchange observers (15 minutes).*
> *c. Report of observers (10 minutes).*
> *d. Exchange of visitors (2 times), and discussion (20 minutes each).*

11. Describe the pre-run operations (decisions and materials).

> *a. Determine amount of time for each activity and how to sequence into days.*
> *b. Make new materials.*
> *c. Obtain second room.*
> *d. Review anthropological concepts and apply these to each culture.*

12. Describe your plan for participant training.

> *Read rules of culture and have students practice each of the activities of the culture as it is introduced. Then pretend I am a visitor and have students use all the rules of the culture at once.*

13. Describe your plan for participant debriefing.

Have one person from each culture summarize what they think the culture is about. Ask other students to do this in terms of major concepts.

Have students discuss their reactions to visiting a strange culture and to being part of a particular culture.

Ask students to relate these insights and feelings to actual experiences they have had.

PLANNING GUIDE FOR THE SIMULATION MODEL

1. Identify the goals of this simulation.

2. Identify and describe the simulation.
    A. Name:

    B. Publisher or developer:

    C. Materials provided:

    D. Is the simulation a model of:

    _____ 1. a social process(es)

    _____ 2. a social system(s)

    _____ 3. the interrelationships among social systems and social processes

    _____ 4. a historical event

    E. How do the rules and limits of the model reflect the realities of the system or process?

3. What skills must the students have in order to understand and perform the activity?

4. Describe relevant aspects of the school or class culture that might enhance or interfere with this activity.

5. What skills does the teacher need to direct this activity?

6. How much time will be required for the activity?

7. What support materials, besides those provided in the game, will you need?

8. Identify and describe the roles or role groups.

9. Identify the learning objectives in this simulation and then describe the specific skill, concept, etc.

_____ 1. skills

_____ 2. concepts

_____ 3. social process

_____ 4. social systems

_____ 5. attitude development

_____ 6. personal growth

10. Outline the stages of the simulation operations (Phase Three) and your role as coordinator during that period. Specifically, what must you do?

11. Describe the pre-run operations (decisions and materials).

12. Describe your plan for participant training.

13. Describe your plan for participant debriefing.

Analyzing the Peer Teaching Lesson

After you have peer taught the simulation lesson, analyze your teaching by completing the Teaching Analysis Guide that follows. Duplicate as many copies of the Guide as are needed to analyze the peer teaching and microteaching of all group members.

TEACHING ANALYSIS GUIDE FOR THE SIMULATION MODEL

Pre-Run Operations

1. Were all necessary decisions made and planned for?

A. number of participants	Thoroughly	Partially	Missing	Not Needed
B. physical logistics	Thoroughly	Partially	Missing	Not Needed
C. timing and sequence of events	Thoroughly	Partially	Missing	Not Needed

2. Were all support materials developed/available?

A. players' support materials	Thoroughly	Partially	Missing	Not Needed
B. supplementary instructional materials	Thoroughly	Partially	Missing	Not Needed
C. scenario presentation	Thoroughly	Partially	Missing	Not Needed

Phase One: Orientation

3. Was orientation provided:

A. for the broad topic of simulation?	Thoroughly	Partially	Missing	Not Needed
B. for concepts?	Thoroughly	Partially	Missing	Not Needed
C. for simulation gaming?	Thoroughly	Partially	Missing	Not Needed

Phase Two: Participant Training

4. Did the simulation manager set up the scenario (explain the game—the rules, roles, procedures, scoring, goals, and types of decisions to be made)?	Thoroughly	Partially	Missing	Not Needed
5. Were role assignments made?	Thoroughly	Partially	Missing	Not Needed
6. Was there an abbreviated practice session?	Thoroughly	Partially	Missing	Not Needed

Phase Three: Simulation Operations

7. Did the gaming activity occur?	Thoroughly	Partially	Missing	Not Needed

238

TEACHING ANALYSIS GUIDE FOR THE SIMULATION MODEL

8. Were the players provided with feedback and evaluation of their performance and the effect of their decisions? — Thoroughly　Partially　Missing　Not Needed

9. Did the simulation manager clarify misconceptions when necessary? — Thoroughly　Partially　Missing　Not Needed

Phase Four: Participant Debriefing

10. Which of the following focuses were introduced in the debriefing?

   A. summary of events and participants — Thoroughly　Partially　Missing　Not Needed

   B. difficulties and insights — Thoroughly　Partially　Missing　Not Needed

   C. projection of future events — Thoroughly　Partially　Missing　Not Needed

   D. comparison of simulation to the real world — Thoroughly　Partially　Missing　Not Needed

   E. relationship of simulation to course content — Thoroughly　Partially　Missing　Not Needed

   F. appraising and redesigning the simulation — Thoroughly　Partially　Missing　Not Needed

11. Was the teacher's role in the debriefing one of an interviewer? — Thoroughly　Partially　Missing　Not Needed

Principles of Reaction

12. Was the simulation manager non-evaluative of players' decisions and moves? — Thoroughly　Partially　Missing　Not Needed

13. Did the simulation manager facilitate the players' understanding and interpretation of the rules? — Thoroughly　Partially　Missing　Not Needed

14. Did the simulation manager encourage participation and help players cope with uncertainty, where necessary? — Thoroughly　Partially　Missing　Not Needed

15. Did the simulation manager keep the game going ("get on with the game") when players digressed or became bogged down? — Thoroughly　Partially　Missing　Not Needed

TEACHING ANALYSIS GUIDE FOR THE SIMULATION MODEL

16. Did the simulation manager maintain the rules (referee the game) when necessary?	Thoroughly	Partially	Missing	Not Needed

AFTER PEER TEACHING: MICROTEACHING

Peer teaching was an opportunity to "walk through" the pattern of activities of the model you are using. It should have helped you identify areas of understanding or performance that were amiss for you!

Aside from the specifics of the Teaching Analysis Guide, we would like you to reflect intuitively on your peer teaching experience. Did you feel that the essence of the Simulation Model was incorporated into the learning activity? Were you able to maintain the teacher's role as you had anticipated?

As you prepare to manage your first simulation with a small group of students, identify aspects of your peer teaching that you want to improve upon or include. Usually, these aspects are such things as being more precise in explaining the procedures, coaching students, and relating the simulation to real life situations. We suggest walking yourself mentally through the microteaching before actually engaging in it.

We suggest audio-taping your first microteaching session so that you can reflect on the lesson afterwards. Students will respond differently from your peers. It is a good idea to use the Teaching Analysis Guide with your microteaching lesson. You may also want to share the experience with your colleagues and receive their comments and suggestions.

The fourth and last component of the Simulation Model suggests ways to use the model over a long-term curricular sequence and ways to combine the model with other models of teaching. The emphasis of your training in this model will gradually shift now from mastering the basic elements of teaching to curriculum design and application.

Component IV

ADAPTING
THE MODEL

CURRICULUM APPLICATION

It is probably apparent by now that the Simulation Model can be used for a variety of teaching purposes. We have already discussed many simulations in the social studies. Simulations have also been developed to help students explore personal values, inter-group relations, economic and political processes, cultural interchange, and a host of other topics, as well as to provide training in many areas.

In the classroom, simulations are generally employed as part of a fairly extensive unit of study. They can be used to introduce a unit of work, to extend and deepen understandings as the unit progresses, or to pull ideas together and insure their application to real-life problem situations. For example, the game of *Hang Up* can be used to open up the area of personal values and racial stereotyping, and a unit can be built from there. Similarly, *Bafa* can be used to introduce the study of the nature of culture and cultural interchange. *The Legislative Game* can be used to bring together knowledge of the legislative process, caucusing, and such.

Essentially, to apply simulation to a unit, we develop a plan that specifies content and scope. We then examine lists of simulations, searching for ones that might be applicable and sifting them for quality. It is wise to try a simulation with a small group of people, whether children or adults, before using it in the classroom.

(The authors have practiced many simulations as parlor games at parties, thereby becoming familiar with the games and having fun at the same time.) Many simulations are very much like board games such as *Monopoly* or a game of charades (some of the elements of which are included in simulation games such as *Hang Up*).

Upper elementary, junior high, and high school students can be prepared for leadership roles in simulations. It is important to note, however, that if students are to be used as leaders, they will have to be coached so that the essential point of the game is quite clear to them. Some game-type simulations have a tendency to go off on tangents if the leader loses focus.

Since simulations teach people to work within a system, it is important to identify the elements of the system that have to be mastered by the end of the game. Political games, for example, require the mastery of a political system, and economic games the mastery of an economic system. This is, of course, why simulations are so good as introductions to and culminating activities of units of study. Used in the first sense, they open up the system for study. Used in the second sense, they induce the integration into a total pattern of the elements that have been learned.

Some simulations are good only for one operation. *Bafa* is such a game. Once you have learned its system, there is little incentive to learn it again. Some other simulations, such as *The Legislative Game*, can be played over and over. Thus, they can be used throughout a unit, and the students can play the game more and more effectively as they acquire information, in this case, about the legislative process.

COMBINING SIMULATION WITH OTHER MODELS OF TEACHING

If the unit or course of study is built on one or more other models of teaching besides Simulation, then Simulation is controlled by those models. Combined with group investigation, for example, Simulation can be used to present a puzzling problem or it can be used as a source of data during the inquiry phases. Similarly, the Advance Organizer Model can be used to present concepts that the students can apply in the course of using a simulation. In *New Strategies for Social Science Education*,[1] we describe an extended unit in which students study India and attempt to send food to an Indian community. The essential model used in that unit is group investigation. If you read the description of this unit you will find that the *Bafa* cross-cultural simulation would have been useful in a number of instances as the students encountered obstacles to their humanitarian project. They did not understand many of the cultural differences that were creating problems of communication, and they had no way of comprehending that what they were dealing with was a system with which they should have learned to interact.

---

[1] Bruce Joyce, *New Strategies for Social Science Education* (Chicago: Science Research Associates, 1972), pp. 155-67).

INDEX